REGIONS
IN THE
EUROPEAN COMMUNITY

REGIONS
IN THE
EUROPEAN COMMUNITY

EDITED BY

MICHAEL KEATING
AND
BARRY JONES

CLARENDON PRESS · OXFORD
1985

Oxford University Press, Walton Street, Oxford OX2 6DP
Oxford New York Toronto
Delhi Bombay Calcutta Madras Karachi
Kuala Lumpur Singapore Hong Kong Tokyo
Nairobi Dar es Salaam Cape Town
Melbourne Auckland
and associated companies in
Beirut Berlin Ibadan Mexico City Nicosia

Oxford is a trade mark of Oxford University Press

Published in the United States
by Oxford University Press, New York

British Library Cataloguing in Publication Data
Keating, Michael, 1950–
Regions in the European community.
1. Regionalism—European Economic Community
countries 2. European Economic Community
countries—Politics and government
I. Title II. Jones, J. Barry
306'.2 JN30
ISBN 0-19-827476-9

Library of Congress Cataloging in Publication Data
Regions in the European Community.

Includes index.
1. European communities—Addresses, essays, lectures.
I. Keating, Michael J. II. Jones, J. Barry (James
Barry), 1938–
JN15.R37 1985 341.24'2 85-13578
ISBN 0-19-827476-9

Set by Colset Pte. Ltd., Singapore

Printed in Great Britain at The Alden Press, Oxford

305802

Preface

The European Community is an association of independent states. Since the Treaty of Rome, national governments have continued to insist that access to the decision-making organs of the Community should be through them and that the Council should remain paramount.

Yet Community policies effect regions within member states in varied ways and the interests of regions in Community matters are not always identical with those of the states of which they form part. Further, the reservation of certain policy areas to the Community has in some states impinged upon the responsibilities of regional administrations so drawing them into the European policy process. Finally, implementation of Community policy is often conducted through regional and other subnational administrations.

In recognition of this, elaborate networks have developed for the articulation of regional interests in European policy-making, through national governments, to some extent through the Commission and its network of advisory committees, and latterly through th European Parliament. This book studies these networks, examines arrangements within states for identifying regional interests and involving regional administrations in Community policy and analyses the regional operation of the various European Funds. We have not attempted to cover all ten member states; and indeed four of our eleven chapters are about the United Kingdom. Nor have we sought to impose a uniform definition of what a 'region' is; we are in the best possible position to know, indeed, that three of our case studies, Scotland, Wales, and the Republic of Ireland, should not really be described as 'regions' at all. However, our purpose was to explore the diversity of policy-making and administrative links between the Community and those areas, usually below the level of the member state, which, from the standpoint of Brussels, can be conceived of as regions and which, indeed, form the framework for the delivery of the Community's own regional policies.

In preparing this book, we have received a great deal of help from institutions and individuals. Our conference in Scotland, at which the draft chapters were discussed, was supported by the Commission of the European Communities, the European Educational Research Trust and the European Cultural Foundation. Our thanks go also to Stanley Budd, Ken Collins, MEP, and David Scott, for help with this. Mike Goldsmith, Mari James, Arthur Midwinter, Rhodri Morgan, John Russell, Vincenzo Santantonio, and Herman Wyts acted as discussants and their comments and criticisms greatly assisted the task of the editors. Without the help of Yvonne MacLeod, it is unlikely that we would all have succeeded in assembling at the right time and place from our various parts of Europe. Finally, our thanks go to the University of Strathclyde and University College Cardiff for their support of us and our project.

Michael Keating
Barry Jones

Glasgow, December 1984

Contributors

Michael Keating: *University of Strathclyde, Glasgow, Scotland.*

Barry Jones: *University College, Cardiff, Wales.*

Mario Ruis Martins: *University of Oporto, Portugal.*

John Mawson: *University of Birmingham, England.*

John Gibney: *University of Birmingham, England.*

Nigel Waters: *Management Consultant, formerly with the Planning Exchange, Glasgow.*

Paul Hainsworth: *University of Ulster, N. Ireland.*

Francesco Merloni: *Istituto di Studi Sulle Regioni, Rome, Italy.*

Hans-George Gerstenlauer: *University of Tübingen, West Germany.*

Yves Mény: *University of Paris, France.*

Joan Hart: *Institute of Public Administration, Dublin, Ireland.*

Contents

List of Abbreviations   x

1 Introduction: *Michael Keating*   1

2 The Development of the European Community
   Regional Policy: *John Mawson, Mario Ruis Martins, and
   John T. Gibney*   20

3 Scotland in the European Community: *Michael Keating
   and Nigel Waters*   60

4 Wales in the European Community: *Barry Jones*   89

5 Northern Ireland in the European Community:
   Paul Hainsworth   109

6 English and Welsh Local Government and the European
   Community: *John Mawson and John T. Gibney*   133

7 Italian Regions in the European Community:
   Francesco Merloni   160

8 German *Länder* in the European Community:
   Hans-Georg Gerstenlauer   173

9 French Regions in the European Community:
   Yves Mény   191

10 The European Regional Development Fund and the
   Republic of Ireland: *Joan Hart*   204

11 Conclusion: *Barry Jones*   234

Index   247

List of Abbreviations

ADP	Agricultural Development Programme
AMA	Association of Metropolitan Authorities
APEX	Association Pour l'expansion du Nord—Pas de Calais
CAP	Common Agricultural Policy
CELIB	Comité d'études et de liaison d'interêts bretons
CFTC	Confédération Française des Travailleurs Chrétiens
CBI	Confederation of British Industry
CGT	Confédération Générale du Travail
CODER	Commission de développement économique régional
COPA	Comité des Organisations Professionelles Agricoles
COREPER	Committee of Permanent Representatives
COSLA	Convention of Scottish Local Authorities
CPMR	Conference of Peripheral Maritime Regions
CRP	Common Regional Policy
CSU	Christian Social Union
DAFS	Department of Agriculture and Fisheries for Scotland
DATAR	Délégation à l'aménagement du territoire et à l'action régionale
DOE	Department of the Environment
DTI	Department of Trade and Industry
EACC	East Anglian Consultative Committee
EAGGF	European Agricultural Guarantee and Guidance Fund
EC	European Community
ECSC	European Coal and Steel Community
ECU	European Currency Unit
ECOSOC	Economic and Social Committee
EEC	European Economic Community
EIB	European Investment Bank
EMS	European Monetary System
EMU	Economic and Monetary Union
EP	European Parliament
EPCs	Economic Planning Councils
ERDF	European Regional Development Fund

ESF	European Social Fund
EUA	European Unit of Account
FEOGA	Agricultural Guidance Fund
FUW	Farmers' Union of Wales
GDP	Gross Domestic Product
HIDB	Highlands and Islands Development Board
ICELA	Irish Council of European Local Authorities
ICFC	Industrial and Commercial Finance Corporation
IDA	Industrial Development Authority
IDP	Integrated Development Programme
IDS	Industry Department for Scotland
IRA	Irish Republican Army
IULA/CEM	International Union of Local Authorities/Conference of European Municipalities
LFAs	Less Favoured Areas
MEP	Member of the European Parliament
MSC	Manpower Services Commission
NECCA	North East County Councils Association
NCI	New Community Instrument
NICS	Northern Ireland Civil Service
NFU	National Farmers' Union
NFUS	National Farmers' Union of Scotland
NIO	Northern Ireland Office
PCP	Public Capital Programme
RDO	Regional Development Organisation
RDP	Regional Development Programme
RSG	Rate Support Grant
SDA	Scottish Development Agency
SDLP	Social Democratic and Labour Party
SFF	Scottish Fishermen's Federation
SNP	Scottish National Party
STAR	Scheme for Textile Area Regeneration
TUC	Trades Union Congress
UFU	Ulster Farmers' Union
UK	United Kingdom
UKREP	United Kingdom Permanent Representative
UWC	Ulster Workers' Council
WCC	Welsh Counties Committee
WOAD	Welsh Office Agriculture Department
YORTAG	Yorkshire Textile Area Action Group

1

Introduction

MICHAEL KEATING

Europeanism and Regionalism

Europeanism and regionalism in post-war Europe have represented twin challenges to the nation-state as a framework for making and delivering public policy. Both concepts are wide and, at times, ill-defined, covering a considerable variety of political movements with varied aims and strategies. Yet both have their roots in the problems of managing the modern industrial state, particulary to stimulate development and growth; and in a complex of political impulses directed towards less material goals. In turn, the interaction of state economic development policies and the political demands of peripheral regionalists or Europeanists has created a new dynamic which further calls into question the European nation-state. To clarify this argument, let us examine briefly the emergence of Europeanism and regionalism and the demands and needs which have inspired them.

The creation of the European Community can be traced to political and economic arguments developed in the context of post-war reconstruction. Politically, European unity provided a framework for Franco-German *entente* and an insurance against future war, as well as bolstering European independence in a superpower age. Economically, it corresponded to the logic of large-scale industrial development, both capitalist and state-owned. Free-trade theory predicted that the removal of tariff barriers would increase efficiency through greater specialization and competition. The creation of a larger home market would provide the basis for European firms to grow and rival the American giants. Political and economic logic came together with the argument that economic integration would lead ineluctably to greater political co-operation and, ultimately, European unity.

For the more idealistic, the dream was of a United States of Europe, a political and economic union to take its place beside the superpowers. In practice, integration was subordinated to the needs of national

governments and the purpose of the Treaty of Rome, to establish institutions with their own integrationist dynamic, effectively thwarted. So
unity only proceeded in those areas where it suited the convenience of
the least European-minded member governments, for instance in agriculture, where France was able to transfer a large part of the political
and economic burden of agricultural support and adjustment to the
Community. For some of the large states, then, Europe became an
element in the economic development policies of *national* governments
rather than an independent force subversive of those governments
themselves. The effective renunciation of the supranationality principle so that it only operates with the consent of member states and the
retention of the veto in all important matters show the resilience of the
state in the face of integrationist pressures.

Regionalism is a more complex phenomenon, taking a wide variety
of forms but it, too, has been a major feature in the post-war development of European states[1] and, like Europeanism, inspired by both
political and economic impulses which, interacting, have produced
their own dynamics. To simplify greatly, we can see regionalism as an
outgrowth four types of impulse. First, there are the technical needs of
the modern state. Regional forms of administration have been introduced by central governments for the convenience of physical and
economic planning. The region has often been seen both as the
appropriate physical, social and economic unit for planning and as
an intermediate level at which intergovernmental differences can be
negotiated and accommodated.[2] It some states, for example the United
Kingdom and France, it is also a level relatively free from either elected
local government control or strong, vertical bureaucratic central
control and thus constitutes a political 'space of uncertainty'[3] in which
public sector professionals and technocrats may have an enlarged
scope. For the central state, regionalism may have the added
advantage of relieving political and administrative overload on the
centre, particularly where it is taken beyond mere administrative
deconcentration to the establishment of elected regional governments.
As in the European case, the question then arises of the extent to which
the state is using the regions for its own political and economic
purposes or, conversely, regions are undermining the basis of the state
itself.

Second, regionalism has emerged in the form of 'regional policy' or,
to spell it out more fully, interregional economic policies. A feature of
all post-war European states, these have been grounded in arguments

of economic efficiency and equity. In the years of growth and Keynsian policies, it was generally accepted that national output could be maximized with minimum inflationary effects by bringing into use idle resources in depressed regions. Steering development away from 'overheated' regions by a 'carrot-and-stick' package of incentives was seen as a non-zero sum game benefiting both the motor regions and the depressed regions, as well as adding to national output.[4] The policy also accorded with the need, on social and political grounds, to secure a measure of territorial equity which, in turn, could reinforce the cohesion and solidarity of the nation state. Policies and techniques varied from the 'carrot-and-stick' British system of incentives to the elabroate French schemes for *l'aménagement du territoire* but all were essentially centralist tools for economic development.

The third source of regionalism is the cultural and economic demands arising from within regions themselves. These are extremely complex and varied. In some cases, regionalist movements represent a protest against the consequences of modern capitalism allowing regional economies to decline. In such cases regionalism looks first to the central state to reverse the process and thus, ironically, becomes a centralist force.[5] In other cases, the protest is more complex, directed not only against economic decline but also against the very policies developed in response to it in so far as these represent a threat to regional cultures and a further incorporation of the periphery into the metropolitan order. Such protests may be purely traditional or backward-looking; or, under the influence of rising local *forces vives*, they may develop their own philosophy of modernization and balanced development in parallel with, or in opposition to, that of the central state.

Fourth, there are demands for regional autonomy; these, too, are complex and varied. In Scotland and Wales 'historic nations' have sustained autonomist and secessionist movements of varying strength. In Northern Ireland, a nationalist movement seeks unity with the neighbouring state while most of the 'loyalist' community seek autonomy within the UK. In France and Italy, 'micro-nationalist' movements exist in some regions, basing their claims on the rights of historic peoples. More widespread in Western Europe is a belief in regional autonomy as a means of enhancing the democratic, pluralist nature of the state. The West German federal system was imposed by the victorious Allies after the war precisely to disperse power and hinder the rise of another totalitarian government. In Italy, too, regional government was written into the post-war constitution as a reaction to the centralist excesses of fascism.

While these four elements may be analytically separate, in any given case there is usually a dynamic at work to link them and to bring into being social movements drawing on more than one element. So, while purely economic demands for more regional aid or regional development may be implicitly centralist, the political movements which they inspire may move quickly to an autonomist stance. This is partly because of the failure, of centralized interventions to meet the demands made on them and partly because effective political mobilization requires both types of appeal. A further complicating factor is that it has often been centralized regional policy interventions which have helped to develop regional consciousness in the first place, by encouraging people to articulate their demands in a regional as opposed to a class, sectoral, or any other framework. So centralized regional policy, regional economic and cultural demands, and the issue of regional autonomy are linked in dynamic and complex ways. Whatever the constitutional arrangements, the confluence of national policy, often delivered on a regional basis, and demands flowing up from below, make the region a key level of political dialogue and action. Several of the chapters in this book make reference to the ways in which European states have attempted to come to terms with this.

So far we have suggested that the typical response of the national state to the development of both Europeanism and regionalism has been to try and preserve its own power intact, harnessing these movements to its own objectives. Nevertheless, the two phenomena have altered the position of the state in two important ways. First, the development of the European Community and of regional political institutions have circumscribed the freedom of action of national governments, albeit not to the extent desired by the more ardent supporters of regional and European government. Second, they have presented the state with opportunities to hive off some of the less gratifying or more burdensome tasks of government to other levels. This has been a common criticism on the left of regionalizing measures of right-wing governments.[6] Without subscribing to this 'dualist' thesis in its entirety, we can see examples of states attempting to externalize problems. Mény's chapter shows the French state doing this with both regions and the European Community, while strongly maintaining the essentials of state power. British proposals for Scottish and Welsh devolution in the 1970s kept the levers of economic power in central hands, while devolving considerable areas of social and environmental policy. Over Northern Ireland there is a temptation for British governments to externalize the problem or at least share the burden with Europe; but, as the row over the European Parliament initiative, mentioned in Hainsworth's chapter, shows, there is still a strong belief that this would touch the essence of the state, its territorial sovereignty. In the case of Corsica, too, the French government has insisted that the matter is purely an internal affair.

Policy Issues

The conjunction of European and regional questions within states adds a further dimension to the question and takes us to the essential concerns of this book. There are three sets of issues here. First, the political logic of the European movement and its practical expression in the Community call into question the nation-state as the basis of political and economic organization. Some European visionaries have looked to the withering away of the nation-state altogether and in such a perspective the importance of regions is enhanced; at its extreme, there are those who dream of a Europe of the regions without nations. More realistically, there have been those who have seen Europe as a framework for the independence of certain regions and small nations, without the risks of political and economic isolation or being tarred with the 'separatist' brush. As Jones shows, a policy of independence within Europe has allowed Plaid Cymru, the Welsh nationalists, both to give an element of realism to the independence policy and to claim a more cosmopolitan outlook than the British parties. In the case of the Republic of Ireland, it is arguable that Community membership was the means of making formal independence a reality by lessening the dependence on Britain. In the case of Scotland, the option of independence-within-Europe has, surprisingly, hardly been considered except, as Keating and Waters show, by the short-lived Scottish Labour Party, though recently there have been signs that the Scottish National Party may be changing its attitude.

Short of independence, regionalist movements have looked to Europe to some degree to protect their interests against the nation-state. The Bureau of Unrepresented Nations, grouping Bretons, Basques, Alsatians, and Welsh, but not Scots, attempts to circumvent unsympathetic national governments, albeit with little success, while the Conference of Peripheral Maritime Regions attempts to push issues of concern to its regional members. Several attempts have been made to bring the Northern Ireland question on to the European agenda to circumvent what is seen as British opposition to the nationalist case.

Second, the free-trade and competition policies to which the Community is committed pose a threat to vulnerable sectors and vulnerable regions, which in many cases coincide. The advantage of the European Golden Triangle *vis-à-vis* the periphery is thus increased, reinforcing the sense of disillusionment in the peripheral regions both with the nation state and with the Community. For this reason, many supporters of European integration have seen a vigorous regional anti-disparity policy as a vital concomitant to the building of the Community. Furthermore, like national governments, the Community has tended to see the region as a basis for plans for economic adaptation and for anti-disparity measures. However, not all European regions have an interest in regional policy. At one extreme, Hainsworth shows us the severe effects of Community competition policy on the economy of Northern Ireland while, at the other, Gerstenlauer shows that the interest of the German *Länder*, with their strong competitive economies, lies precisely in dismantling barriers to trade and competition.

Third, it is a fact that specific Community policies have an uneven spatial impact, depending on the distribution of affected sectors. The chapters show the importance of the fisheries policy for Scotland, the wine policy for the south of France, textile, coal, the steel policies for Northern Ireland, Scotland, Wales, and northern and eastern France. The initial response to crises in these declining sectors has been to demand help and protection from national governments, so reinforcing the legitimacy of the nation-state. In some cases, though, sectoral crises afflicting specific regions have come to be seen in territorial terms and so have fed the regionalist dynamic. So the crisis in agriculture in the French Midi has developed into a *regional* crisis, while the threat to steel production at Ravenscraig became a *Scottish* issue, mobilizing a broad coalition of defence. Where the threat to regional interests comes from European rather than national policies, it is not surprising that attention turns to means of influencing policy at that level. It is possible, indeed, that regional, national, and European interests may be mutually divergent, raising the question of how each is to be articulated in the process of Community decision-making and how Community decisions are to be implemented.

Three sets of issues are examined in the chapters. First, the influence of regional interests, both governmental and private, on the Community's decision-making process. This involves tracing channels of influence, direct and indirect, and assessing their importance. Second, the administration of the Community's own regional policies and, in the chapter by Martins and Mawson, the framing of these policies in Brussels. Third, the use made of Community regional policies by regional interests, national governments, and the Community itself. It must be emphasized that we have not attempted an economic evaluation of the *impact* of Community policies which would be beyond our scope. We would, in any case, further emphasize that the weight of our analysis is on the first set of issues, the way in which regional interests are articulated in the Community. Much publicity has been given to the Community's regional and social funds and much argument has raged around them. They are, however, extremely small in size and there is a danger of their distracting attention from the wider question of the thrust of general Community policy and its uneven regional impact.

Policy Networks

To locate the points at which regional influence might be felt, it will be useful to sketch out the decision-making institutions of the Community. These bring together, first and foremost, states, though they also give expression to a wider 'European' interest and, to some extent, sectoral and constituency interests. The most important decision-making body is the Council, commonly known as the Council of Ministers, which promulgates Community laws and approves the budget and other major decisions. Consisting of ministers sent from national governments according to the subject on the agenda of any particular meeting, it expresses essentially national interests, bargaining and compromising as necessary to reach agreement. It is because of the importance of the Council of Ministers that the most promising route for regional interests to gain expression is through national governments.

The Commission is appointed by member governments for a fixed term of four years but, once appointed, members become custodians of the 'European interest', cutting their ties of loyalty to their own national governments. In practice, matters may not be as clear-out as this and Commissioners have been known to take a keen interest in the affairs of their native regions. It is the Commission which has the responsibility for initiating Community policy, formulating proposals for decision by the Council of Ministers. This involves an elaborate process of consultation with national governments, advisory bodies, and interest groups at national and European levels, giving opportunities in principle for regional interests to have a say, if they are able to find a way through the complexities. However, pressures from a single regional interest group would be unlikely to carry weight and the Commission encourages approaches through national and, especially European-wide groupings. We examine the position of interest groups below. The other roles of the Commission are in policy implementation and law enforcement. All the contributions to this volume show that subnational administrations have been drawn into the implementation of European policies, in varied ways depending on the territorial division of functions in any given state. Such arrangements are at the discretion of national governments, particularly where the Commission is acting through directives, addressed to member states. Though the chapters do show that approaches have from time to time been made by subnational administrations directly to the Commission, for example by Scottish local authorities, these are virtually doomed without the support of the national government.

The Committee of Permanent Representatives (COREPER) consisting of ambassadors from the member states, acts as a link between member governments and the Commission and often settles issues of a less contentious nature before they come to the Council of Ministers. There is no place here for the articulation of regional interests, though COREPER my be a useful way to find out what is happening or about to happen in the Community.

The European Court of Justice is the final authority on questions of European Law. It raises no issues of regional influence, though concern has been expressed from time to time about the need for it to include members of the Scottish bench.

The European Parliament, directly elected since 1979, is a natural focus for subnational pressures as it is quite independent of member governments and highly politicized. However, the extent of territorial representation varies from France, where there is a single national constituency with voting for party lists, to the United Kingdom which elects MEPs for single member constituencies using the first-past-the-post system, except for Northern Ireland which is a single constituency electing three members by proportional representation.

Table 1.1. Methods of Election to European Parliament, 1984

Belgium	Regional list system of PR. Country divided into one Flemish and one Walloon constituency, with Brussels voters able to vote in either.
Denmark	National list system of proportional representation.
France	National list system of proportional representation. No party with under 5% of vote can qualify.
W. Germany	Parties can choose between national or regional lists for proportional representation.
Greece	National list system of proportional representation.
Ireland	Single transferable vote system in four multi-member constituencies.
Italy	Regional list system of proportional representation, with five regional constituencies.
Luxembourg	National list system of proportional representation.
Netherlands	National list system of proportional representation.
United Kingdom	First-past-the-post system for 78 constituencies in Britain. Single transferable vote system for three-seat constituency of Northern Ireland.

[handwritten left margin: non probabilian]

[handwritten annotation below United Kingdom row: PR (PMS)]

Clearly, where there is a territorial basis to representation in the Parliament, the opportunities for subnational administrations and pressure groups to influence members are enhanced though, as Mény's chapter shows, even in France a convention has developed to provide effective regional representation on national party lists.

The major limitation on the Parliament as a vehicle for effectively articulating subnational interests is its lack of powers. It has extensive debating and scrutiny functions and can reject the budget or, by a two-thirds majority, dismiss the whole Commission. However, it lacks power to amend policy or budgetary proposals where these involve 'compulsory' spending or to hold the Council of Ministers accountable. Direct elections were intended to bolster the Parliament's political weight and it has undoubtedly become more assertive in recent years but, in the absence of formal powers, it must remain marginal to the centres of decision-making.

Finally, there is the elaborate network of consultative committees surrounding the institutions of the Community. The Economic and Social Committee, established by the Treaty of Rome, groups industrialists, trade unionists, farmers, consumers, and others appointed on the nomination of member governments. Other consultative committees have since been established to cover specialized aspects of Community affairs. Draft Commission proposals are submitted to these consultative bodies before consideration in the Council of Ministers. In effect their membership is nominated by national interest groups though where, as in Scotland, there is a well-developed network of independent groups below the level of the member state, these may gain representation. Interest groups also gain expression through European federations which may have direct consultative status with the Commission. Once again, these bring together national groups though, where there are several groups in one state, all may be represented. In agriculture, for example, several states have more than one farmers' union, all seeking access to Community decision-makers. However, the UK is unusual in having *geographically* separate farming unions so allowing territorial agricultural interests to be articulated.

Although the Commission has traditionally favoured the formation of Europe-wide interest groupings to encourage a *communautaire* perspective on policy issues, these have often found great difficulty reaching the necessary consensus. Consequently, the Commission has relaxed its rule and started to talk more with national groups.[7] These in turn are often in tune with the views of national governments. This weakening of the European, as against the national, dimension of policy-making may have reduced the scope for distinct regional interests to gain expression where they differ from those of national governments and national groups.

In the chapters which follow, we show states with a variety of regional institutions and means for articulating regional interests. To simplify matters somewhat, we can group them into three types. First, there are those states, namely West Germany and Italy, where elected regional government has been established. Here regional interests have, potentially, a variety of channels of influence: (a) through the regional (or *Land*) government, and then the national government, to Brussels; (b) through the national government only to Brussels; (c) through the regional government and then directly to Brussels; (d) directly to Brussels, perhaps via a national or European interest grouping. Regional governments themselves also have the choice of channels. Given the predominance of national governments in Community decision-making, channels (a) and (b), where available, are likely to be the most fruitful. Indeed, it may be that a high degree of functional decentralization to regional governments could, in the absence of linkage mechanisms, reduce the scope for regional influence on Community affairs. In practice, the trend in states with systems of federal or regional government has been for functional differentiation between tiers of government to give way to complex patterns of co-operation, negotiation, and accommodation.[8]

In the Italian case, as Merloni shows, functional differentiation has never become a reality and regional government has developed from the start as a means of channelling regional demands to the centre rather than as a source of independent policy-making. Membership of the Community may simply have reinforced this trend by requiring agriculture, formally a largely regional responsibility, to be handled nationally to provide the Italian input into Community agricultural policy and to ensure the implementation of that policy within Italy. In Germany, too, Community membership has probably had a centralizing effect but one which went in the direction of existing trends. The implications of this are examined in Jones's conclusion. In Germany the need for *Land*-Community links has been recognized in the institution of the *Landerbeobachter* though, as Gerstenlauer shows, his role is necessarily limited, with complex patterns of intergovernmental relations developing informally. Potential problems in the German arrangements have also been avoided because few of the *Länder* have the same interest in shifting Community policy radically as the vine-growers of Languedoc, Scots fishermen, or textile producers in Northern Ireland.

Second, there are those countries which have neither elected regional governments nor powerful decentralized arms of central government—the Republic of Ireland and England. Ireland is included in this volume, though it is a member state and not a region of one because, in the *European* perspective, it shows some parallels with regions of the larger states. For the purposes of the European Regional Development Fund, the whole of the Republic is an assisted 'region', allowing the government, as Hart shows, to break down the distinction between national and regional policies. Having gained its independence from Britain, Eire is also a model for separatist movements in other parts of the European periphery, who may jealously eye its seat in the Council of Ministers and generous representation in the European Parliament. In England the weak articulation of regional interests and their lack of an institutional expression has meant that, as Martins and Mawson show, the Community has had to push the

EC responsible for devolution? [handwritten marginalia]

national government into adopting a regional framework for the delivery of European policies. France is a case apart. Indirectly elected regional Councils have existed since 1972 with planning and economic responsibilities but until recently the French state has rigorously excluded them from any involvement in European policy; conversely, France has gone further than any other state in effectively excluding the Community from any influence in its regional policy, regarding not only regional but also social fund moneys as simply part of the national pool. However, Mény suggests that the current decentralization programme, which includes provision for the direct election of regional Councils, will change the picture.

Third, there is the case of the peripheral nations of the United Kingdom with special arrangements for decentralized administration in the form of the Scottish, Welsh, and Northern Ireland offices. The offices are an integral part of UK central government, represented in Cabinet and its committees and so able to play a part in the making of European policy. Their role here is to defend and promote the interests of their own areas, as they do in domestic policy, forming a part of a policy network linking Scottish, Welsh, and Northern Ireland concerns to the UK political arena.[9] Their effectiveness varies, being greatest in the case of the Scottish Office which is well represented both on Cabinet committees and in UK ministerial teams at the Council of Ministers. This has allowed important Scottish interests, for example those of the fishermen, an effective voice in Community policy. The existence of the Scottish Office has also encouraged the development of a range of Scottish interest groups which in turn can approach Europe through it or through UK or European interest-group federations. In Wales and Northern Ireland this phenomenon is much less developed. This is not, of course, to say that the Scottish arrangements are ideal. Privileged access to UK government and thence to Brussels is a valuable asset for those groups who have the government's ear and are able to present a 'Scottish' case which does not contravene the political line of the government of the day. The responsiveness of the Scottish Office to Scottish demands, however, is constrained by the fact of its being a department in an essentially centralized system of government, subject to powerful 'policy leadership' from other departments and, of course, to the policy line of the governing party.

The Community and Regional Policies

In the early years, it was widely assumed that the Common Market would generate enough growth to solve regional economic problems without specific measures.[10] The only regional policy instrument specifically included in the Treaty of Rome at Italy's insistence was the European Investment Bank. However, as early as the Treaty of Paris, establishing the European Coal and Steel Community, it had been recognized that exceptions would have to be made to the provision banning in principle all subsidies to the coal and steel industries[11] and in practice subsidies have been allowed on regional grounds. Since then, European regional policies have been developed along three main lines: first, the co-ordination of national regional policy measures to ensure their conformity to the treaties; second, the creation and development of Community funds for the purposes of regional economic development; third, a series of halting moves towards a positive European regional policy, taking into account the regional impact of general Community policy and drawing together the various regional policy instruments behind coherent and purposive programmes.

As we have noted, the Treaty of Paris in principle banned national aids to the coal and steel industries. The Treaty of Rome, establishing the European Economic Community, was less restrictive. National regional aids could be introduced with the consent of the Commission provided these were aimed at regions with an abnormally low standard of living or high unemployment or aimed at promoting regional development.[12] Significantly, it is the Commission Directorate for Competition Policy which, with the advice of the Regional Policy Directorate, takes the lead role in this. In 1971 the system was formalized, with a requirement for aids to be transparent and quantifiable and in 1975 ceilings were fixed for specific regions of the community. As confirmed in 1979, these were: 100 per cent of the cost of investment up to 13,000 ECUs for the Italian Mezzogiorno, the Republic of Ireland and Northern Ireland, 30 per cent up to 5,500 ECUs for Scotland, Wales, Northern and South-West England, South-West France and central Italy: 25 per cent up to 4,500 ECUs for the eastern border regions of the German Federal Republic; 20 per cent up to 3,500 ECUs elsewhere.

The European Investment Bank has a capital subscribed by member states and can borrow on the open market. It makes loans at commercial rates for three types of project. In order of priority, these are: projects in underdeveloped regions; projects concerning more than one member state; and industrial reconstruction, for example in coal, steel, and shipbuilding areas. Although the EIB operates on a commercial basis, it is often able to borrow at favourable rates on the international markets, passing the benefits on to its clients. It can be approached directly by public authorities in member states and has been used particularly heavily for projects in the Italian Mezzogiorno and in Scotland.[13]

The European Social Fund (ESF) was established by the Treaty of Rome in order to help deal with the employment consequences of industrial change, notably by retraining. From 1972 it was developed to tie in more closely with the needs of sectoral and regional reconstruction. It was laid down that priority regions should get 50 per cent of the funds, though in the event they have received something like 80 per cent. Applications to the Fund are presented by member states which must agree to provide matching funds but there are no national quotas. This means that energetic users of the Fund can gain a disproportionate advantage, though at the risk of some political backlash. As the chapters show, member states very considerably in their use of the ESF. In France the moneys disappear into the general revenue; in the UK, on the other hand, they are treated as 'additional' but only when they go to local authorities. This has led some British local authorities to make quite heavy use of the Fund for employment subsidy schemes, making up the matching funding from the limited rate poundage which they are free to spend on the general benefit of their areas. This enabled them to do so well out of the Fund that in 1983 it was only with great difficulty that that money was found to meet all the requirements. Recent reforms give priority to schemes tackling youth employment but with 40 per cent earmarked for six 'super priority' regions. Submissions will still have to come through national governments, but subnational authorities will be able, as at present, to initiate projects and to make informal contacts with the Commission to sound out the possibilities for funding.

The European Regional Development Fund was established in 1975 following the accession of the UK, Ireland, and Denmark. In principle, it awards grants to public or private organizations in depressed or underdeveloped regions for industrial or infrastructure investment. It is administered by a Fund Management Committee which vets applications for conformity to the Fund regulations. In practice, the

Fund's work has been governed by the existence of national quotas and national 'additionality rules'. The bulk of the Fund is distributed according to a formula giving a fixed percentage to each member state. The regions which can benefit from the Fund are those in which member states themselves grant regional aid.

However, the additionality principle, applied by all member states, means that moneys received from the fund are not allowed to be added to national aids but, rather, are used to reimburse them. So generally it is the national government and not the region itself which benefits; though there may be some advantage to local governments if they receive a proportion of capital expenditures as a grant rather than having to borrow. In defence of the additionality rule, it is argued that the ERDF, by reimbursing national governments for regional policy expenditures, allows the latter to be higher than they would otherwise have been. This, of course, is unprovable; it is equally plausible to argue that the extra funding allows a reduction in the Public Sector Borrowing Requirement or increases in some other item of spending. It is also argued that to allow additionality would risk allowing some projects to exceed the Community's own aid ceilings, by cumulating national and European aids.

Certainly, the question of additionality has vexed all discussions of the working of ERDF and given rise to both confusion and controversy. In some member states, such as the UK, great publicity is given to the award to ERDF grants to industrial projects, though the firm receives no extra money, or to infrastructure projects funded by central government, though the budget of the recipient department remains unaltered. Keating and Waters point to some of the confusion this has caused in Scotland. In France, on the other hand, Mény shows that ERDF funding is not given prominence, in order to avoid taking credit from the national government.

While member states have striven to retain control of ERDF moneys and to treat them as part of their own national budgets, the Commission has sought to develop the Fund as an instrument for a genuinely European regional policy, as Martins, Mawson and Gibney show. Projects are vetted by the Fund Management Committee, advised by the Regional Policy Directorate and it does happen that some infrastructure projects are regarded as not related to regional development and some industrial projects are regarded as ineligible for sectoral reasons. In these cases the member state may be advised to withdraw the application or it may be turned down by the Committee.

The degree of choice in projects open to the Commission and the Fund Management Committee, however, is limited by the fact that states tend to put in projects up to the amount of their quota, with only perhaps a small margin to ensure a continuous throughput. Even the priority and timing of projects is largely to suit the convenience of member states, whose major interest is in getting the money back as soon as possible. As money is only paid when the projects have started, their priority is dependent on the date of commencement of already scheduled programmes.

Another way in which the Commission tries to control the policy is through the requirement for Regional Development Programmes (RDPs), to which individual applications must conform, though Mawson, Martins and Gibney show, these have been of limited value. The most recent changes in the ERDF are described in the next chapter.

The European Coal and Steel Community (ECSC) is concerned with mitigating the effects of change in those industries and providing alternative jobs for redundant workers. In designated areas, it can make available a wide range of benefits relating to retraining, housing, and support for redundant workers.

The Guidance Section of the European Agricultural and Guidance Fund (EAGGF) provides assistance for the modernization and improvement of agriculture, fishing and related industries. This is of particular value in declining agricultural regions.

Further, the Community has developed other major facilities to enable loans to be obtained at low interest rates for major national and regional development projects which promote Community integration and attack unemployment, low levels of industrial investment and weak economic performance. Such loans are raised and distributed under the provisions of the New Community Investment (NCI or Ortoli Facility). Members of the European Monetary System (EMS) which the UK has not yet joined, qualify for interest subsidies on these loans.

There are also a number of schemes for assisting research and development in such technical fields as nuclear energy, environmental and climatological research and recycling of waste.

Finally, there are the efforts by the Commission to develop a more active regional policy of its own and to develop a wider appreciation of the regional impact of Community policies as a whole. There is a Task Force in the Regional Policy Directorate which has the responsibility for monitoring the regional impact of the various funds and proposing ways in which they can be better integrated. Their data base employs three levels: 'regions', such as Scotland or English standard regions, a level corresponding to English counties, and travel-to-work areas. Work has also been done on the regional impact of the Agricultural Guarantee Fund, concluding that its impact was 'anti-regional' and regressive. So far, however, this work has involved only input studies of the destination of Community funds rather than impact studies on the effect of policies.

Another initiative has been Integrated Operations, pioneered in Naples and Belfast and now being proposed in other parts of the Community. These have not so far involved the commitment of extra resources but rather the co-ordination of existing funds behind programmes of work. It has, however, been possible in the case of Belfast to use the Integrated Operation to extend the use of funds to cover previously ineligible matters such as housing. Since 1983 a spate of approaches for Integrated Operations has come to the Commission, notably from industrial areas in the UK but also from rural areas in France and Italy. As the only new money available has been for feasibility studies for the Integrated Operations, there has been no objection by national governments to direct approaches from regional and local governments, though the co-operation of the national government will invariably be essential for the launching and running of the Operations themselves.

So far, as we have said, Integrated Operations have not involved any extra funds or, indeed, radically new policy initiatives. They will assume greater importance in the context of the reform of the ERDF and ESF currently under way, as shown by Mawson, Martins and Gibney in Chapter Two.

There are also Integrated Development Programmes, in the Western Isles, Lozère in France and south-east Belgium. There has been some money available in these programmes which might otherwise have gone elsewhere, though it has not proved possible to relax the eligibility requirements of the main funds or to get round the national 'additionality' rules.

In 1983 the European Council (that is, the summit meeting) asked the Commission to formulate proposals for increasing the effectiveness of the Community's structural funds; these were defined as the Guidance Section of the Agricultural Fund, the Social Fund, and the Regional Development Fund. The Report[14] published in July 1983, insisted that the funds should henceforth be used in order to further

Community policies and not simply to serve to finance national policies or redistribute resources between states. So the Commission, representing the 'community interest', must have a role in decision-making on aided schemes. To make this possible, it was recommended that future fund assistance should be given on the basis of programmes and not individual projects; that assistance should be targeted on key regions and key policy priorities; and that the level of Community financing of joint projects should be increased in order to enhance the Community's influence in them. Policy priorities for each of the three funds were suggested and proposals already tabled for reform of the Social Fund (see above) and the Regional Development Fund (see Chapter 2) reiterated. Proposals were made for co-ordinating the work of the funds, to ensure complementarity and avoid waste; and for monitoring, ex-ante assessment, and evaluation of schemes. Finally, an increase in the size of the funds was called for. The lengthy nego-tiations on the reform of the Regional Development Fund are described by Mawson, Martins and Gibney in Chapter Two. As they show, member states have continued to oppose the development of a genuine Community regional policy, fearing that this could strengthen the European and regional as against the national perspective and bring regional and local levels of administration more closely into European policy formulation, an issue taken up in the final chapter of this volume.

Community funds, their significance, and the use made of them have generated a great deal of controversy, as all our chapters show. Their importance should not be exaggerated. It has been calculated[15] that Community assistance is equivalent to the following proportions of national expenditure in the relevant fields:

Agricultural Fund, Guidance Section	6.5 per cent
Regional Development Fund (Productive Investment)	4 to 6 per cent
Social Fund (Vocational Training)	10 to 12 per cent

The more important theme of the book is the articulation of regional interests right across the Community's policy field and it is to this that we have asked our contributors to give their main attention.

Notes

1. Y. Meny (ed.), *Dix ans de régionalisation en Europe* (Paris: Cujas, 1981).

2. M. Keating, 'The Debate on Regional Reform', in B. W. Hogwood and M. Keating (eds.), *Regional Government in England* (Oxford: Clarendon Press, 1982).

3. M. Crozier and E. Friedberg, *L'Acteur et le système* (Paris: Seuil, 1979).

4. Regional Studies Association, *Report of an Enquiry into Regional Problems in the United Kingdom* (Norwich: Geo, 1983).

5. J. B. Jones and M. Keating, 'The British Labour Party. Centralisation and Devolution', in P. Madgwick and R. Rose (eds.), *The Territorial Dimension in UK Policies* (London: Macmillan, 1982).

6. e.g. J.-P. Worms, 'La Décentralisaiton: Une Stratégie Socialiste de Changement Sociale', *Recherche Sociale*, 75 (1980).

7. A. Butt Philip, 'Pressure Groups and Policy Making in the European Community', in J. Lodge (ed.), *Institutions and Policies of the European Communities* (London: Frances Pinter, 1983).

8. K. Hanf and F. W. Scharpf (eds.), *Interorganisational Policy Making* (London: Sage, 1978). D. S. Wright, *Understanding Intergovernmental Relations* (Massachusetts: Duxbury Press, 1978).

9. M. Keating and A. Midwinter, *The Government of Scotland* (Edinburgh: Mainstream, 1983).

10. S. George, 'Regional Policy', in J. Lodge (ed.), *Institutions and Policies of the European Communities* (London: Frances Pinter, 1983).

11. P. Romus, *L'Europe et les régions* (Paris: Cujas, 1979).

12. Ibid.

13. Ibid.

14. Commission of the European Communities, *Report and Proposals on Ways of Increasing the Effectiveness of the Community's Structural Funds*, COM (83) 501 final (Brussels, 1983).

15. Ibid.

2

The Development of the European Community Regional Policy

JOHN MAWSON, MARIO RUIS MARTINS, and JOHN T. GIBNEY

Introduction

In seeking to understand the nature of EC Regional Policy it is important to appreciate as the Commissioner for Regional Policy has observed some years ago that the programme has always been an 'accompanying measure' developed to cope with the detrimental effects or negative consequences of the main Community policies.[1] The existence of regional disparities in the Community has never in itself been a sufficient reason for the development of a Common Regional Policy (CRP). Significant geographical variations in the level of development were apparent from the inception of the community but it was not until the mid-1970s that an explicit regional package emerged. The development of the CRP must therefore be interpreted within the context of the evolution of the Community as a whole and in particular in terms of the internal decision making process, or 'Community method' by which conflicts between member states are resolved. Given this perspective, it is apparent that two sets of factors are of significance in explaining the development of the CRP. On the one hand, the first process of enlargement of the Community in the early 1970s, to include Denmark, Ireland and the United Kingdom, which was accompanied by efforts to achieve an economic and monetary union. Secondly, the current process of restructuring of the Community budget, which occurs against the background of a severe economic crisis and has to anticipate the financial consequences of the second enlargement of the Community to include Greece, Portugal and Spain. In this chapter we examine the evolution of the CRP in this wider political context.

The Period Leading to the Creation of the ERDF

The original treaties of the European Communities (ECSC, EEC, and

20

Table 2.1. Financing Instruments — Main Characteristics

Instrument	Legal Basis	Aim	Type of Aid
EAGGF Guarantee Section	EEC Treaty art. 40 Regulations EEC 17/64 and 355/77	Purchasing of agricultural products at a guarantee price. Rebates on exports of agricultural products to third countries	Subsidies to cover guarantee prices decided annually by the Council of Ministers
EAGGF Guidance Section	EEC Treaty art. 40 Regulations EEC 17/64 and 268/ to 276/75	Improvement of production and commercial agricultural structures. Aid to hill-farming and less favoured agricultural areas	Subsidies ranging from 25 per cent to 50 per cent of eligible investment
European Investment Bank (EIB)	EEC Treaty arts. 129 and 130	Projects for: developing less developed regions; modernising or reconverting undertakings; the common interest of various member states	Loans of up to 50 per cent of the cost of the investment eligible and made at commercial interest rates
European Social Fund (ESF)	EEC Treaty arts. 123 to 126 Decisions EEC 66/71 and 801/77	Vocational retraining and payment of wages to workers affected by conversion or closures of industrial undertakings	Subsidies of up to 50 per cent of the costs involved in the operation
ECSC Fund	ECSC Treaty art. 54.1	Projects for restructuring the coal and steel industries	Loans with interest rebates of up to 3 per cent on commercial rates of interest
ECSC Fund	ECSC Treaty art. 54.2	Construction and modernisation of coal and steel workers' dwellings	Loans at 1 per cent interest rates
ECSC Fund	ECSC Treaty art. 56.2a	Creation of new economic activities in areas of reconversion of coal and steel industries	Loans with interest rebates of up to 3 per cent on commercial rates of interest
ECSC	ECSC Treaty	Payments of tide-over resettlement allowances and vocational training to redundant coal and steel workers	Subsidies of 50 per cent of the cost involved

Source: Local Government Studies: July/August 1980 [33].

EURATOM) contained a number of features which reflected the desire for positive integration. These elements were particularly evident in the EEC treaty where explicit provisions were made for common policies in the field of agriculture, transport, monetary, and social services (articles 1, 2, and 3). However, despite the fact that the Treaty of Rome stated that the signatories were: 'anxious to strengthen the unity of their economies and to ensure their harmonious development by reducing and differences existing between the various regions and the backwardness of the less favoured regions', no specific reference was made to the establishment of a Common Regional Policy.[2] Instead, during the period up to enlargement of the Community in 1972, efforts were restricted to the co-ordination of national/regional policies and to the application of Community financial instruments which had a regional impact. These instruments included the European Agricultural Guarantee and Guidance Fund (EAGGF), the European Social Fund (ESF), and the loans and subsidies provided by the European Coal and Steel Community (ECSC). The Treaty of Rome also created the European Investment Bank with the specific aim of assisting projects in less developed regions (see Table 2.1).

In 1973 the European Commission published the results of a study which examined the geographical distribution of these various forms of assistance in relation to the overall levels of prosperity in the Community. This work was significant because it examined not only those instruments which had an explicit geographical allocation but also estimated the regional distribution of the ESF and the guarantee section of the EAGGF (from 1954 to 1972 the Guarantee Section of the EAGGF accounted for 70 per cent of total Community financial commitments).[3] The overall picture which emerged from the EEC report was one of a set of relatively disconnected instruments in which: 'the regions which benefited the most from Community financing were not always the ones most in need of regional development assistance' (Table 2.2).[4] The need to develop policy instruments more specifically related to regional problems was emphasized in various reports and documents prepared by the European Parliament and Commission in the period prior to enlargement. It was not, however, until the mid-1970s that the CRP finally emerged and this can be attributed to wider political pressures, particularly the process of enlargement. At the Summit meeting in the Hague in 1969, the Heads of State of the six countries accepted as a goal for Community development, the creation

Table 2.2. Per Capita Distribution of Community Financing

Country	Loans per head Units of account	Loans per head EEC 6 = 100	Subsidies per head Units of account	Subsidies per head EEC 6 = 100	Total per head Units of account	Total per head EEC 6 = 100	GDP[a] per head Units of account	GDP[a] per head EEC 6 = 100
Federal Republic of Germany	17	81	47	67	64	70	3,114	129
France	18	86	93	132	111	122	2,770	114
Italy	31	147	52	74	83	91	1,653	68
Netherlands	11	52	160	228	171	188	2,505	104
Blegium	21	100	86	122	107	119	2,650	110
Luxembourg	49	234	38	54	87	96	2,935	116
Community	21	100	70	100	91	100	2,529	100

[a] Current prices and exchange rates, 1971.

Source: EC Commission (1973): Final Report of the Study on the European Communities Interventions with Regional Impact (1954–72) (Batelle, Centre de Recherche de Genéve).

of an Economic and Monetary Union (EMU) and the opening of negotiations with various EFTA member states to enlarge the Community.
These key decisions brought a new political focus to bear on the Community and were important in determining the form and content of the
CRP which finally emerged in 1975.

By the end of the 1960s it was clear that previous attempts to co-
ordinate the economic and monetary policies of the independent
member states had largely failed. The 1969 devaluation of the French
franc and the revaluation of the German mark threatened not only
Community monetary stability but also undermined its corner-stone,
the Common Agricultural Policy. There was, moreover, a lobby
within the Community which strongly supported the move towards
stricter co-ordination of monetary and economic policies as a step
towards overall political integration.

The Werner report which considered the mechanics of integration in
1970, argued that two processes were necessary in order to achieve
EMU: firstly, a narrowing of the margins of adjustment of the
exchange rates between member states' currencies and, secondly, an
increased co-ordination of national economic policies.[5] As far as
regional problems were concerned the move towards EMU was seen as
having serious consequences unless countervailing action was taken.
To begin with, it would prevent the member countries from devaluing
their currencies in order to protect low-productivity sectors and
regions. Furthermore, according to the conventional theory of
economic integration, factor prices (labour and capital) would tend to
equalize between various regions and therefore discriminate not only
against low productivity areas but also undermine the chances of
natural self-correcting mechanisms (emigration, etc.). Not surprisingly in the final communiqué of the Paris Summit in 1972 the reaf-
firmation of the commitment to EMU was coupled with strong support
for a CRP.

The Paris Summit was the first occasion when the representatives of
the three new member states were included in the process of Community decision-making and it is clear that the British Prime Minister,
Edward Heath, played a major role in shifting the emphasis towards
regional policy. The reasons for this are not difficult to see. At the time
of enlargement the Community was introducing a new system of
budget financing which was heavily biased towards levys on agricultural imports. With more the 70 per cent of Community's financing
commitments allocated to the Guarantee Section of the EAGGF it was

clear that Britain would soon become a heavy net contributor to the Community budget. The creation of a regional development fund provided one means of alleviating the detrimental effects of the Community's financial mechanisms and of counteracting the anti-EC lobby in the UK. The regional development fund was also strongly supported by another new member state, Ireland, and so the issue seemed resolved.

In the event, however, the only recommendation of the Paris Summit communiqué which was immediately implemented was the preparation of the Thomson Report on the 'Regional Problems in the Enlarged Community'.[6] The move towards monetary union and co-ordination of national and regional economic policies was delayed by the aftermath of the Yom Kippur War and the energy crises. Attention was diverted from the regional question towards more urgent issues such as the need for a common energy policy. The failure to achieve a united front, in this field, undermined the relations between member states and the Community's ability to develop common policies.

A second factor which delayed the introduction of the CRP was the particular difficulty of resolving the conflicting interests of member states in this area of policy. Although the Treaty of Rome established that decisions on a wide range of issues could be taken by majority vote in the Council, a subsequent decision meant that in practice there was a unanimity rule for almost every decision (budget and agricultural issues excepted). This was the direct result of the French walkout from the Council meetings in 1965 for a period of seven months because of its disagreement with a package of proposals submitted by the Commission. In the end the French were only persuaded to return after a compromise was reached by which a unanimous agreement was required for every decision 'where very important interests are at stake'. The unanimity rule presented major problems in a discriminatory policy field, such as regional policy, where it was not easy to identify clear advantage for all member states. The situation was further complicated because arguments over the net direction of financial flows were coupled with a concern about the mechanisms controlling resource allocation.[7]

Eventually, after two years of negotiation, a Community regional policy came into being with the establishment of the European Regional Development Fund. The detailed process of negotiation had revolved round three main issues; the size of the fund, the definition of the areas eligible for assistance, and the mechanism for allocating assistance among the member states. Taking first of all the question of the fund itself, it was held by the proponents of Regional Policy that it should be of sufficient size to counteract the negative consequences of economic and monetary union. The original suggestion by the Commission of 3,000 m. units of account for a three-year period, was of an order of magnitude appropriate to the nature of the problem. However, the hard line adopted by the Germans resulted in a final figure of 1.300 m. units of account at the Paris Summit in December 1974.[8] On the question of which regions should receive assistance, the Thomson Report had suggested areas with either high emigration, persistent unemployment, declining industries, or agricultural employment above the Community average. The German proposals of 1973, on the other hand, recommended concentrating aid in regions with GDP per capital 20 per cent below the Community average. In the end it was clear that the only politically acceptable solution would be to take advantage of those areas defined by member states for their own national regional policies.

On the process of allocating the fund between countries, there was also a shift from the original proposals which had given the Commission a considerable measure of discretion. This was unacceptable to the French and so the final solution was to establish a system of fixed quotas negotiated periodically by Member States. As far as the operation of the fund was concerned, applications made by the appropriate departments of the member governments were to fall within one of a specified number of categories, broadly, industrial investment and infrastructure. Decisions concerning which projects were to be supported were vested in the Fund Management Committee, comprising representatives from Member States and the Commission (see next section).

The package adopted by the Council during 1975 and 1976 also involved the setting up of a Regional Policy Committee[9] whose primary function was to seek a co-ordination of the regional policies of the member states. Its tasks in particular were to examine problems relating to regional development, progress in tackling these, and policy measures required to achieve the Community's regional objectives. In this context the Regional Policy Committee approved in October 1975 the outline for Regional Development Programmes.[10] These documents were to be submitted on a regular and updated basis by national governments in order to be eligible for ERDF support for their assisted regions. By setting out in a common format the nature of regional problems and specifying the regional measures being pursued (in each member state) it was hoped that they would provided the Commission with an overall and coherent perspective on regional imbalances in the community and a mechanism for the more efficient allocation of ERDF assistance.

Evolution of the Common Regional Policy from 1975 onwards

By the mid-1970s the basic elements of the Community's regional policy had emerged. In summary three interrelated strands of development can be identified: first, the co-ordination of the national regional policies of member states; second, the attempt to make other Community policies and financing instruments more sensitive to regional disparities; third, the establishment of specific Community regional policy instruments.

On the co-ordination of regional policy, Community efforts have been concerned with the design and enforcement of general rules with which national-regional systems of aid are to comply. These rules establish aid ceilings for various parts of the Community territory as well as a method for evaluating the level of assistance to industrial firms. The first set of rules was introduced in 1971 and modifications were made in 1975 and 1979 (see Table 2.3.).

Another aspect of the co-ordination activities of the Community concerns the role of the Regional Policy Committee which since 1975 has played a significant role in all aspects of the CRP. Most significantly from the point of view of co-ordination, it has been responsible for the development of the system of Regional Development Programmes (RDPs) as mentioned above. A further element in the co-ordination activities of the Community concerns the sponsorship and publication of a number of comparative studies of the national-regional policies operated by member states.[11]

In relation to the second evolutionary strand in the CRP, successive modifications have been introduced in the *modus operandi* of the Community's major financing instruments such as the European Social Fund and the European Investment Bank in order to ensure that Community activities in general are sensitive to regional problems. These changes have sought to enhance the regional impact of the main instruments against a background of criticism that their use was neither adequately co-ordinated nor directed to the most needy areas.[12] A recent attempt to take such initiatives a stage further has involved the intro-

Table 2.3. The Community Ceilings for Regional Aid
(Ceilings are expressed as percentages of the initial investment or a fixed amount of EUA per job created.)

Ceiling	Regions
None	Greenland
75 per cent or 13,000 EUA per job created[a]	Ireland, Mezzogiorno, Northern Ireland, West Berlin, and the French Overseas Departments.
30 per cent or 5,500 EUA per job created (where not exceeding 40 per cent of the initial investment)	French territory which receives Regional Employment Premium, aided Italian areas of Friulia-Venezia, Giulia, Trentino-Alto Adige, Val d'Aosta, Lazio, Marche, Toscana, Umbria and Veneto, British Development and Special Development Areas (other than Northern Ireland)
25 per cent or 4,500 EUA per job created (where not exceeding 30 per cent of the initial investment)	Federal Republic of Germany 'Zonenrandgebiet'; Danish-assisted areas (North Jutland and the islands of Bjornsholm, Acro, Samso, and Langeland)
20 per cent or 3,500 EUA per job created (where not exceeding 25 per cent of the initial investment)	Other regions of the Community

[a] Plus an additional of 25 per cent or 4,500 EUA per job created spread over the minimum of the first five years of the investment for projects exceeding 3 m EUA.

Source: Commission Communication to the Council of 21 Dec. 1978, OJC in 31/79 of 3 Feb. 1979.

duction of planning exercises known as 'integrated operations' which seek to secure the co-ordination of various financing instruments in a few selected areas which are in receipt of substantial Community support. In line with this development the Community is also undertaking a series of systematic regional impact assessments of its main policies.

The first in the series, on the Common Agricultural Policy (CAP) has shown that the distribution of expenditures under the CAP clearly discriminates against the weaker agricultural regions of the Community which are, at the same time some of its poorer areas. This is the result of two main factors. On the one hand, the support prices for the Guarantee section of the EAGGF are biased in favour of the products (cereal milk, sugar) from the northern regions at the expense of those southern areas whose economy is based on fruit, vegetables, and wine production. On the other hand, the systems of such support prices directly link EAGGF support with productivity levels which is, in turn, related to general economic development. Thus, as an expert commentator recently observed, 'the only substantial policy operated by the EEC which takes 75 per cent of its budget—has an inbuilt bias towards the richer regions'.[13]

The final strand in the development of the CRP concerns the attempts to develop common regional policy instrument. In this respect the establishment in 1975 of the European Regional Development Fund, 'intended to correct the principal regional imbalances within the Community resulting in particular from agricultural preponderance, industrial change and structural unemployment', was a turning-point. The ERDF was designed to finance investments in industrial, handicraft, or service activities, thereby creating new jobs or protecting those already existing; it also covered investments in infrastructure directly linked with the previous activities or in less-favoured mountainous areas. With regard to infrastructure the Fund was limited in practice to financing 'economic' projects such as roads, ports, airports telecommunications, water and sewerage, electricity, gas, and industrial sites.

The legislative developments of 1975 constituted a crucial moment in the development of the CRP and it is, therefore, necessary to reiterate that the ERDF was set up initially as a financing mechanism of support for the national-regional policies operated by the member states of the Community. Assistance from the fund could only be granted to investment projects submitted by national governments and located in areas eligible for national–regional policy assistance. Furthermore, aid from the ERDF had to be granted according to a system of fixed national quotas, with all member states receiving some assistance, irrespective of their relative prosperity. Several consequences have stemmed from this approach, perhaps the most significant being, that national control has prevailed over all the major aspects of the policy (designation of assisted areas, quotas, management of the Fund, etc.). A further consequence has been that regional problems have been seen primarily as residing within rather than between member states.[14]

From the outset the CRP, and the ERDF in particular, were subject to criticism. The fund was held to be too small and spread over too wide an area of the Community (covering some 60 per cent of the geographical area and 40 per cent of the population). The system of national quotas was considered too rigid and, moreover, inadequately related to the nature and seriousness of existing disparities. To many observers the ERDF was 'inadequate to a derisory degree'.[15]

The first years of operation of the ERDF revealed further shortcomings. The narrow 'economic' definition of infrastructure investment eligible for assistance proved too restrictive given the varying nature of regional problems throughout the Community; procedural difficulties in payments from the ERDF quickly gave rise to an increasing gap between payments authorized and those actually made. More fundamentally, it became obvious that national governments were using the ERDF as a partial reimbursement of their expenditure on regional policy instead of engaging in additional expenditure. Local authorities in certain member states, notably in the United Kingdom, complained of a lack of involvement in the operation of the CRP, and, moreover, the existence of a minimum size threshold (50,000 EUAs) for projects to qualify for the ERDF assistance proved unsatisfactory.

In 1979, in response to the criticisms and following a lengthy process of negotiations initiated some two years earlier, the Council of Ministers introduced a decision on guide-lines for the development of the CRP and a number of amendments to the regulation governing the CRP. The guide-lines, which did not carry the same statutory force as items contained within the ERDF Regulation itself, comprised three major features. First, a comprehensive system of analysis and policy formulation was to be introduced. For this purose the Commission would prepare a regular report on the social and economic development of the regions of the Community, which would serve as a basis for discussing the priorities and measures proposed by the Commission. Second, the Council recognized the need for a more detailed assessment of the regional impact of the main Community policies, when making its own decisions. Third, the Council considered that it was necessary to achieve closer co-ordination of the regional policies of individual member states. In this respect the new guide-lines recognized that the largely experimental system of RDPs created in 1975 provided the most appropriate framework for co-ordination between the national-regional policies of individual member states, and between these policies and the CRP.

The amendments to the ERDF regulation implied that the system of preparing these documents would play an increasingly important role in the operation of the CRP, since it was felt that this would enable the Community institutions to determine the priorities for assistance from the ERDF with more precision. However, the major innovation introduced by these amendments was the creation of a new 'quota-free' section of the ERDF which could be applied outside the nationally-designated areas of assistance. The size of this 'quota-free' section was fixed at 5 per cent of the total ERDF resources and it was decided that responsibility for the allocation of aid ought to rest with the Council of Ministers on the basis of unanimous decisions. One of the most important features of this non-quota section was that aid would be made available through the implementation of Community-defined special programmes (i.e. an integrated package of investment projects) rather than on the basis of nationally-submitted individual investment projects. The only major condition attached to this aid, which could be used outside the areas eligible for national–regional policy assistance, was that the programmes had to be jointly financed with national governments. Within the context of special regulations setting out types of problem region eligible for support and types of measures to be pursued, member states were required to forward applications to be examined by the Fund Management Committee and sent to the Council for final approval. With the creation of this new section, it was claimed that the ERDF was no longer merely a mechanism of support for national–regional policies but had taken on a specific Community dimension.

The amendments to the ERDF regulation also met some of the criticisms of the efficiency of its operation. The eligibility criteria for ERDF assistance for infrastructure investments were relaxed, opening up the possibility of financing such investments as hospitals, schools, technical colleges, and environmental improvement. The proportion of investments in infrastructure that could be financed by ERDF was raised from 30 per cent to 40 per cent in regions suffering from the most serious difficulties. Further, a system of accelerated payments was introduced with the aim of ensuring that claims for ERDF assistance were dealt with as rapidly as possible.

However, the amendments to the CRP introduced in 1979, while overcoming some of the procedural difficulties of the 1975 package, can be seen as marginal adjustments rather than a major step forward. The basic characteristics of the ERDF were not substantially altered by the introduction of the 5 per cent 'quota-free' section. Moreover because Community aid under this section of the fund has to be unanimously approved by the Council of Ministers, the approval of individual programmes has involved considerable political bargaining and compromise between member states and contributed to delays in their introduction.[16] There have been questions raised about effectiveness of the RDPs in strengthening the role of the CRP. To date there has been a tendency for member states to attach relatively little importance to the documents except in as far as their preparation is legally required by the Community to secure ERDF assistance.[17]

It is against this background that the Commission presented late in 1981 its proposals for a further revision of the ERDF regulation based on the statutory requirement to undertake a regular review every three years. The proposals were to go through two principal phases between 1981 and 1984. Before considering these developments it is useful to consider regional trends in the EEC and specifically the findings of the First Periodic Report on Socio-Economic Trends in the Regions of the Community as the intention of preparing these documents was to provide an input into the Commission's review process.[18]

Regional Trends in the European Community

In recent years there has been no shortage of research studies and reports on the issue of regional disparities in the Community although fewer offer significant insights into the causes of the problem. While the studies are not unanimous in their conclusions, some degree of consensus has emerged about the broad regional problems which the Community is experiencing and will have to face in the foreseeable future. The first periodic report usefully draws together the findings of a number of these studies, describing the principal economic trends in

Community regions and the deterioration in the situation of the weaker regions over the past decade.

It argues that these trends have to be seen within the context of the economic reversal of the 1970s and that the problems of the weaker regions are likely to persist. This is due not only to the poor growth prospects of member states but also to a number of new factors which it is argued are likely to threaten the cohesion of the Community as a whole. These include rising energy costs, rapid advances in technology, the increasing competitiveness of newly industrializing countries, and the impact of further enlargement.

In examining recent demographic trends in the Community the report notes three major developments. In the first place, there has been a slowing down in population growth due primarily to a fall in the birth rate. Second, reflecting the worsening economic climate, there has been a marked turn-about in migration flows from the backward agricultural regions of the Community which have traditionally exported their surplus labour. A final noticeable trend has been the shifting pattern of urbanization within Community regions. While urban population continues to grow in some of the peripheral regions such as southern France, southern Italy and Ireland, large cities throughout the Community are declining, either absolutely or relatively, in relation to their surrounding hinterlands. This decline is associated in the northern countries with forces of industrial restructuring and to a certain extent deindustrialization in which many of the major urban industrial areas have witnessed factory closures, contractions, disinvestment, and steeply rising unemployment.

Turning to the labour market, the most significant feature in the past few years has been the rise in unemployment from 2 per cent in 1970 to more than 8 per cent in 1981 (in August 1984 the level of Community unemployment stood at 11 per cent), due, according to the Report, not only to the present recession but also to the rapid increase in the labour force. In terms of the structure of employment, the 1970s saw a decline in the share of agricultural employment and output, a decline in manufacturing employment, static manufacturing output, and a compensating increase in employment and output in the tertiary sector. Before the mid-1960s increased manufacturing investment paralleled rising employment. However, since the early 1970s, while investment has continued to rise, manufacturing employment has fallen dramatically (2.5m. between 1970 and 1977). Looking to the future it is argued the outlook is gloomy, as the substitution of capital for labour is likely to continue and the report suggests that the tertiary sector will not create jobs on the same scale as it has done in the past. This forecast is consistent with the conclusions of various studies which have examined the employment impact of the introduction of new technologies.[19]

As far as the geographical pattern of unemployment is concerned, with the exception of certain Belgian regions, the highest levels are to be found in the peripheral regions of the Community, that is, Ireland, southern Italy, south-west France. The *Second Periodic Report* found that for 1981 the highest regional unemployment rate levels were to be found in Southern Italy, North and West Great Britain including the West Midlands, Northern Ireland, Ireland, Denmark, and some Dutch and Belgian regions. Although unemployment during the 1970s increased most rapidly in the economically stronger areas, mirroring the forces of industrial restructuring, these increases came from a lower base and the actual level of unemployment remains higher in the depressed weaker peripheral regions. The First Periodic Report predicts that these areas will experience more severe unemployment in the future, as they will have a much higher proportion of young people entering the labour force than in the prosperous regions.

In the analysis of regional disparities the Commission uses gross domestic product (GDP) as the prime indicator of Community regional problems. Apart from the obvious need to select an indicator commonly available throughout the Community, the selection of regional GDP is a reflection of the Community's overall approach to regional policy. This approach may be summarized as one which seeks to raise regional incomes through the development of productive capacity rather than through income transfers. The figures quoted in the Report for 1977 reveal that at that time all Italian regions (except Valle d'Aosta), all British regions, the whole of the Republic of Ireland, all the regions of west and south west France and the Massif Central, together with Lüneburg in Germany, Friesland in the Netherlands, Luxembourg, and Hainault in Belgium had GDP figures below the Community average (these regional trends were confirmed in the recently published Second Periodic Report.) By far the worst situation existed in the Mezzogiorno and Republic of Ireland where GDP per head was less than 50 per cent of the Community average. At the other extreme were the strongest regions, including most of the major cities of northern and central Europe all with a GDP more than 150 per cent of the Community average. The overall picture of the changes in regional prosperity is revealed by comparing the situation in 1970 with that for 1977 (Map 1). Such a comparison shows that regional disparities in GDP per head widened during the 1970s (at least until 1977).

The interpretation of these trends has been the subject of debate in recent years. At one extreme, there are those who see regional disparities in the Community in terms of a centre–periphery model and insist on the 'motion of cumulative disequelibria' in economic development because of the centre's inherent and derived comparative advantage for investment in advanced forms of economic activity. These central comparative advantages relate to maximum accessibility to markets and minimization of distance costs of all kinds, leadership in innovation and technological change, agglomeration economies and more favourable labour market characteristics.[20]

Without denying the appeal of centre-periphery models there is now a growing number of analysts who prefer to see the evolution of regional disequilibra in the Community 'as a complex scenario of multiple and diverging forces operating at different spatial levels'.[21] However, in this complex scenario there have been contradictory trends. Thus, while disparities have increased at the Community level, when looked at in terms of the aggregate of Community regions, trends within member states have not involved a widening of disparities. Regional disparities in the Community have increased as a result of the varying economic performance of individual member states.[22] Camagni and Cappellini suggest that the increase in disparities does not stem, in the main, from diverging employment or productivity levels; but rather from increasing differences in the exchange rates and sectoral price trends.[23] Even so, it is a worrying fact that over the period 1970-7 investment per head was very much lower in those countries which had below average GDP—the United Kingdom, Italy and the Republic of Ireland—than in the rest of the Community. Thus the gap between the productive capacity of the three weakest countries and the remainder of the Community was widening substantially during the 1970s.

A further significant macro-economic issue considered in the First Periodic Report concerns the impact of the second enlargement of the Community on regional disparities. The report shows that with the accession of Greece the GDP ratio of the ten richest to the ten poorest regions in the Community increased from 4.0 to 1 in 1977 to 5.1 to 1 in 1981. The addition of the Greek regions raised the number of regions

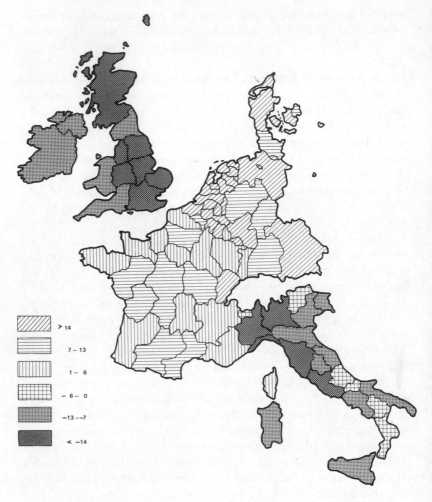

/////	> 14
≡≡≡	7 – 13
‖‖‖	1 – 6
⊞⊞⊞	– 6 – 0
▦▦▦	–13 – –7
▓▓▓	< –14

Map 1. Change in GDP per capita 1970–7 UCE.
          (EC = 100)
Source: *EUROSTAT* 1980.

with GDP per head below 50 per cent of the Community average from
nine to seventeen. In other ways Greek entry has added to existing
Community regional problems. It has increased, for example, the
number of mountainous regions experiencing rural depopulation,
added to the number of Mediterranean regions with a weak agricultural structure, and increased the number of industrial areas with

high unemployment. Clearly, however, the main challenge in this regard will emerge with the accession of the two Iberian countries.[24] This will not only dramatically increase disparities but will also aggravate some of the major problems facing the weaker regions of the existing Community. It is therefore safe to conclude that, on the basis of present trends, the odds point to greater regional dsparities in the Community for the forseeable future.[25]

The Commission Proposals for the Revision of the ERDF Regulation 1981–4

We have charted the emergence of the CRP and set out some of the major regional trends up to the early 1980s. Since then the Community has engaged in a lengthy further review of the policy which has only recently been resolved. The debate surrounding the revision is highly instructive inasmuch as it exposed some of the key issues and problems surrounding the operation and future development of the policy. It is therefore useful to consider the debate in more detail. The Commission's proposals went through two stages; the initial proposals appearing in October 1981, being superseded by a reworked set of Commission initiatives in November 1983.[26] The adopted regulaton finally appeared in the official journal of the Community in June 1984. The procedures which are followed to introduced or revise Community law involve the Commission drafting proposals which in turn are examined by the Parliament and negotiated with officials and ministerial representatives before being accepted by the Council of Ministers.

From the perspective of the Commission the main objective was to alter the ERDF in such a way that the Commission's regional responsibilities were to evolve from those of a financing body to those more clearly identified with a European-wide regional development agency. In other words the object was to break away from the tight national control of the policy towards a genuine supra-national European programme of action. It was also recognized that more needed to be done to improve the effectiveness and efficiency of the policy which in part the Commission felt could be accomplished by a more centrally-directed approach.

The First Phase

In the initial phase of the ERDF review, the Commission suggested a number of wide-ranging amendments to the ERDF regulation (COM

(81)589) including the definition of rules for the coordination of nation–regional policies; major changes in the geographical distribution of assistance from the quota-section of the ERDF and in its methods of opeation; a significant expansion in the size of the quota-free section of the Fund coupled with fundamental procedural changes; and the inclusion within the regulation of the concept of integrated development operations. These proposals were far broader in their scope than anything considered in the previous review and not surprisingly proved controversial and politically charged.

As far as the issue of coordination was concerned, the Commission proposed to include in the ERDF regulation the substance of the guidelines issued by the Council of Ministers 1979. In doing so, it is clear that the Commission intended to reinforce the existing mechanisms for co-ordination, namely: the periodic report on the social and economic conditions in the regions of the Community; the system of Regional Development Programmes; and lastly, the regional impact assessment studies of the main Community policies. In relation particularly to the RDPs, the Commission sought to strengthen member-state committment to the documents in two ways. First, by involving local authorities in their preparation. Second, by firming up the annual report on the implementation of the RDP for the previous year. Member states would now be obliged, for example, to provide quantified information on the results of regional development measures carried out in terms of investment and jobs.

In regard to the actual operation of the ERDF, the proposals maintained the distinction between a quota and a quota-free section but at the same time contained procedural and substantive policy changes which had significant political ramifications. Thus, the Commission proposed to concentrate aid from the quota-section of the ERDF in regions suffering from serious structural underdevelopment defined on the basis of Community criteria, aid being restricted to those regions in which per capita GPD at current prices and long—term unemployment rate were less than 75 on an index where the Community average was 100. The regions involved were to include all Irish and Greek regions (with the exception of the Athens and Thessalonika regions) as well as the Italian Mezzogiorno, Greenland, the French Overseas Departments, Northern Ireland and the assisted areas of Scotland, Wales and the North and North-West of England. The restriction of quota-section funding to these areas would have involved changes in the existing national quotas (see Table 2.4). Pcrhaps more significant it meant taking the allocation of Community aid away from the political negotiation process in which member states had previously fixed quotas and instead placing it in the hand of a supra-national bureaucracy operating a supposedly rational techocratic allocation mechanism.

Table 2.4. ERDF National Quotas

	1975–7(%)	1978–80(%)	1981(%)	Proposals (%)
Belgium	1.49	1.39	1.11	—
Denmark	1.29	1.20	1.06	1.30[a]
Germany	6.34	6.00	4.65	—
France	14.87	16.86	13.64	2.47[b]
Greece	—	—	13.00	15.97[c]
Ireland	6.46	6.46	5.94	7.31
Italy	40.00	39.39	35.49	43.67
Luxembourg	0.10	0.09	0.07	—
Netherlands	1.69	1.58	1.24	—
United Kingdom	27.60	27.03	23.80	29.28
	100.00	100.00	100.00	100.00

Notes:
[a] Greenland only.
[b] French Overseas Departments only.
[c] Athens and Thessalonika areas excepted.
Source: EC published sources.

The first set of Commission proposals also contained major alterations to the method of financing development from the ERDF. In particular, over a three-year transitional period, the Commission wished to replace progressively the system of financing individual projects by the financing of programme-contracts. These programmes were intended to be interrelated packages of investment projects set within the context of an overall regional development strategy based on a common format which included objectives and a finance schedule for implementation (see Table 2.5). They were intended to cover a period of no less than three years and were to be concluded between the Commission and the member state concerned having the force of a legally binding contract. Following the three-year transitional period it was intended that all quota-section aid proposals would be presented through the medium of programme-contracts.

Table 2.5.   Percentage of Resources to be devoted to Projects and Programmes

	1982	1983	1984	1985
Individual infrastructure:	90	less than 70	less than 40	nil
Project schemes programmes	probably 10	30	60	100

Source: House of Commons Ninth Report from the Select Committee on European Legislation. European Regional Development Fund 10443/81.

The Commission suggested that programme contracts should be drawn up by national governments in close co-operation with the authorities (local, regional), or agencies responsible for their implementation and that, instead of ERDF assistance being handed to national governments, future grants of infrastructure investments should be paid directly to the authority or agency commissioning that work. As a further innovation, it was proposed that the quota-section of the ERDF should in part be used for financing operations aimed at exploiting the indigenous development potential of the regions. Such operations were not necessarily to be related to tangible investments and they were to be directed to help small and medium-sized locally-based firms in activities such as handicraft, business, and rural tourism. In the context of these operations assistance would be made available to conduct sectoral studies, to improve management facilities, to diffuse information on product and technological innovations, to create shared facilities for several businesses, etc. The Commission also suggested that assistance should be given to regional and local authorities in working out, and implementing, operations that might qualify for ERDF assistance. All grant applications, however, would need to be submitted to the Community via the member state concerned.

Underlying this set of proposals was clearly a desire on the part of the Commission to become more closely involved in the formulation of regional policy initiatives and to break out of the stranglehold of national control of Community funded measures. The preparation of regional programmes was seen as a mechanism to facilitate such a dialogue as was the emphasis on a closer relationship with regional and local agencies. In advocating the support of measures to encourage indigenous development potential, the Commission regarded itself as being in the forefront of developing new approaches to regional development, at a time when traditional infrastructure measures such as a road-building and advance factory construction were becoming less effective, with little mobile industry available to attract to declining areas.

Turning now to consider the proposals for the support of specific community regional development measures (the so-called quota-free section) here again there was evidence of the Commission's desire to develop a genuine European wide regional policy. Three aspects in particular are worthy of mention: first, the suggestion that the share of the ERDF allocated to these measures was to be enlarged from its 5 per cent level, up to a limit of 20 per cent of the ERDF total resources (the exact amount being annually fixed within the framework of standard budget procedures); second, the proposal that measures under this heading were to be aimed at Community regions and zones seriously affected either by recent problems of industrial decline or by certain Community policies or measures; and third, the recommendation that these measures were to be adopted by the Commission, according to the procedure of the Management Committee of the ERDF, and not through the unanimous vote of the Council of Ministers as was the case under existing system.

The last proposed change concerned the special provision for the promotion of integrated development operations. Given that there were at the time two experimental integrated operations (Naples and Belfast) in progress without any formal legislative basis within the ERDF regulation, it is not surprising that the revised proposals should have proposed their formalisation as part of the Community's effort to secure co-ordination in regional development. There were, however, two features worthy of particular consideration: first, the recommendation that priority treatment was to be accorded to measures included in integrated operations; second, the proposal that ERDF contributions to investments and measures that form part of integrated operations might be increased by 10 per cent, though subject to a general ceiling of 80 per cent of the total expenditure incurred.

By the summer of 1983 the Council had been discussing the advantages and disadvantages of the Commission's original package for almost two years without any consensus emerging.[27] In the Commission's view its wider objectives had become bogged down in debates amongst member states about the amount of funding to which they were entitled. Unwilling to accept that negotiations were primarily about the financial redistributive dimension of the ERDF and conceeding that little was likely to be achieved by continuing to press with the original set of proposals, the Commissioner for Regional Policy, Antonio Giolitti, drew up a new proposal which marked the debut of the second phase of the review.[28]

The main stumbling block in the negotiations up to summer 1983 had been, first, the Commission's intention to concentrate ERDF resources in those member states where the more severe regional problems existed. This would have meant that certain member states, specifically Germany and Holland would have been effectively excluded from the quota section of the ERDF, while France and Denmark would have only received regional assistance for certain non-metropolitan areas. A second problem concerned the Commission's proposal to raise the ceiling of ERDF non-quota appropriations from 5 per cent to 20 per cent, thus passing effecting control of the allocation of the section from the Council of Ministers to the Fund Management Committee and yielding the Community a substantially increased degree of control over the ERDF. Not surprisingly, these two aspects of the review proved unattractive to various member states. The revised proposal which appeared in November 1983 can be seen as an attempt to overcome the former and more contentious issue of concentration of fund assistance in only certain member states with severe regional problems.

The Second Phase

The two main features of the second proposal package were, first that the distinction between quota and non-quota funding would be abolished, to be replaced with a set of 'quantitative guidelines'; second, that the programme-contracts approach set out in the original review package should be refined and extended.

On the 'quantitative guidelines', the Commission sought to merge the concept of geographical concentration of ERDF resources with the more politically acceptable notion of an allocation of the Fund to all member states, as in the previous quota system. To this end the Commission suggested that each member state should receive a flexible ERDF quota allocation with upper and lower limits to the total amount of aid allocated. The average ERDF allocation would remain approximately equivalent to the quotas as determined under the original regulation, but the creation of upper and lower limits would mean that aid would therefore no longer be allocated to member states according to inflexible national quotas (see Table 2.6). The margin between the upper and lower limits was to be made available to the member states on condition that they put forward regional measures in the spirit of a Community-based approach.

Table 2.6. The Commission Proposal for a System of 'Quantitative Guidelines'

Member State	Lower Limit (%)	Upper Limit (%)
Belgium	0.85	1.20
Denmark	0.81	1.14
Germany	3.55	4.81
Greece	11.05	15.60
France	10.44	14.74
Ireland	5.05	7.13
Italy	30.17	42.59
Luxembourg	0.06	0.08
Netherlands	0.95	1.34
United Kingdom	20.23	28.56

Source: Com (83) 649. final.

The upper and lower limits were to provide basic guide-lines only. Individual member states would obtain the lower limit of ERDF assistance if applications for finance met the conditions of the new regulation. They would obtain resources between the lower and upper limits by submitting packages of investment projects in the form of regional programmes based on a format and guidelines set by the Commission. This latter development, linking a flexible system of national aid allocation to the submission of programmes, was essentially a reflection of the Commission's desire to change from financing individual projects to a method of programmed submission. Arguably, the system of flexible regional aid finance through programmes instead of projects represented the adaptation and extension of the original non-quota section of the ERDF previously fixed at 5 per cent of total resources. In all, it was hoped that within four years at least 40 per cent of ERDF resources would be reserved for this type of programme development.

In extending the concept of programme-contracts, included initially in the first review package (October 1981) the Commission in fact proposed two types of programmes. Community programmes and National programmes. Community programmes were defined by the Commission as 'a co-ordinated series of multiannual measures directly serving Community objectives and the implementation of Community policies.'[29] They were to be drawn up in consultation with the authorities of the member states concerned, and would constitute a programme agreement.[30] Where a programme was undertaken in a region of a member state not covered by the RDP, an RDP for the region would have to be prepared. Community programmes could therefore be carried out in areas which did not have national regional development priority status (non-assisted areas). Crucially, the programmes, although a collaborative effort between member states and the Commission, would be instigated on the initiative of the latter. Further, the programmes were to be set out specific objectives and expected results. National programmes of Community interest would be prepared by national government in collaboration with the authorities concerned within the limits laid down by national legislation. They would be limited to the nationally-defined assisted areas but would have to be of 'Community interest', a concept which was relatively ill-defined in the Commission's proposals. The Commission proposed to examine the programmes in order to assess whether they were consistent with Community regional development objectives. As with Community programmes, national programmes were to include detailed information on objectives, means, and results. The Commission hoped that within four years at least 40 per cent of ERDF resources would be reserved for these measures, with rising priority given to Community programmes. The Commission envisaged the level of ERDF participation in programmes being fixed at between 60–65 per cent. It was the Commission's intention that Community programmes would provide the link between the minimum and maximum quota ranges. Moreover, expenditure on national programmes would be additional. The programme approach therefore threatened to have an important impact on previous operating practices of the ERDF centred around project submission. Despite problems encountered in the Council concerning the inclusion of integrated operations in the ERDF Regulation the Commission reaffirmed its intention to give integrated operations formal legal status. The proposal confirmed that priority ought to be given to measures included in integrated operations and that there should be a 10 per cent increase in the overall Fund resources devoted to these measures. Finally, the second phase of proposals included one other important adjustment to the original proposals. Further to the introduction of the notion of indigenous development potential the Commission explicitly linked its measures to exploit the potential for internally generated regional development with the programme approach by requiring that such measures could only be supported if set out within the context of a programme. In terms of the percentage of fund intervention, this was set at 65 per cent.

The Revision of the ERDF Regulation: Assessment of the Proposals

The delay in coming to an agreement about the Commission's review proposals is an indication of their political sensitivity. In the following discussion an attempt is made to highlight the points of debate surrounding the proposals as they moved through to the formal acceptance of the regulation.

One central theme running throughout the exercise has been the desire on the part of the Commission to emphasize the importance of co-ordination of member states and the Community's own measures in this policy area. Clearly if one accepts the legitimacy of a Community-wide regional policy then such a concept takes on particular importance. This very point was recognized in 1979 when the Council of Ministers published its guide-lines for the future development of the CRP in which the various largely experimental co-ordination measures which had been undertaken before that date were set out in such a way as to emphasize both their centrality and cohesion. The Commission had already published the first Periodic Report and a commitment to their regular preparation emphasized by inclusion in the ERDF regulation could hardly be regarded as exceptional given the acceptance of a Community based approach to regional policy. Likewise a start had already been made in preparing impact studies. In this case the real question concerned the extent to which other Commission Directorates were willing to take necessary action in line with the findings, something not capable of resolution within the confines of the ERDF regulation. Undoubtedly the item relating to the RDPs was the part of the co-ordination proposals which drew most attention in the negotiations, focusing as it did on the role of local authorities.

The Commission has always seen these documents playing a particularly important role in the CRP by providing a regular source of information on regional trends, the policies being pursued by member states, and highlighting the role and effectiveness of Community funded resources. It was for this reason that the Regional Policy Commission in 1975 produced a RDP outline requesting member states to submit on a regularly updated basis information concerning their development activities in assisted regions in a common format (analysis, objectives, measures, financial schedules, evaluation). By 1978 the first round of documents had been prepared and it was possible to make a judgement about their usefulness. Unfortunately it was apparent that the documents had failed to live up to their expectations of the Regional Policy Committee. While the quality of the documents was variable, it is nevertheless possible to reach some general conclusions: analysis of regional trends was superficial, there was little precise information about the regional measures or their financing, and only cursory attention had been given to the role and effectiveness of Community measures. In operational terms matters were made worse by the failure of certain member states to prepare a regular update of their programmes.

In 1979 the Commission published its own review of the first round of RDPs which included a formal statement of the Commission's opinion on the RDPs and recommendations to member states concerning preparation of the programmes. The veiled criticism of national governments was backed up by a clear statement re-emphasizing and further elaborating the need to prepare the documents in line with the RDP outline. It is worth commenting that Commission opinion does not carry the full force of Community law. Significantly, in commenting on the second round of RDPs in August 1984, the Commission found that although the documents represented an improvement on the first round, they still did not identify the relative priority of regional development measures. Further the documents failed to link infrastructure investment to regional development; nor did they indicate the total resources available for regional development at a regional level.[31]

In the light of these difficulties, it is not surprising that the Commission should propose the firming-up of the RDP outline in the ERDF regulation, along with a requirement that they should be regularly updated, and that local authorities should be closely involved in their preparation. In assessing the reaction of member states to these proposals it is clear that they were regarded as an attempt by the Commission to involve itself, on behalf of the Community, in decisions about domestic regional policy which were best left to national governments. For a number of member states, preparing information in line with the structure of the RDP outline poses problems since their administrative structure and financial planning mechanisms are not designed to fit into an explicit regional development approach. However in the past, member states have somewhat grudgingly been willing to prepare the documents, despite a certain amount of administrative difficulty, because of the requirement that projects eligible for ERDF have to be continued within assisted areas designated within the national RDP document. The fact that member states have not been required to spell out individual projects in the RDP documents has enabled then to adopt a somewhat cavalier attitude, going through the motions of the exercise without putting much effort into detail. The inclusion of the requirement to conform specifically to the RDP outline in the ERDF regulation does not overcome this basic problem. Indeed it is significant that it was not so much this aspect of the proposal which generated opposition to the proposal but rather the requirement closely to involve local authorities in the preparation of the documents.

As far as the proposed changes in the geographical distribution of aid from the quota section of the ERDF was concerned, the most important issue was not only the question of the precise geographical boundaries of areas of assistance, but also the fact that the proposals implied that these areas should be defined on the basis of 'objective' Community criteria. A number of points need to be made in this regard. To begin with, the attempt by the Commission to define the areas of assistance on the basis of Community criteria can be sen as a return to the approach recommended in the Thomson Report in 1973. The definition of areas on this basis was rejected in the negotiations which led to the establishment of the CRP, as it implied a direct intervention by Community institutions in the mechanisms through which member states operate their national-regional policies. Similar arguments surfaced in the most-recent round of negotiations.[32] In a period of economic recession it was difficult for non-recipient Member States to justify a major redistribution of fund resources to their electorates. Furthermore queries were raised as to the availability and comparability of regional data at the Community level. In a period of rapid economic change statistics quickly become out-of-date, and it was somewhat disturbing that the original proposals relied on 1977 data. The consistency of the overall criteria employed by the Commission was therefore, brought into question. Given the political and technical problems which these proposed changes raised, it is not surprising that they were to prove unacceptable to the Council of Ministers.

Turning to the proposal to move to a programme approach, the Commission's arguments in favour of such a shift included the claim that it would increase the effectiveness of the Fund's assistance by concentrating aid on coherent sets of measures rather than isolated investment projects; that it would reduce the bureaucratic burden of assessing a large number of projects, leaving more time to be devoted to the vital question of co-ordination and coherence of the measures; and that it might increase the chances of ensuring the 'additional' character of the Fund's assistance by involving Community institutions in the process of formulating and implementing the programmes. It was also argued that a programme approach would facilitate the development of new forms of aid such as the measures to encourage indigenous development potential and so contribute to a higher degree of community specificity in the CRP measures. Finally it was claimed that the way programme contracts would be prepared would allow for more participation by local and regional authorities in the operation of th CRP and that it would secure greater publicity for ERDF assistance.[33]

While these were undoubtedly laudable objectives, they were not received with overwhelming enthusiasm by all member states.

The proposals were interpreted in some quarters as a device to secure increasing Community involvement in the operation of national regional policy. Further, they were seen not only as a political intrusion on domestic policy-making but also as excessively bureaucratic and unnecessary device for dispensing Community funds. Indeed the complexity of preparing and approving the programmes was seen as threatening what was regarded as a relatively simple and straightforward system of periodically forwarding to Brussels blocks of single investment projects. Member states were also concerned about the possible lack of flexibility inherent in legally binding contracts when regional development measures might stretch over several years. In administrative and professional terms there was a certain amount of scepticism, particularly in the case of the UK, about the validity of the rational normative approach to economic development based on the concept of preparing a regional plan which contained: analysis, objectives, financial measures, final schedules, and also evaluation. Matters were made worse by an apparent lack of clarity amongst Commission officials concerning the nature and form of programme contracts. Underlying all these objections, of course, lay a fundamental difference of opinion as to what the Community's regional policy was about: on the one hand, a simple and relatively efficient device for financial transfers from Brussels to national treasuries to underpin national expenditure on regional policy, as against, on the other, an attempt to secure a common European-wide approach to regional development in which the Community played an important role.

In relation to the Community's hopes for the programme approach, the limited experience of the non quota programmes in the early 1980s had not been auspicious.[34] Taking the UK as an example, the British Government had proved reluctant to allow local authorities much say in the preparation of the non-quota programmes. In the case of these programmes and those prepared for regional development purposes as part of the UK budget rebate known as the Supplementary Measures, it was made absolutely clear that the UK would not accept additionality. Moreover because of auditing problems in Brussels and misunderstandings and disagreements between British and Community officials there had been long delays in the acceptance of the non-quota measures for Steel and Shipbuilding areas.

Turning to the Commission's suggestions for the quota free section of the fund in COM 81 (589), the proposed expansion of the section was again interpreted as a device to increase Community control over the policy and certain member states were therefore concerned as to the uncertainty which would arise in regard to their receipt of moneys from the ERDF as distinct from the certainties of the existing system. This concern was heightened by the suggestion that the Commission (subject to procedure of the Fund Management Committee which acts by majority voting) should determine the major features of the measures. The Commission proposals for the revision of the ERDF in 1977 made precisely the same recommendations. They were subsequently rejected by the Council in 1979, which insisted that the non-quota measures should be unanimously agreed by the Council of Ministers. The move towards supranationalism in the 1981 proposals seemed destined to suffer the same fate.[35]

Finally it is necessary to comment on the proposals to include in the ERDF regulation provisions concerning integrated operations. Up till the early 1980s integrated operations had only operated as an experimental exercise, and as well as their formal recognition within the ERDF regulation, the Commission had suggested that ERDF assistance to projects included in them might be increased by ten percentage points in order to provide an additional incentive for their preparation. Given that the Commission was placing the burden of securing the co-ordination of Community measures upon the local authorities and agencies of member states, such an incentive seemed sensible. However in the process of negotiation it was pointed out that the introducton of this additional aid might result in a certain amount of confusion and controversy. Projects included in integrated operations would be receiving greater assistance than identical projects, in similar problem areas, merely because of their inclusion in a scheme designed to secure greater co-ordination of Community aid.

The second round of Commision proposals, COM 83 (649), which appeared in November 1983 can be regarded as a skilful redrafting and reformulation of the first round of Commission initiatives. It has already been argued that the Commission had become seriously disillusioned with the pace and nature of the discussions in Council concerning its original proposals. However, it is important to note that, far from presenting before Council a set of conciliatory proposals which responded to previous criticisms, the second round with some reservations tended to heighten many of the issues that had surfaced previously.

In relation to co-ordination, the new proposals remained in very much the same form as in the original. The RDP proposals, while posing limited administrative problems for certain members and to some extent representing an infringement on domestic planning, were not seen as presenting any serious difficulties except in respect of local authority involvement. Interestingly, in the second set of proposals, the reference to local authority involvement in the elaboration of the RDP's was watered down. Instead of RDPs being 'prepared in close association with the regional authorities concerned', the co-ordination proposal now stated that local authorities were only to be 'involved as much as possible in their preparation'. This reflected a reticence on the part of certain member states to engage in a more intimate dialogue with local and regional authorities on regional development activities.

The Commission's 'quantitative guidelines' were interpreted by the Council as the concentration proposal under another guise. As a proposal it proved in some ways more difficult to resolve than that based on concentration of ERDF moneys in the worst-affected regions and countries. Clearly, as with the original concentration issue, there was a split between those member states who were likely to benefit financially and those who were likely to lose out. However, because the Commission had decided to link the allocation of moneys between upper and lower limits to the submission of Community programmes, the issue became more complex than a straightforward split between donors and receivers. While certain member states found the concentration of fund resources in the regions of greatest need to be a logical step forward in Community regional planning, there remained concern about the emphasis on programme submission in order to obtain additional resources from the Fund. It was not certain how the Community might operate this link between resource allocation and programme submission or for whose benefit. In short, for certain member states, the quantitative guide-lines threatened to put too much authority in the hands of the Commission. The Commission view, on the other hand, was that, without the link between resource allocation and programme submission, it would be unable to prevent member states from operating unconditional drawing rights on the new flexible quotas and so have the fund continue as a simple instrument of budgetary transfer.

The programme concept in the second round of proposals, although redefined and extended by the Commission, remained a contentious issue. Member states interpreted the suggestion relating to Community programmes as the resurrection of the non-quota section in a different guise. Moreover, the Commission had envisaged that the Community programmes would account for some 40 per cent of total ERDF expenditure, and that these measures would eventually take priority over projects. Given that member states had previously objected to the increase in the proportion of the Fund allocated to the non-quota section to 20 per cent, it is hardly surprising that they should find unacceptable the proposition that 40 per cent of ERDF resources be allocated to programmes which would be identified and selected by the Commission itself.

Finally, there was doubt over the inclusion of integrated operations in the revised Regulation for the reasons outlined above; that is to say the prospect of increased priority for these measures as well as 10 per cent increase in allocated resources. Given that the second set of proposals suggested no significant change in the stance of the Commission *vis-à-vis* integrated operations, the negotiations surrounding their inclusion in the regulation remained problematic throughout.

Adoption of the Review

The ERDF regulation was finally adopted by Council in June 1984 with the prospect of the imminent direct elections to the European Parliament, and hence the possibility of a relatively fresh and perhaps more vociferous parliamentary lobby, providing the incentive for a rapid conclusion to be negotiations after almost three years of debate.[36] Bearing in mind the issues discussed above, it is useful to comment on some of the main aspects of the adopted regulation.

On the principle of co-ordination the adopted text differed only slightly from that proposed by the Commission in its second set of proposals. The Periodic Report, the RDPs and the regional impact assessment remained central to the attainment of co-ordination. However, the Commission proposal that member states should supply a detailed report on the implementation of the RDP for the preceeding year was notably diminished.

As far as the more contentious issue of quota ranges was concerned, the member state minimum shares had been agreed under the French Presidency of the Council in May 1984 (see Table 2.7). Originally, the Commission had envisaged that a member state would not receive an unconditionally guaranteed minimum share. In Article 4 (4) of the adopted text member states succeeded in obtaining their guaranteed minimum if an adequate volume of applications for assistance were submitted which satisfied the conditions in the regulation. The

Table 2.7.   The Quota Ranges

Member State	Lower Limit (%)	Upper Limit (%)
Belgium	0.90	1.20
Denmark	0.51	0.67
Germany	3.76	4.81
Greece	12.35	15.74
France	11.05	14.74
Ireland	5.64	6.83
Italy	31.94	42.59
Luxembourg	0.06	0.08
Holland	1.00	1.34
United Kingdom	21.42	28.56
Total	88.63	116.56

Source: 1984 ERDF Regulation.

adopted regulation, however, failed to clarify satisfactorily how the difference between minimum and maximum shares was likely to be achieved; whether, for example, through programme or project submission or a combination of both.

It should be remembered that Community programmes were at the outset to have provided the link between minimum and maximum ranges. Given the downgrading of these measures during negotiations it was unlikely in practice that the Commission would be able to use them for this end.

Indeed, the adopted regulation stated that programme financing would only account for 20 per cent of total ERDF resources after three years. Moreover, in the preamble to the regulation that experimental nature of the measures was underlined: 'Whereas to improve the impact of ERDF assistance: it is necessary to ensure, *on a trial basis*, that part of the Funds' resources are used in the form of programmes, including Community programmes.' (author's emphasis.)

The dilution of these measures was taken further in Article 7 (3) which stated that member states would inform the Commission of regional problems likely to be the subject of a Commission programme. In short, Community programmes would not be identified by the Commission as had been the original intention. These measures, therefore, were placed firmly under the control of member states.

In regard to National programmes, Article 11 (e): was retained from the original proposals, yet in a different form, 'the Commission shall assess programmes on the basis of their consistency with regional development programmes and their contribution to the attainment of the Community's objectives and priorities . . .,' reference to the additionality of payments included in COM (83) 649, Article 13 (1)(e) was omitted. The adopted regulation also fixed the levels of fund intervention for programmes. For the Community programmes the level of intervention was reduced from 65 per cent to 55 per cent of total public expenditure. In the case of national programmes the level was set at 50 per cent rising to 55 per cent in exceptional circumstances. These levels represented reduction in the level of intervention (60–65 per cent) originally envisaged by the Commission. For indigenous development measures, the rate was from 50–55 per cent (originally 65 per cent) but total finance devoted to these measures could not exceed 10 per cent of the minimum quota range of individual member states.

Integrated operations succeeded in being accorded priority treatment. However, the nature of their priority remained unclear. Finally, the exact extent of local authority involvement partcularly in regard to programmes was not clearly spelt out. There was limited provision, however, for their involvement in drawing up the RDPs and integrated operations.

Conclusion

In charting the evolution of the Community's approach to regional policy it is clear that the policy has always been inextricably linked with the political bargaining process which is the essence of Community decision-making, reflecting the conflicts of interest between member states as well as the wider tensions between them and the Commission. In regard to the latter point, the CRP is generally seen as involving the establishment of common rules and procedures which require the transfer of certain controls to a supranational authority. However, regional development is a highly visible and politically sensitive policy area and thus most member states are less than willing to relinquish their prerogatives in this field particularly at a time of recession.

While the persistence of severe regional problems in certain member states, allied with the political pressures for economic and monetary union and enlargement of the Community have kept up the monentum for development of the CRP, progress had nevertheless been marred by national control over all the major aspects of the policy (quotas, designation of assisted areas, management of the fund etc.). Moreover, the proportion of the EC's budget devoted to the CRP has always remained small and seems likely to remain so while the Community continues to be obsessed with agricultural questions.

In seeking to assess the position of the Commission towards the development of the policy, it is clear that it has sought to pursue a number of underlying, and some would argue not very clearly thought out objectives. To begin with, the desire to secure a uniform approach towards tackling regional problems across Europe (e.g. aid ceilings, RDPs, the programme approach, measures to promote development) reflects a perspective that there are common regional problems and solutions which merit a Community-wide response. Admittedly, forces of economic centralization have to be taken into account when national frontier controls are removed. There are, moreover, regional problems which can be directly attributed to Community legislation (e.g. Coal and Steel Treaties).

Nevertheless, it has to be remembered that the trends towards increasing disparities are more apparent between the nations of the EEC than between the Community's regions. Further, the difficulties the Community has had in reaching agreement about the eligibility criteria for ERDF support is in part a measure of the diversity of regional problems which are to be found amongst the Ten. The assumption that the Community can and ought to become more closely involved in the creation of regional development measures is questionable. It is difficult to see how the small number of staff in DG XVI could make a useful contribution at a time when member states themselves are recognizing the significance of a decentralized approach to the administration and implementation of regional policy. Measures aimed at fostering the indigenous development potential of regional economies are becoming more common across the Community, and claims that the Community is leading the way in this regard should be treated with caution. It is perhaps more a case of following rather than leading.

There are, of course certain powerful economic forces operating at an international level, multinational companies, whose investment activities have significant geographical consequences where international co-ordination of measures would make sense. Moreover, current efforts to ensure that the geographical dimension of the Community's main policies are more sensitive to regional problems, and pressures to shift the balance of Community expenditure towards policies concerned with industrial and new technology investment, unemployment, and social support measures, are encouraging. However, the speed of progress in this direction is marred by the current political balance with the Community and there remains the ultimate problem of the 'unanimity rule' which effectively precludes radical shifts in direction.

This brings us back therefore to the funding of specific regional development measures. Here the Commission, supported by the European Parliament, has fought a continuing battle with member states to secure additionality in respect of funds provided by the Community.

While member states remain determined to use the fund to reimburse their own regional expenditure and insist on the joint funding of projects, the policy is little more than a financial transfer mechanism, and a rather cumbersome one at that, given the small amount involved. Attempts to secure additionality through the identification of EC measures within RDPs and regional programmes can easily be overidden if member states so choose.

This leads to another important objective which the Commission has sought to pursue, namely that of co-ordination. If it is accepted that there is a need for a Common Regional Policy, then it clearly makes sense to seek cohesion both at the Community level and between the policies of member states and the Community. Co-ordinating the impact of the EC's various financial instruments is largely an issue that has to be tackled within Community institutions, although in geographical terms integrated operations are also important. However, the question of the co-ordination of the policies of member states poses major problems. In the debate about the reformulation of the ERDF regulation the Commission has regularly made reference to securing a more efficient and effective policy through co-ordination measures but such statements never go beyond generalities. There appears to be a somewhat naïve belief that the acceptance of the rational model of planning as set out in the RDP outline and in the various regional programmes proposed by the Commission will inevitably lead to a more efficient policy. While there is of course some truth in the proposition, there is little evidence that the question has been thought through, let alone considered in terms of the practical difficulties of seeking to impose a common approach across ten member states with varied administrative and political structures. Given this backcloth it is instructive to consider what real progress the Community has made in the revision of the regulation.

Clearly, the Commission has succeeded to some extent in initiating the move towards programme based regional development through Community and National programmes. However Community programmes which were the main supranational element of the review, appear to have been hijacked by member states. Progress in the move towards programmed regional development must also be balanced against other less welcome aspects of the review. First, concentration of ERDF resources has not been obtained. The quota ranges can be viewed simply as a second-best to a genuine concentration of fund resources in the areas of greatest need. It is likely that these limited resources will continue to be spread far too thinly between member states to have any real impact on regional disparities. Second, the extent and nature of local authority involvement in the RDPs, programmes, and integrated operations has not been sufficiently clearly spelt out. This may allow member states to continue present practices without a process of genuine consultation with local and regional authorities. Finally, the additionality issue, which at the outset of the review was to be clarified by the programme approach, seems to have been ignored in the revised regulation.

Looking to the future, the Commission has recently published the second Periodic Report[37]. According to the report regional disparities in Europe have continued to increase over the last decade, in terms of production, output, and unemployment levels. In the light of these trends, it would be wrong to assume that the revised ERDF regulation commanding extremely limited funds will have any significant impact. What is on offer is largely procedural changes to a marginal policy of the European Community. Moreover, it is important to stress that the revised regulation does not represent any attempt to come to terms with the new patterns of regional disparity in the Community which will follow the accession of Spain and Portugal.

At this stage it is, obviously, impossible to foresee how that particular challenge will be faced. At present the guiding principle of Community decision-making is one of strict attention to the interest of individual member states. As the restructuring of the CRP requires a unanimous decision of the Council of Ministers, it seems unlikely that the more prosperous member states would agree to a policy which would significantly increase their net financial contribution to the poorer countries of the EC, during a period in which all countries are experiencing acute economic and financial problems. In this respect, the Community is confronted with a major dilemma. On the one hand, the introduction of institutional or policy innovations by the Community can be interpreted in part at least as an attempt to overcome the lack of co-operation and commitment of member states to certain aspects of the policy. On the other hand, however, the nature of the relations between national governments and Community institutions is such that the successful implementation of the innovations depends on the consent and commitment of the very member states whose behaviour the innovations are supposed to regulate in the first place. This clearly presents a formidable obstacle to fundamental policy changes.

58   *Regions in the European Community*

Notes

1. Giolitti, A., 'We must get a balance in our Community relations', *Municipal and Public Services Journal*, 4 May 1979, pp. 459–60.
2. Preamble to the Treaty of Rome.
3. EC Commission, *Final Report of the Study of Community Financing for Regional Policy Purposes* (1954–72), Battelle-Genève Research Centre, Brussels, 1972.
4. EC Commission, op. cit., p. 15.
5. EC Commission, *Economic and Monetary Union in the Community* (Werner Report), Brussels, 1970.
6. EC Commission, *Report on the Regional Problems in the Enlarged Community* (Thomson Report), Brussels, 1973.
7. A detailed discussion of the negotiation period can be found in R. Talbot, 'The European Community Regional Fund: a study in the politics of redistribution', *Progress in Planning*, Pergamon Press, vol. 8, Part 3, 1977.
8. EC Council Regulation 724/75 creating the European Regional Development Fund, *Official Journal of the European Communities*, no. L73 of 21 Mar. 1975.
9. EC Council Decision 185/75 setting up a Regional Policy Committee, OJ no. L73 of 21 Mar. 1975.
10. Outline for Regional Development Programmes, OJ no. L69 of 24 Mar. 1976.
11. EC Commission, *Regional Incentives in the European Community—a comparative study*, Regional Policy Series, No. 25, Brussels; 1979; idem, *The Role of the Tertiary Sector in Regional Policy—a comparative study*, Regional Policy Series, no. 19, 1981 Brussels; *Deglomeration Policies in the European Community—a comparative study*, Regional Policy Series no. 18, Brussels, 1981.
12. Cuddy, M. 'European Agricultural Policy—the regional dimension', *Built Environment*, vol. 7, No. 3/4 pp. 2200–10, 1982.
13. Martins, M. R., and Mawson J., 'The Evolution of EEC Regional Policy—cosmetics or major surgery', *Local Government Studies*, vol. 6, no. 4, pp. 29–56 (1980).
14. Martins, M. R. and Mawson, J. op. cit., pp. 49–54.
15. Fitzgerald, G., 'EEC Regional Policy: A Re-appraisal', paper presented at the Regional Studies Association Conference on The Financing of Regional Development in the EEC, 26–7 June 1979, Trinity College, Dublin, 1979, p. 1.
16. Martins, M. R., and Mawson, J., 'The Development of the Programme Approach in the CRP—an evaluation of the British Experience', *Town Planning Review*, vol. 54, no. 1, pp. 63–92, 1983.
17. Martins M. R., and Mawson, J., 'The Programming of Regional Development in the EC', *Journal of Common Market Studies*, vol. XX, no. 3, pp. 229–44, 1982.
18. EC Commission, *The Regions of Europe*, COM (80) 816, Brussels.
19. Molle, W., *Prospects of Regional Employment, Scanning of Technological Options—synthesis*, Netherland Economic Institute, 1982.
20. Keeble, D., Owens, P.L., and Thompson, C., 'EEC Regional Disparities and Trends in the 1970s', *Built Environment*, vol. 7, no. 3/4, p. 154, 1982.
21. Camagni, R., and Cappellini, R., 'European Regional Growth and Policy Issues for the 1980s', *Built Environment*, vol. 7, no. 3/4, p. 164, 1982.
22. Martins, M. R. and Mawson, J., op. cit., 1980; Molle, op. cit.
23. Camagni, R., and Cappellini, R., 'Policies for Full Employment and Efficient Utilization of Resources and New Trends in European Regional Development', paper presented to the XXI European Congress of the Regional Science Association, Barcelona, 1981.
24. Musto, S., 'Regional Consequences of the Enlargement of the European Community', *Built Environment*, vol. 7, no. 3/4, pp. 172–81, 1982.

25. Molle, W., op. cit.

26. EC Commission, *Proposal for a Council Regulation amending Regulation (EEC) 724/75*, COM (81) final, 26 Oct 1981 and, EC. Commission, Proposal for a Council Regulation amending Regulation (EEC) 724/75, COM (83) 649 final, 18 Nov. 1983.

27. COM (81) 589 final, op. cit.

28. COM (83) 649 final, op. cit.

29. Ibid., p. 8.

30. COM (83) 649, Article 14.

31. 'Commission Opinion of 19 June 1984 on the Regional Development programmes', *Official Journal of the European Communities* No L 211/18 of / Aug. 1984.

32. See House of Lords, *Revision of the European Regional Development Fund Regulation*, Select Committee on the European Communities, 12 th Report, Session 1981-2.

33. Wilson, J., 'The European Community's Regional policy', *Local Government Studies*, vol. 6, no. 4, pp. 11-28, 1980.

34. Martins, M. R., and Mawson, J., op. cit., 1983.

35. House of Lords, op. cit.

36. OJ No. L. 169/1, 28 June 1984.

37. EC Commission, 'The Regions of Europe; Second Periodic Report on the social and economic situation and development of the regions of the Community', COM (84) 40, Brussels, 4 Apr. 1984.

3

Scotland in the European Community

MICHAEL KEATING and NIGEL WATERS

The European Issue in Scotland

In Scotland, as elsewhere in the United Kingdom, membership of the European Community has long been a contentious issue. Public opinion has been fickle but, in the years in which membership has been in debate, there is consistent trend for Scottish opinion to be less favourable than that of the UK as a whole and specifically of England. In the 1975 referendum, Scotland recorded a vote in favour of staying in the Communities but by a smaller margin than either England or Wales (Table 3.1). Indeed it is interesting to note that, given the relatively low turn-out, Scotland failed to vote in favour of EC membership by the margin (40 per cent of the electorate) later required for the establishment of a Scottish Assembly. Further, the only two areas in the UK to vote NO were in Scotland—Shetland and the Western Isles. Since then polls have consistently shown Scots less enthusiastic about membership. A 1979 ORC poll in the *Glasgow Herald*[1] showed Scots in favour of withdrawal by 50 per cent to 38 per cent (12 per cent Don't Knows), while 22 per cent considered that Britain benefited from membership and 54 per cent that it was harmed. The *Herald* contrasted this with a poll published shortly before in the European Communities' Bulletin showing that in the UK as a whole 39 per cent considered the Communites a 'good thing' and 37 per cent a 'bad thing'. A further Scottish twist in the ORC poll was that, while those who thought that Britain benefited from membership were as likely to see Scotland doing worse than the rest of the UK as better, those who thought that Britain did not benefit did show a certain tendency to see Scotland faring particularly badly. In 1982 a Marplan poll for the UK showed 51 per cent in favour of withdrawal against 41 per cent in favour of staying in.[2] In the North of England and Scotland, the figure for withdrawal was said to be 54 per cent against 35 per cent, while the South favoured staying in by 50 per cent to 47 per cent. This

Table 3.1. European Referendum Result, 1975

	Turnout (%)	YES Vote (%)
UK	64.5	67.2
England	64.5	68.7
Scotland	61.7	58.4
Wales	66.7	66.5
Northern Ireland	47.7	52.1

Source: D. Butler and U. Kitzinger, *The 1975 Referendum* (London: Macmillan, 1978).

accords closely with a contemporary MORI survey[3] showing 56 per cent of Scots voters in favour of withdrawal against 35 per cent for staying in.

Interpreting Scottish hostility to the Communities is more difficult. In 1975 Michael Steed[4] calculated that most geographical differences in the referendum result could be accounted for by the varying pattern of party support, two exceptions being the Highlands and Borders of Scotland where support was respectively lower and higher than predicted. However, Steed's predictions of support were based on party voting in the 1974 General Elections when there was a high level of support for the Scottish National Party; and it is difficult to infer to what extent it is partisanship which determines attitudes to the EC or vice versa. Certainly supporters of the main parties divide sharply. Most favourable to the EC are Conservative voters shown to be in favour of staying in by 51 per cent to 38 per cent in the 1982 *Scotsman* poll and 49 per cent to 37 per cent in the 1979 *Glasgow Herald* poll. Polls since 1979 have shown Liberal supporters more evenly divided (we do not have data on Scottish Social Democrats), with Labour voters strongly against membership. SNP voters are consistently shown to be massively opposed to the Communities. However, even among Conservatives, support for staying appears less in Scotland than in England. Indeed, it has been widely suggested that opposition to the EC was one factor in the loss of Conservative seats to the SNP in fishing areas in the north-east of Scotland in 1974.

Partly attitudes in Scotland generally follow those in the rest of the UK. The Conservative Party has consistently supported membership. The Labour Party, reluctantly pulled into supporting membership by Harold Wilson in the 1960s, reverted to hostility after entry and only after the 1983 General Election began to soften its approach. If anything, the Labour Party in Scotland has been more implacably opposed, though with a significant pro-EC element. The SNP has opposed membership, ostensibly on the grounds that Scotland should be able to decide the question for itself, but in practice showing a degree of opposition in principle at least as great as that of Labour.

Among MPs, a trend in attitudes to the EC becomes apparent in the 1970s. In the vote on principle of entry in 1971, Scottish MPs in each party divided more or less in the same proportions as did their English and Welsh colleagues. In the vote on direct elections in 1977, however, there was a marked divergence. While Scottish Conservatives, like those elsewhere, were overhwelmingly in favour, Scottish Labour MPs divided 16–10 against, in contrast to non-Scottish MPs who voted 122–110 in favour. Significantly, perhaps, six of the Scottish opponents of direct elections but only one of the supporters had been elected since 1970. SNP Members, though opposed to EC membership in principle, voted for direct elections.

While the EC and devolution/independence issues might seem to have something in common, both being concerning with constitutional change and shifting the territorial framework of decision-making, in practice they have developed separately. The SNP uses antipathy to the EC to bolster its case for independence but has made little serious attempt until recently to formulate a European strategy, preferring to defer the question until after independence. Among MPs there is no observable relationship between attitudes to devolution and attitudes to the Community and neither the Labour nor Conservative nor even the Alliance parties have attempted to link the two. The only party to do so was Jim Sillars's short-lived Scottish Labour Party. In the early 1970s Sillars, then a Labour MP and an opponent of the EC, was converted to the cause of Scottish Home Rule. He founded a Scottish Labour 'watchdog committee' to monitor EC decisions as they affected Scotland and came round to the view that, *if* the UK were to remain in the Community (which he opposed) then Scotland would need as much Home Rule as would give it independent representation. The position, in effect Scottish independence within the EC, became the policy of the Scottish Labour Party but has died with the SLP since 1979. Although some Labour left-wingers in Scotland toyed during the 1979–83 Parliament with the idea of independence should the next General Election fail to return a Labour government at Westminister, they share the opposition to the EC Of the rest of the Labour left. So they, like the SNP, are unable to use Europeanism as a defence against the charge of 'separatism'.

The EC issue also takes on a different hue in Scotland because of the different impact of Community policy and the distinctive Scottish issues in Community-related fields. As a 'peripheral region', Scotland is potentially at risk from integrationist policies and the removal of trade barriers, unless special measures can be taken in matters such as industrial incentives and the attraction of investment. Parts (until 1979 the whole of) Scotland have development area status and, in common with other assisted areas, have an interest in protecting national regional policy measures and trying to secure a genuinely redistributive Community regional policy. Scotland's considerable coal and steel industries have faced major problems of adjustment, creating a major interest in Coal and Steel Community (ECSC) matters. Unemployment levels and difficulties of structural adjustment have created an interest in the Social Fund. Scotland has over half the UK fishing industry so giving it, as we shall see, a major stake in any Common Fisheries Policy; and there are distinctive features of Scottish agriculture, such as the importance of sheep-farming and the incidence of hill-farming ('less favoured areas' to use the Community parlance). Finally, there is a wide range of consumer, legal, social, and educational matters in which Scotland has distinctive traditions, institutions, or needs.[5] Many of these come within the remit of local authorities.

The best examples of EC legislation affecting local government functions, in Scotland as in the rest of the UK, are in the area of environmental health and consumer protection. In the former, directives on food law, including labelling and inspection, whilst being of direct benefit to consumers, have necessitated considerable changes in the duties of local-authority staff. Difficulties over the role of environmental health officers in relation to that of veterinary surgeons have illustrated the difficulty of harmonization across different national systems of professional qualifications, standards, and procedures. In consumer protection, directives on metrological standards have also had major implications for local government.

An example of legislation on which there was inadequate local government input is the 'Seveso' directive on Major Industrial Accident Hazards. This was identified recently by the Chief Executive of Strathclyde Regional Council as a major concern.[6] It will require changes in the Health and Safety at Work Act to provide for the drawing up of hazard surveys and emergency plans and for the dissemination of information to the public. Much of the responsibility for these is likely to fall on local authorities, and there will also be implications for land use planning, particularly in respect of existing hazardous sites in densely-populated urban areas. The Seveso directive is an example of inadequate awareness and lobbying by local government—little advantage was taken of the opportunities offered during the lengthy discussions between the Commission and central government. As a result, local authorities are faced with the need for far-reaching changes required by legislation taking effect in 1984.

Local authorities are also brought into contact with EC matters through their developing economic role, particularly in relation to Small and Medium sized enterprises and regional policy. This has led to a concern with the effects of Community regulations in this area and a search for ways in which EC funds can be used most effectively.

The Policy Network

With the policy-making structure of the European Community so firmly based upon national governments, Scotland is potentially favoured by having, in the Scottish Office, a decentralized form of administration with a limited territorial remit but which is *an integral part of the central government.*

The Secretary of State for Scotland is a member of the Cabinet and heads a department which deals, for Scotland, with a range of functions which in England would be the responsibility of several 'functional' departments. These include the responsibility for the supervision of local government and for regional (Scottish) economic development. He can be seen as having three principal roles:[7] first, to administer those functions which, for historical reasons, have been organized separately in Scotland; second, to modify government policy in Scotland or develop distinctive Scottish policies; and, third, to lobby for extra resources for Scotland. For the purpose of this paper, we are interested in the last two roles. The Secretary of State's role in policy-making has been analysed[8] in terms of (a) policy autonomy and (b) policy leadership. Policy autonomy occurs when the conditions are such that the Scottish Office is allowed to develop policy independently, merely keeping other departments informed of what it is doing. Policy leadership is more common and occurs when policy is made interdepartmentally between the Scottish Office and other departments, with one department taking the 'lead', drafting papers summoning meetings and preparing legislation. As EC matters involve the UK government presenting a common position in Europe, policy autonomy is not relevant here. Rather EC matters are subject to policy leadership.

Which department takes the lead on EC, or on other matters, and the balance of influence between the Scottish Office and 'Whitehall' departments will depend on a range of factors. The first of these is the administrative responsibility of the departments concerned. On fisheries, the Scottish Office has a major role because, over half the UK fishing industry being in Scotland, its fisheries section is as large as that of the Ministry of Agriculture, Fisheries and Food. On energy, on the other hand, the Secretary of State for Scotland's administrative responsibilities are limited to electricity and, while this does give the Scottish Office representation on interdepartmental committees on energy policy, its role is responsive rather than leading. On Community matters, the lead department, usually a Whitehall department, will play the main role in defining the UK negotiating position, deal with the Commission and represent the UK in the Council of Ministers. When there is a particular Scottish interest at stake, however, there will be a Scottish junior minister on the negotiating team. Sometimes the Secretary of State for Scotland himself will be on the team and occasionally, on some agriculture and fisheries matters, he has taken the lead.

Influence in policy leadership will depend on a range of factors analysed by Keating and Midwinter.[9] There is the political weight of the Secretary of State, his closeness to the Prime Minister and the importance of Scotland to the Government's electoral position. There is the scope for the Secretary of State to make bargains with his colleagues at Cabinet level; and there is the question of seniority. Given the Scottish Office's breadth of responsibilities and relatively small size, it is likely that a Scottish official or junior minister dealing with any matter will be faced with a Whitehall counterpart who is senior to him and may be better briefed on the details of the particular item under discussion. This inevitably reduces the Scottish impact on policy and means that the Scottish Office role is more often one of responding than leading—though care is taken to ensure that the Scottish Office response makes a contribution to the policy as a whole and is not merely special pleading for Scotland.

In addition to his specific functional responsibilities, the Secretary of

State has a general role as 'Scotland's Minister', looking after Scottish interests wherever they arise. This is particularly important on the occasions where a matter of importance to Scotland (but which is not part of his administrative responsibilities) comes to Cabinet—for instance the proposed closure of the Ravenscraig Steel Works. Occasionally, this may impinge on EC matters. His work in defending Scottish interests is particularly important in relation to finance, which, given the complexities of European finance, is worth exploring.

At one time, Scottish Office expenditure was bargained for, function by function, with the Treasury and Cabinet. Given the strong position of the Secretary of State and political circumstances, this had by the 1970s produced expenditure levels for Scotland well above those for corresponding functions in other parts of the United Kingdom. In the late 1970s, the devolution debate publicized Scotland's relative advantage and sparked off an English backlash. Together with the pressure for public expenditure cuts, this led to the introduction of the 'Barnett formula'[10] whereby Scottish Office expenditure is determined by taking a fixed, population-weighted proportion of any expenditure increases or decreases for corresponding functions in England. Such changes in expenditure levels are allocated among England, Scotland, and Wales in the ratio 85:10:5. So the Secretary of State, in theory at least, can only increase his own spending by supporting the case of the appropriate English ministers. Since 1979 a block sum has been allocated to the Scottish Office which the Secretary of state is free to distribute as he chooses, though in practice his room for manœuvre is tightly constrained. Most of the Secretary of State's expenditure falls within this block though key items of relevance to our present subject do not. Rate Support Grant to local authorities is part of the block allocation but industrial aids paid by the Scottish Office to private firms are not.

The Interest Group Network

Scottish interest groups and local authorities have potentially several channels of access to the organs of the Community. Some interest groups are purely Scottish and deal with matters covered by the Scottish Office. This is the case, for instance, in law and education. Others are Scottish branches of UK-wide groups which are thus able to act at both UK and Scottish levels. Others again are independent Scottish groups but are linked or affiliated to UK-wide groups. So the

Confederation of British Industry is organized on a UK basis and has close links with Whitehall departments but has a Scottish organization with close links with the Scottish Office. It is thus able to take matters up at both levels. Trades unions are organized nationally in the Trades Union Congress but there is also a separate Scottish TUC to which both the few remaining independent Scottish unions and UK unions operating in Scotland affiliate (in addition to their TUC affiliation). Scottish farmers are organized in the National Farmers Union of Scotland (NFUS) which has close working links with the National Farmers Union in England and Wales. On matters of UK and EC agricultural policy negotiations take place between the government side, comprising the four agriculture departments (for England, Scotland, Wales, and Northern Ireland) and the three agricultural unions (England-and-Wales, Scotland, and Northern Ireland). Usually, the England-and-Wales union takes the lead, but occasionally, on matters such as hill farming, the NFUS does so. On matters such as hops, where there is no Scottish interest, NFUS may choose not to attend. Fisheries interests are represented in the Scottish Fishermen's Federation (SEF) but, as we shall see below, this is very prone to splits and has great difficulty in agreeing a common line, in contrast to the professionalism of the NFUS. Nor has the SFF close links with similar organizations in England and Wales.

Both Scottish and UK interest groups are usually members of European-wide federations and/or formal EC consultative committees. The NFUS is a member of COPA, the *Comité des Organisations Professionelles Agricoles*, a European-wide body, along with the NFU, giving them access to the Commission. It is also represented in the Brussels office established jointly by the UK farming unions. The Scottish Fishermen's Federation is a member of *Europêche*, the European fisheries organization and on various advisory committees. Employers and trade union organizations are represented through the UK bodies, as these operate in Scotland and in any case distinctive Scottish interests are less apparent than in agriculture and fishing. For instance, the Economic and Social Committee (ECOSOC) is made up of 156 members, including twenty-four from the United Kingdom (two from Scotland), divided into three equal groups representing employers, labour, and other interests. ECOSOC works through nine sections and is consulted on all Commission proposals, providing a technical/professional input to policy formation.

Unlike its English counterparts the Convention of Scottish Local

Authorities (COSLA) does not have a special EC or international committee, although the Secretary keeps track of Community matters through IULA/CEM and the European Joint Group (see below). COSLA is represented on the British sections of IULA/CEM, the international grouping of local authority associations. The small secretariat of the British sections is based in London and provides a useful guide and initial contact for any approach to Brussels, Luxembourg, or Strasbourg. An IULA/CEM office in Brussels was closed in 1976 due to lack of finance and inadequate usage, but there is currently a proposal for several local authorities in Scotland to share representation in Brussels under the auspices of the Conference of Peripheral Maritime Regions (CPMR). This could help to overcome some of the criticisms of badly briefed and expensive approaches by individual authorities.

The Consultative Committee of Local and Regional Authorities of Member States of the EC was initiated by IULA/CEM in 1976 and includes members representing the British sections. It is consulted regularly by the Commission on matters relating to regional policy. The work of the Committee has been beset by procedural difficulties and problems, but it is hoped that it will extend its influence to other areas of Community policy in future. It continues to be a useful forum for the airing of general common issues.

The European Joint Group was established before accession to act as a forum for local and central government dialogue on Community matters. Revived after accession, the Group now meets at six-monthly intervals, bringing together representatives of the local authority associations (including COSLA), with relevant central government departments. A briefing paper on progress with Community proposals of concern to local government is regularly updated and forms the basis of the Group's discussions. The meetings are chaired and serviced by the Department of the Environment, and the usefulness of the Group is therefore very much dependent on the level of central government interest. IULA/CEM's British Sections co-ordinate the local-authority side input and are permitted to submit three items for the agenda of each meeting. The Joint Group is useful as a channel of communication but has no real influence and is definitely not a negotiating forum. Brief reports of the meetings are carried in EIS, while the full papers come to COSLA through the Secretary, who attends EJG meetings. Unfortunately this information does not seem to penetrate very far into the individual Scottish authorities.

From the point of view of local government in Scotland, these formal channels and mechanisms for participation in Community affairs have serious limitations. The difficulty of the local authority associations reaching anything other than the lowest-common-denominator view is well known, and magnified at the international level. Although the associations are justified in feeling that the UK central government is not willing to take local authority particiaption seriously, local authorities can strengthen their case for participation by becoming more knowledgeable about Community affairs through other channels. Awareness by Scottish authorities of EC matters has improved considerably in recent years, and most of the larger authorities have officials charged specifically with monitoring developments in EC funding, though the remit of most such officials does not yet extend to the wider scanning of Community policies. Indeed, because of this pre-occupation with the Funds, authorities still often miss out on the early stages of proposals which will eventually affect them, such as the 'Seveso directive' already mentioned.

Two or three years ago some of the Highlands and Islands authorities could fairly have been said to be the most advanced of the Scottish authorities in their contacts with Brussels and internal awareness and organization, and this paid dividends in the successful campaign for derogation of aid ceilings, the Integrated Development Project for the Western Isles, ERDF grant aid for tourist infrastructure, and innovative pilot projects in training and social work. This lead can be partly attributed to support from the Highlands and Islands Development Board which has close links with the Scottish Office, Whitehall, and Brussels, and the staff resources to exploit them, not least through a secondment to the Commission. Dumfries and Galloway Regional Council also managed to send an official on secondment to Brussels, with the result that it was one of the first local authorities to take advantage of European Investment Bank loan finance. The rural authorities have also benefited from membership of the Conference of Peripheral Maritime Regions, which offers another channel of contact and influence.

More recently, however, other authorities in the more urban central belt of Scotland have markedly improved their awareness and contacts. In particular, Strathclyde Regional Council, with all the advantages of influence inherent in its size (2.5m. people and a budget of over £1,500m.), has seized the initiative in developing contacts with Brussels, to a certain extent bypassing the formal channels through central government. In 1982 Stratchclyde arranged for secondment of an official to Brussels (in fact by hiring the existing Highlands and Islands Development Board official already in post) and won its first £1m. grant from the Social Fund towards its employment subsidy scheme which has continued since. As mentioned earlier, Strathclyde has also responded directly to the Commission on the Development of Community regional policy, and with Glasgow District is lobbying for an Integrated Operation for Glasgow along the lines of the scheme already operating in Belfast. With the help of a £70,000 Commission grant a feasibility study was completed in 1984. The integrated Operation will not itself produce any 'new' Community money for Scotland but is intended to co-ordinate and make the best use of existing funds. If, however, the proposals for the reform of the ERDF are adopted (see Chapters 1 and 2) then the existence of an Integrated Project may put the region in a strong position to exploit it. Tayside Region has followed the example of Strathclyde in successfully seeking Social Fund support and lobbying for ERDF non-quota aid for areas of textile industry decline.

In the European Parliament, Scotland has eight MPs. It is a grievance to Scottish nationalists that Scotland, with its larger population, has fewer representatives than the Republic of Ireland. However, the MEPs, who each have a territorial constituency, do provide a channel to decision-makers in Brussels and a means for airing grievances. The MEP for Strathclyde East, Ken Collins, chaired the Parliament's Environment, Public Health and Consumer Protection Committee in the first parliament and brought the Community to Strathclyde in 1981. The South of Scotland MEP, Alasdair Hutton, also arranged for a delegation from the Regional Policy Community in the same year, while James Provan, the MEP for North-East Scotland was very active during 1982 in promoting an Agricultural Development Programme for the Highlands. Over the last five years the Parliament has increasingly sought to exercise a greater influence with the Council and the Commission, with some success, and the MEPs will almost certainly become a more important channel of influence in the years ahead. A new development in 1980 was the establishment of an Inter-Group of nineteen British MEPs who have local-government interests, and who hope to be able to promote those interests within their political groups in the Parliament. The group is, however, short of administrative support and has not been well attended to date. It could also run into opposition from other established committees if it seeks to take policy initiatives.

There is also a Commission Office in Edinburgh which is able to provide information about the Communities and guide interested parties to sources of finance and other benefits though the Commission representative does not play a 'political' role in lobbying for Scotland and does not participate in any of the Community's decision-making processes. Some organizations, such as the Scottish Council (Development and Industry) have sent staff on secondment to Brussels to 'learn the ropes'. Others have secured the services of former British and Community civil servants in helping them approach the Communities. Other points of influence are the *cabinets* (personal staff) of the Commissioners, the secretariat of the European Parliament, and, of course, Commission officials with specific responsibility for policies of concern to Scottish interests.

Not all these channels of influence are of equal importance. For distinctively Scottish issues the most important and effective channel is undoubtedly via the Scottish Office through the UK government to the Council. Success in using this channel depends partly on the closeness of the organization concerned to the Scottish Office. The NFUS has close and frequent links with the Scottish Office which enable it not only to argue its own case but to provide ammunition for the Scottish Office to use in putting a Scottish case at UK and European levels. So the lobbying of the Scottish Office by Scottish interests can help the former in its own lobbying. Representatives of the NFUS accompany Scottish ministers to Brussels when they go there as part of the UK negotiating team and are on hand for continuous consultation. They claim to have had a considerable influence on policy on Less Favoured Areas. The importance of well-organized interest groups to the Scottish Office is shown by the case of the fisheries groups. After a split in the SFF and the resignation of four of its constituent bodies, officials of the Scottish Office were reported to be playing a role in talks to heal the split.[11] For local government in Scotland, the Scottish Office provides both a channel of influence and, given the close links between the Scottish Office and local authorities, a source of support in dealing with EC matters.

The other channels are useful mainly for information purposes, to find out what is available from the EC or to get advance notice of items which are about to come up so as to be able to lobby Scottish and UK departments. The better-organized and more skilful groups have occasionally been able to operate at both European and Scottish levels. So the NFUS has tried to promote the proposed Agricultural Development Programme for the Highlands (see above), based on experience in Ireland and with the Western Isles IDP, in Brussels as well as in the Scottish Office. Their assumption has been that, if such a proposal were to come from the Commission, the Scottish Office would take it up and seek to have UK representatives promote it in the Council. However, this approach has to be sustained over a long period of time, as the protracted negotiations over the Western Isles project showed. When the European Regional Development Fund was being constructed, a team of former ambassadors was assembled by the Scottish Council (Development and Industry) to influence the formulation of policy. These however are exceptions. Direct access to the Commission is mainly useful for information, while influence is exercised primarily through the national government.

Scotland's Success in Europe?

To make an assessment of how Scotland has exploited Community membership, it is necessary to consider two aspects. First, there is the extent to which Scottish interests have influenced Community policy. Second, there is the use made in Scotland of available Community aids. As an example of the former, let us take, first, fisheries, possibly the area of Community policy of most direct interest to Scotland. There has been a protracted series of negotiations going back ten years to try and agree a Common Fisheries Policy. On some occasions in the past the British fisheries team had been led by the Secretary of State for Scotland but under the present Government the lead has been taken by the Minister of Agriculture and Fisheries or his deputy. There has always been a Scottish minister in the negotiating team and sometimes and Secretary of State for Scotland has attended alongside the Minister for Agriculture and Fisheries.

Negotiations came to a head in 1982 with crucial talks in Brussels in June. As the *Glasgow Herald* put it:

Mr George Younger, Secretary of State for Scotland, will represent Scottish interests and, with Scotland now taking more than 66 per cent of the UK catch, any deal will have to be acceptable to the leaders of the industry in Scotland. Mr Gilbert Buchan, president of the Scottish Fishermen's Federation, will be on hand with his colleagues for immediate consultation with the British negotiators. Any agreement must be acceptable to them. 'If they say they would rather have no agreement at all than what is on offer, then there will be no agreement' said Mr Younger.[12]

In fact the Commission's proposals at that time represented considerable concessions to Scottish interests. There would be a 12-mile exclusive zone in Scotland—as opposed to six miles elsewhere—and a 'box' around Orkney and Shetland limiting access for boats over 80 feet (local boats are nearly all under this length). Scottish fishermen were said to be fairly happy about this but tension was developing between Scottish fishermen, some of whom wanted the exclusive zone to exclude English fishermen, and the Englishmen who resented the advantages gained by the Scots.

When the stalled negotiations were resumed in the Autumn, dark rumours began to spread that the (English) Minister for Agriculture and Fisheries might be prepared to make concessions to the Danes at the expense of the Scots. The Minister did, in fact, get the reluctant agreement of the Scottish Fishermen's Federation (and presumably of the Secretary of State for Scotland) for a partial concession to the Danes on access to mackerel grounds off the west of Scotland and on the numbers of foreign boats allowed into the Orkney and Shetland 'box'. This, however, contributed to a rift in the Federation itself. The Shetland fishermen, already outside the Federation, rejected the agreement and in late 1982 four of the SFF's constituent member organizations resigned. It was only Danish rejection of the proposed Common Fisheries Policy which allowed time to try and re-establish some consensus in the Scottish industry.

What the fisheries case shows is that, where a Scottish interest can be identified and agreement reached between the Scottish Office and organized interests, then these interests can be effectively represented in the EC. Where Scottish interests are conflicting or disorganized, the Scottish Office's own position is made more difficult. It is not surprising, then, to find officials of the Department of Agriculture and Fisheries for Scotland making efforts to heal the breach in the Scottish Fishermen's Federation.

Another example of Scottish interests influencing Community policy making is the Regional Development Fund, set up in 1975 as part of the deal over UK entry. As well as the lobbying of the Scottish Council already mentioned, the UK government's case for the Fund drew heavily on Scottish Office has been remarkably successful in the past in defending development area status and regional aid for Scotland, this influence can be seen to have waned under the present government;[13] large parts of Scotland have lost assisted-area status since 1979.

The Commission has clearly stated its desire to have a closer relationship with local and regional authorities in the development of regional and social policies. Highland Regional Council, aided and abetted by the Highlands and Islands Development Board, has taken advantage of this to extract significant changes/concessions from the Community, albeit with the approval of the Scottish Office. Other UK local authorities are increasingly going on the offensive in putting proposals direct to Brussels without waiting for invitations and without clearing them with central government. Strathclyde Regional Council for instance, commented on the First Periodic Report, lobbying for the proposed repetitive Integrated Operation for Glasgow.[14]

The Integrated Development Programme for the Western Isles must also be seen as an example of the new Community policy, though it is modelled on examples elsewhere in the Community. It was proposed by the Commission in 1979 and steady pressure was maintained by local and farming interests both on the Commission and on the Scottish Office to keep it on the agenda. The Scottish Office (or perhaps the Treasury) was extremely cautious because of the commitment required from national funds and the precedent that might be set for other parts of Scotland and Britain. In 1980 the Project was blocked by the Germans but by mid-1981 it was given the go-ahead, albeit in much reduced form. The Regional and Social Funds declined to contribute, leaving it as a largely agricultural project and the Scottish Office contribution consisted largely of spending to which it was already committed in any case. The reluctance of the Scottish Office to be drawn into extra expenditure even to extract Community funds was confirmed by the Secretary of State's refusal to allow the Highlands and Islands Development Board to put up £380,000 towards the resuscitation of the Breasclete fish processing plant, although 40 per cent of this would be reclaimable from Community sources.[15] Finally, it is worth mentioning the less Favoured Areas Directive in agriculture, in which the Scottish Office played a key role, championing the interests of Scottish hill farmers.

The position with regard to the use in Scotland of existing Community funds is more complex. It is notoriously difficult to trace the effect of EC funds on particular areas. The European Regional Development Fund has received a great deal of publicity in Scotland, with regular press reports announcing the 'award' of a grant to a firm or a local authority for such and such a project. This is largely illusory. Apart from a small 'non-quota' section, a fixed proportion of ERDF money is allocated to the UK Government which, operating on the principle of 'non-additionality' deducts an equivalent amount from national expenditure so there is no additional regional expenditure as a direct result of the ERDF. Within the UK, the benefit to the under-takers of these projects varies. In the case of private firms, there is no benefit; ERDF funds are simply deemed to replace existing national aids and the Treasury keeps the money. Similarly, in the case of grants awarded to departments of the Scottish Office itself (for example for the Scottish Development Department's trunk road programme), the money stays in the Treasury, deducted from the Secretary of State's block allocation.

In the case of local authorities there is a real benefit in that money is made available as a grant for projects for which they would otherwise have to borrow. However, no extra spending is possible as these projects must be accommodated within existing capital expenditure limits. Further, the saving on loan charges is reduced in that the allowance for them is deducted from their Rate Support Grant (RSG). So that saving amounts, depending on the level of RSG to the authority concerned, to an average of only 44 per cent of the loan charges. For the poorest authorities, with a high level of RSG, the benefit is even less.

Applications from Scotland for ERDF funding are handled through the Industry Department for Scotland (IDS) (in the Scottish Office), which is informally allocated a share of the UK quota. IDS assembles a list of schemes including the Scottish Office's own projects such as trunk roads, to meet the Fund's criteria. Local authorities may put in bids to the Scottish Office. In the case of private firms, which receive no direct benefit from being designated as recipients of ERDF funds, IDS selects firms already receiving national aids.

In recent years, EC budget refunds have been received by the UK government to be spent on 'supplementary measures' of regional policy. As the government regards these as national rebates, however, all the money remains in the Treasury, while parts of the existing work of grant aided bodies like the Highlands and Islands Development and the Scottish Development Agency are simply labelled as 'supple-mentary measures'.

The quota section of the ERDF has been well used by Scottish

Table 3.2.   European Regional Development Fund (ERDF)
Grants to Projects in Scotland, Quota Section only (£'000)

	Infrastructure			*Industry*	*Total*
	Local Authority	*Other*	*Total*		
1975	719	2,579	3,298	6,554	9,852
1976	5,973	3,244	9,217	5,389	14,607
1977	3,064	3,191	6,255	7,672	13,927
1978	9,690	8,697	18,287	6,439	24,826
1979	26,896	5,797	32,693	4,439	37,133
1980	10,204	5,689	15,893	10,794	26,687
1981	33,013	19,247	52,260	15,417	67,680
1982	n/a	n/a	82,012	1,914	83,926
1983	n/a	n/a	62,820	20,330	83,150
1984 (2nd round)	9,500	17,244	26,744	3,075	29,819
TOTAL to date	—	—	—	82,046	528,624

Source: Planning Exchange, Glasgow and Industry Department for Scotland.

authorities, which have taken up a large and increasing share of the
informal quota available to Scotland (which they share with other
public agencies—Table 3.2). All nine regional and all three islands
councils have received grants from the Fund (Table 3.2a), reflecting
their substantial infrastructure programmes, many of which qualify
for ERDF aid, especially since broader eligibility criteria were introduced in the 1979 Fund Review. District Councils, in contrast, tend to
be involved only intermittently in projects—such as industrial
estates—which qualify for Fund support, and the pattern of grant aid
shown in Table 2a reflects this.

The dominance of regional and islands council receipts is also in a
sense self-reinforcing. Most have now developed procedures, on an
annual cycle, for applications to the Fund via the Industry Department
for Scotland. This allows them to take full advantage of the Fund,
whereas the districts, which cannot justify devoting much staff time to
ERDF claims, may miss opportunities as a result.

The small non-quota (quota-free) section of the ERDF, after several
years of negotiations, is now funding both local authority and other
projects in steel and shipbuilding areas of Strathclyde region (see Table
3.2b) and should in due course be making small amounts of grant aid
available in textile areas of Tayside region. Strathclyde council was

involved in the protracted birth of this new form of aid, and its significance lies mainly in its role as a pilot for new types of development project—focused on the encouragement of small and medium sized enterprises—and new Fund procedures.

Scottish authorities have undoubtedly benefited in their dealings with the ERDF from a close working relationship with IDS in Edinburgh. On the basis of experience built up over several years, the officials concerned were, at least until 1982, particularly skilled in extracting the maximum benefit, and testing the limits of the Fund's eligibility criteria, and also took the trouble to go out and talk to local authority officials on their home ground, explaining and even seeking out suitable projects for applications.

One of the consequences of widened eligibility criteria (and these are likely to be wider still after the ERDF reform) together with restricted budget allocations has been the tendency to favour traditional, large, clearly eligible projects—roads, industrial site servicing, port and harbour improvements, etc. This tendency is reinforced by IDS's control over applications, since central government is understandably interested in maximizing the return to the UK as quickly and easily as possible. This pressure, together with some adverse experiences several years ago in trying to get marginal or new types of project accepted by the Fund Management Committee, has led to a retrenchment around mainstream projects—to the frustration of authorities such as Dundee district council, which had hoped for ERDF aid for a leisure and conference facility.

Other marginally eligible projects not currently being accepted by the Fund Management Committee, and therefore not forwarded by IDS include movable infrastructure such as ferries and railway rollingstock. Advance factories, in small units suitable for Small and Medium seized enterprises, have however recently been admitted after several years in which they were rejected by the Fund Management Committee.

In anticipation of a change from project to programme based submissions in the forthcoming Fund regulation, IDS officials are currently presenting some projects to the Fund Management Committee in the context of the Scottish Development Agency's Area Projects. These involve a co-ordinated programme of infrastructure, environmental improvement, and business development by the SDA and the local authorities[16] and may come to lend themselves particularly well to the new ERDF procedures outlined by Mawson,

Table 3.2a. ERDF Commitments in Scotland (less decommitments) by Agent

Agent	Total	1975	1976	1977	1978	1979	1980	1981	1982	1983	1984
Total	327,665,137	6,037,977	10,330,873	6,255,461	18,387,294	35,358,425	15,892,634	53,628,427	59,560,411	62,841,425	59,372,210
Borders RC	1,774,348	—	200,314	79,650	—	469,080	1,579,766	222,478	−776,940	—	—
Central RC	8,077,373	—	233,093	266,400	492,180	1,793,400	28,800	1,449,300	1,291,500	1,541,700	981,000
Dum. and Galloway RC	2,276,663	—	40,905	164,311	120,000	251,964	535,573	203,610	72,600	175,200	712,500
Fife RC	10,121,568	—	300,000	278,300	585,955	1,162,800	—	1,297,091	1,452,644	1,827,278	3,217,500
Grampian RC	10,481,493	—	1,209,786	52,200	—	2,284,870	2,851,352	3,497,653	300,450	240,182	45,000
Highland RC	18,070,850	120,900	52,958	49,252	—	3,149,795	1,029,354	848,940	4,533,283	4,458,238	3,828,130
Lothian RC	17,262,104	—	482,625	316,660	2,486,961	3,764,926	—	3,317,486	4,683,166	845,280	1,365,000
Strathclyde RC	63,761,292	888,634	1,601,919	784,825	4,779,548	11,730,440	3,760,777	12,693,358	3,235,020	13,722,421	10,564,350
Tayside RC	13,569,640	—	624,492	216,600	810,750	1,184,955	189,300	3,403,665	1,924,447	2,781,131	2,434,300
Orkney Isles IC	2,155,671	42,600	157,788	—	—	322,644	441,000	69,000	426,539	222,700	473,400
Shetland Isles IC	6,123,615	189,000	148,155	15,690	—	—	51,000	1,683,000	818,730	2,134,740	1,083,300
Western Isles IC	11,727,751	—	195,540	—	111,000	2,110,140	—	2,009,071	460,000	3,917,600	2,924,400
Dunfermline DC	91,650	—	37,590	21,690	—	—	−6,630	—	—	—	39,000
Kirkcaldy DC	225,081	—	—	—	—	—	—	—	36,000	162,081	27,000
North-East Fife DC	16,500	—	—	—	—	—	—	—	—	16,500	—
Inverness DC	673,196	—	—	98,325	—	—	—	151,871	—	423,000	—
Lochaber DC	38,600	—	—	—	—	—	—	—	—	38,600	—
Ross and Cromarty DC	149,184	—	—	—	—	—	—	—	—	149,184	—
East Lothian DC	113,520	—	—	—	—	—	—	113,520	—	—	—
Edinburgh DC	853,646	—	443,246	45,900	525,000	−160,500	—	—	—	—	—
West Lothian DC	249,000	—	—	—	—	—	—	—	249,000	—	—
Argyll and Bute DC	92,376	—	—	—	—	33,228	30,000	—	29,148	—	—
Clydebank DC	152,700	—	—	32,700	—	—	—	—	—	120,000	—
Clydesdale DC	233,269	—	—	15,000	32,100	96,452	31,567	—	58,150	—	—
Cumnock and Doon DC	47,700	—	—	91,200	—	—	−68,700	—	—	13,200	12,000
Cunninghame DC	178,012	—	—	—	—	—	—	104,055	—	73,957	—
Dumbarton DC	63,329	8,021	60,000	—	—	—	—	—	−4,692	—	—
East Kilbride DC	39,000	—	—	—	—	—	—	—	—	39,000	—
Eastwood DC	15,000	—	—	—	—	15,000	—	—	—	—	—
Glasgow DC	2,955,859	92,068	98,200	—	—	—	—	—	−37,109	2,802,700	—
Hamilton DC	79,712	—	—	17,400	—	31,316	—	—	—	9,996	21,000
Inverclyde DC	22,800	—	—	—	—	—	22,800	—	—	—	—
Kilm. and Loudon DC	35,000	—	—	—	—	—	—	—	—	35,000	—
Kyle and Carrick DC	155,100	—	—	—	—	155,100	—	—	—	—	—
Monklands DC	499,000	—	50,000	—	—	—	—	233,400	—	50,000	165,600
Motherwell DC	96,581	29,277	90,000	—	—	—	37,500	—	−60,196	—	—
Renfrew DC	195,200	—	—	—	—	—	—	—	—	150,200	45,000
Angus DC	153,745	—	—	—	—	—	46,200	52,270	15,675	39,600	—
Dundee DC	219,702	—	—	93,450	—	—	—	—	—	40,452	85,800
Perth and Kinross DC	16,406	—	—	—	—	16,406	—	—	—	—	—

Organisation	Total									
Cumbernauld Dev. Corp.	720,570	—	—	147,000	424,830	14,700	—	46,140	87,900	—
E. Kilbride Dev. Corp.	1,272,000	—	—	—	—	—	—	—	—	1,272,000
Glenrothes Dev. Corp.	339,501	—	16,350	—	—	136,620	—	103,566	82,965	—
Irvine Dev. Corp.	663,780	—	162,990	—	315,000	—	—	48,000	125,790	12,000
Livingston Dev. Corp.	4,214,622	—	156,989	17,460	1,678,020	—	-4,647	775,800	163,000	1,428,000
British Rail	18,843,854	—	—	1,053,000	—	—	12,779,800	—	2,096,554	2,914,500
British Telecom	24,524,210	—	—	—	261,000	4,472,100	4,708,800	7,390,590	2,970,720	4,721,000
Cal. Mac. Ltd.	3,406,000	—	—	—	—	126,000	—	—	—	3,280,000
Cen. Scot. Water BD.	2,051,085	—	—	—	—	—	—	1,082,685	968,400	—
Civil Aviation Auth.	3,693,000	1,035,000	—	2,460,000	—	—	—	—	—	—
Forestry Com.	390,527	—	—	—	456,600	—	—	—	-66,073	—
Freightliner	533,220	—	—	75,000	114,900	341,850	—	-58,530	—	60,000
HIDB	1,287,672	—	—	60,000	44,772	—	—	—	150,000	1,032,900
NSHEB	19,225,000	—	—	1,763,700	—	—	6,114,600	2,700,000	5,996,700	2,650,000
SDA	12,128,032	1,638,050	1,704,899	9,167	-195,993	—	-14,080	224,109	6,786,500	1,975,380
SDD	27,125,159	—	173,400	—	3,100,000	—	7,002,109	8,893,650	4,527,000	3,429,000
Scott. Gas Board	2,615,400	—	900,000	—	—	—	92,700	—	265,200	1,357,500
Scot. Sports Council	16,500	—	—	16,500	—	—	—	—	—	—
Scot. Tourist Board	9,450	—	—	—	—	—	—	—	9,450	—
Scot. Trans. Group	72,338	—	137,213	—	—	-64,875	—	—	—	—
SSEB	2,836,100	—	28,191	25,500	—	1,008,555	—	—	830,204	943,650
Strath Pass Trans Ex.	9,469,500	—	—	—	—	69,000	—	7,609,500	—	1,791,000
SBG – Alex(Fife)	117,000	—	—	—	—	—	—	—	—	117,000
Aberdeen Harbour BD.	2,221,125	938,100	—	—	163,800	809,400	—	309,825	—	—
Ass. Brit. Ports.	493,500	—	—	48,000	86,700	85,800	—	42,000	207,000	24,000
Clyde Port Auth.	5,053,770	3,164,100	657,000	1,307,400	27,249	-572,000	299,100	-79	—	171,000
Dundee Port Auth.	411,000	—	—	—	180,000	—	—	—	—	231,000
Forth Port Auth.	2,055,756	—	525,000	—	149,756	120,000	250,000	21,000	669,000	321,000
Fraser. Harbour Comm	261,750	—	—	—	—	—	261,750	—	—	—
Lerwick Harb Trust.	3,483,078	816,078	27,000	1,110,000	—	—	—	—	—	1,530,000
Mallaig Harb Board.	724,648	—	124,380	—	-13,225	—	—	34,000	-29,507	609,000
Montrose Harb Trust.	379,500	—	—	109,500	—	—	270,000	—	—	—
Peterhead Harb Trust.	649,642	—	—	—	—	—	649,642	—	—	—
Scrabster Harb Trust.	336,515	—	87,515	—	—	—	—	—	—	249,000
Storn Pier and Harb Co	61,600	—	—	—	—	—	—	61,600	—	—
Ullapool Pier Trust.	327,765	—	61,765	—	—	—	240,000	—	—	26,000
Inverness Harb Trust.	660,000	—	—	—	—	—	—	—	660,000	—
Crom. Firth Port Auth.	538,432	—	—	—	—	—	—	—	58,432	480,000
Wick Harbour Trust.	42,000	—	—	—	—	—	—	—	—	42,000
Shetland Amen. Trust.	39,000	—	—	—	—	—	—	—	—	39,000
Brit. Airports Auth.	552,000	—	—	—	—	—	—	—	—	552,000
National Trust.	281,100	—	—	—	—	—	—	42,000	239,100	—
Piloc. Fest. Theatre.	475,200	—	475,200	—	—	—	—	—	—	—

Source: Planning Exchange, Glasgow and Industry Department for Scotland.

Table 3.2b.   ERDF Non Quota Section Assistance to Scotland
Under the First Two Programmes (Steel and Shipbuilding) October
1980-December 1984 (£ Sterling)

Article 4 (1)	Aid to public and local authorities for environmental improvements and conversion of industrial property
Article 4 (3)	Consultancy services to SMEs
Article 4 (4)	Common service from SMEs
Article 4 (5)	Information and Implementation of Technical Innovation
Article 4 (6)	Risk Evaluation Studies

Recipient	Art. 4 (1)	Arts. 4 (3)-(6)
Strathclyde Regional Council	552,652	93,225
Glasgow District Council	207,578	—
Cunninghame District Council	221,000	—
Monklands District Council	54,552	—
Motherwell District Council	340,893	—
Inverclyde District Council	576,127	—
Clydebank District Council	45,151	—
Joint Public Authorities	372,500	—
Other Public or Industry Bodies	210,500	255,665
Private Sector	—	1,631,910
Nationalised Industries	362,878	—
TOTAL	2,988,982	1,980,800
	= **4,969,782**	

Note: A further £4.2 m was approved in 1984 for an extension of the non quota programme to include textile areas within Tayside Region over the period 1985-7.
Source: Planning Exchange, Glasgow, and Industry Department for Scotland.

Martins and Gibney (Chapter Two).

Scotland has benefited disproportionately from the lending operations of the European Investment Bank, accounting for about 25 per cent of the total UK borrowing since 1973. Because of their responsibility for eligible water and sewerage infrastructure, Scottish regional and islands councils have accounted for a good proportion of the Scottish total, although there is no consistent pattern over time (Table 3.3), reflecting the 'lumpy' nature of these large capital projects. Apart from water supply and sewerage, the majority of the EIB lending to local authorities has been for road constructions and other construction work associated with industrial development projects.

The project based lending of the EIB does not fit easily into the con-

Table 3.3.   European Investment Bank (EIB) Loans for Projects in Scotland (£ million)

	Local Authority	Other	Total
1974	—	24.8	24.8
1975	16.9	80.0	96.9
1976	25.0	41.2	66.2
1977	—	103.9	103.9
1978	18.5	40.7	59.2
1979	51.6[a]	8.7	60.3*
1980	52.2	50.5	102.7
1981	25.0	—	25.0
1982	46.8	34.7	81.5
1983	59.2	—	59.2
1984	13.1	—	—
TOTAL to date	308.3	384.6	692.9

[a] In addition, Lothian Regional Council received at £16.3 m loan in 1979 for water supply and sewerage schemes under the New Community Instrument (NCI, or Ortoli Facility), administered by the EIB.

Source: Planning Exchange, Glasgow.

solidated fund borrowing system of British local government, and it took authorities some time to take full advantage of the lower interest rates offered by the Bank. Some of the financial benefit has been reduced by the operation of an exchange-risk cover-scheme operated by the UK government, and this scheme was revised in 1981 in such a way as further to reduce the interest rate advantage, in a deliberate attempt to restrain external borrowing. Authorities elsewhere in the UK have chosen to dispense with the exchange-risk cover and carry the risk themselves, but the natural conservatism of most local government finance officers has prevented this from becoming a common initiative.

Applications for EIB loans from District authorities are relatively infrequent, partly because the £2.5m. lower limit on direct loans exceeds the value of most district council projects. Proposals for an 'agency' scheme for retailing smaller loans to public authorities have so far foundered for the lack of any suitable intermediary. One solution, adopted by local authorities in Central Region, is for the upper tier (regional) council to package a set of projects on behalf of itself and the lower tier (district) councils.

Despite these problems and the relatively narrow financial

incentive, demand from local authorities for EIB loans has remained strong, and seems likely to increase with the expansion of the Bank's resources, both from its own borrowing (the ceiling on which was doubled in 1981), and from the Ortoli facility (New Community Instrument) which the Bank administers on behalf of the Commission. Also of interest to local authorities are the lending operations of the EIB to private sector firms, particularly through agency agreements with, in Scotland, the Scottish Development Agency (SDA), the Clydesdale Bank, IDS and ICFC (Industrial and Commercial Finance Corporation). Local authorities' growing intervention in their local economies involves signposting firms to suitable sources of finance, including EC grants and loans.

The recent changes in the assisted areas have a somewhat lesser effect on the availability of EIB loans than they do on ERDF grant aid, since they can lend on projects of regional significance and 'common interest', and on energy-related investments, even outside assisted areas, and the exchange-risk cover-scheme has recently been extended to allow private firms in non-assisted areas to take advantage of EIB finance. Within the development areas, the scope for joint ERDF/EIB financing will increase with the adoption of a programme approach by the Regional Fund, and closer liaison between the Bank and the Commission, particularly in respect of the non-quota section and integrated operations being piloted in Naples and Belfast, and suggested for Glasgow.

The Social Fund has been a major focus of local authority interest since 1982. UK wide, the number of local authority applications to the Fund rose dramatically from twenty-five in 1981 to seventy in 1982. In Scotland, there were only two minor grants to local authorities before 1982 (Table 3.4), but seven in 1982 itself, including major allocations to Strathclyde and Tayside regional councils for wage subsidy schemes. This new found interest is partly due to the introduction in 1981 of this new category of employment grant schemes, but partly also to a belated recognition by authorities that their existing training activities for a range of client groups—women, young people, immigrants and the handicapped—were eligible for grant aid. Previously Scotland had benefited substantially from the Fund, but only through UK-wide Manpower Services Commission or Industrial Training Board schemes, or through the Scottish Development Agency or Highlands and Islands Development Board (HIBD). The 'discovery' of the Social Fund by local authorities has increased its conspicuous and per-

Table 3.4. European Social Fund (ESF) Grants to Projects in Scotland, 1978–82 (£000)

	Local Authority	Other Public	Private	Total
1978	127[a]	—	137	264
1979	—	524	10	534
1980	—	1,038	209	1,247
1981	22[b]	375[c]	250	647
1982	1,767[d]	1,416	216	3,399
1983	4,298[e]	1,149	1,210	6,657
TOTAL from 1978 to 1983	6,065	2,565	1,426	10,056

Notes:

[a] Cunninghame District Council – Article 4, Young Persons – Training
[b] Lothian Regional Council – Article 4, Migrants – Training
[c] Including Grant of £28,000 to Inwork, a training company set up by Fife Regional Council

[d] Strathclyde Regional Council – Article 5, Regions – Wage Subsidy			£1,014,000
Tayside Regional Council	- " " "		£507,000
Highland Regional Council	- " " "		£49,000
Dumfries & Galloway R.C.	- " " "		£4,000
Lothian Regional Council	– Article 4, Migrants – Training		£31,000
Glasgow District Council	– Article 4, Young People – Training		£50,000
Lothian Regional Council	– Article 4, Handicapped – Training		£113,000
[e] Highland Regional Council	– Article 5, Regions – Training		£202,450
Strathclyde Regional Council	- " " "		£239,950
" " "	" " "		£708,400
" " "	" " wage subsidy		£1,870,050
Highland Regional Council	" " " "		£107,250
Central " "	" " " "		£273,000
Tayside			£250,000
Lothian			£120,000
Western Islands Council	" " " "		£58,500
Orkney " "	" " " "		£19,500
Lothian Regional Council	– Article 4, Migrants – Languages		£48,900
Central " "	" " "		£164,500
Lothian " "	" Handicapped – Training		£242,817
Strathclyde " "	" Technical Progress "		£115,000

In addition to these grants which are clearly applicable to Scottish projects, Scotland has benefited from large amounts of Social Fund aid to programmes organized on a UK basis by the Manpower Services Commission, Industry Training Boards, BSC (Industry) Ltd., Nationalised Industries, and private firms.

Source: Planning Exchange, Glasgow.

ceived impact, although the total benefit to Scotland, or the UK, is not significantly changed.

Like the ERDF, the Social Fund was under review in 1982/3, and a new Regulation, entering force in September 1983 governs the operation of the Fund from 1984 onwards. The revised guide-lines place more emphasis on measures to asssist the employment and training of young people (under 25), and on job creation and innovatory projects. Local authorities will have to adjust their activities and submissions to reflect these new criteria. One change in the Social Fund regulation which would seriously reduce the funding available for recruitment-premiums schemes by local authorities in Assisted Areas was proposed by the Commission in August 1983. Scottish local authorities led by Strathclyde and Central regions were quick to respond and helped to organize a UK wide lobby to resist the change, which was in fact a side effect of the Community's wider budget crisis.

The Department of Agriculture and Fisheries for Scotland (DAFS) and the Highlands and Islands Development Board have been active in promoting the use of the Agricultural Guidance Fund (FEOGA) for restructuring and modernization of farms and food processing industries. Scottish local authorities have themselves made sporadic use of the Fund for marketing improvements and for municipal processing facilities in Kilmarnock, Orkney, Edinburgh, Falkirk, and Highland region but the majority of aid has predictably gone to the private sector.

The potential for Community financial aid in rural areas has however assumed a new dimension, and a new level of interest for local authorities with the emergence of the Integrated and Agricultural Development Programme (IDP and ADP respectively). The Western Isles Islands Council has been closely involved in the planning and administration of the IDP for their area. Early hopes that the Programme would be truly integrated, with ERDF, EIB, and ESF aid complementing FEOGA assistance have been disappointed. Nevertheless, the experimental programme, involving farm improvements, rural infrastructure, shelter afforestation, training, and other developments promises to be of considerable benefit to the Islands (£20m. is committed over five years—40 per cent of it from FEOGA), and also to pioneer some interesting new approaches to rural development. This is even more true of the proposed large-scale ADP for the Highlands, with which Highland Regional Council and the area's MEPs have been closely involved. These developments form part of a much wider debate about the desirable future both for remote rural areas and for the common agricultural policy itself. Authorities such as the Borders and Dumfries and Galloway Regional Councils will be watching developments in FEOGA with interest.

The European Coal and Steel Community and Steel Community provides financial assistance for restructuring and retraining and for alternative employment in areas of decline in the coal and steel industries. Central Scotland has a long tradition of both mining and steelmaking. Both industries, despite years of contraction and massive job losses, remain under threat from the continued recession and lack of competitiveness. Closure of collieries in Lothian and Strathclyde regions, and threats to the integrated steel complex based on Ravenscraig in Strathclyde are only the most recent symptoms of a continuing crisis. Since accession to the Community, Scotland has benefited from considerable amounts of ECSC aid, although as with the Social Fund, the amounts cannot always be clearly identified since they are channelled through the national (UK) organizations of the National Coal Board and the British Steel Corporation.

Local authorities responsible for areas of coal and steel decline have maintained a close interest and involvement in restructuring within the industries, and in the development of alternative job opportunities. A good example is the Steel Industry Working Group organized by Strathclyde Regional Council, with representation from BSC management, the relevant trades unions, and the district councils concerned. Strathclyde officials played a major part in preparing the recent defence of Ravenscraig, and help to monitor ECSC developments as they affect the Scotish steel (and coal) industries.

The other aspect of ECSC operations of interest to Scotland is the lending to the private sector in coal and steel closure areas, similar in terms and administration to the EIB agency loans. In the case of the ECSC scheme, agents in Scotland include the SDA, the Industrial and Commercial Finance Corporation (ICFC), Industry Department for Scotland, and the Clydesdale, Co-operative, and Royal Banks. The industrial or business development staff of local authorities include ECSC loan finance in the packages of aid which they promote within their areas and advertise as incentives externally.

The accompanying Tables describe the destination of the main Community Funds in Scotland. The total impact of Community spending would also include the regional impact of agricultural price support.

Conclusion

Scotland's position in relation to UK government has, as we have seen, allowed Scottish interests, through the Scottish Office, access to European levels of decision-making. On occasions this had led to observable results. On the other hand, Scottish influence in Europe should not be exaggerated. Except in relation to fisheries, the Scottish Office is a junior department in UK government and its role is more that of a lobby, to gain concession within the limits of UK policy than to set the policy itself, and there is always the suspicion that in any cross-functional trade-offs in Europe, Scottish interests might be neglected. Moreover, in the government's two stage attack on traditional regional policy (1979 and 1984), even the combined influence of the Scottish Office and other Scottish interest groups has failed to protect Scotland's interests against the claims of the English regions. Even with these qualifications however, Scotland is still relatively well placed, as a peripheral region, to influence decisions as long as Community decision making remains the prerogative of national governments.

Additionality of EC finance remains, as it has been since accession, one of the dominant issues in Community/member state relations. The intention of the Community, as set out in numerous Regulations and supported by the Commission, if not the Council, is clear—that aid from the various Funds should be additional to national government expenditure, in the sense of allowing new or expanded projects to go ahead, which would not otherwise be possible. Local authorities do, in fact, as we have seen, derive a positive, if small net benefit from ERDF and ESF grants. In practice, however, even these gains are constrained and in some cases outweighed by tight government control over both capital and revenue (current) expenditure. ERDF grants and EIB loans are non-additional in the sense that they do not bring an increase in the allocations or capital spending limits set by the Scottish Office.

Any advantage of Social Fund grant aid has been more than undermined in recent years by reductions in rate support grant, and the suspicious mind could easily reach the conclusion that the Treasury was taking ESF receipts to local government into account in arriving at the RSG settlement.

The additionality issue has taken on a new dimension and prominence during the negotiations over the UK budget refund since 1979. It was agreed by the Community that refunds to the UK should be paid partly as a straight cash reimbursement, but partly as a contribution to new public sector investment projects such as road building, water and sewerage works, housing, and land reclamation. As with the ERDF assistance, the British government claims that the budget rebates have allowed existing programmes to continue at a level that would not otherwise have been possible. Both the European Parliament and the Court of Auditors have recently rejected this claim, finding that the rebates have been financing projects that were not only committed, but in many cases even well under way before the refunds were agreed.[17] At a major Conference of Local Authorities in Edinburgh in November 1982, Commissioner Ivor Richard, departing from his prepared text, indicated that the Commission viewed the abuse of the additionality principle (by all member states), as a serious problem, and that they intended to make resoluion of this issue a priority.

Overall, the Funds, though publicly highly visible, are in practice a relatively less important aspect of Scotland's relationship with the EC. The prominence given to them by central and local government and the controversy over additionality has tended to obscure the more important ways in which Scottish interests have been able to influence Community policy, the results which have been obtained, and the problems of access which remain.

Were Scotland to receive a devolved government, the picture would change. Unless the Scottish Office were retained in some form, access to Community decision-making could be made more difficult. Alternatively, means could be found for the direct articulation of Scottish and other 'regional' interests in the Communities. This proposal, which would no doubt be resisted strongly by national governments, is thus a corollary of proposals to devolve power to regions from national governments. Devolution would, in any case, open up to public scrutiny much of the bargaining that currently takes place among Scottish, UK, and European levels of decision-making. Certainly, if the merits and drawbacks of EC membership in Scotland are to be debated and public opinion informed, there does need to be much more openness about the way in which EC issues are handled within the UK.

Notes

1. *Glasgow Herald*, 24 Apr. 1979.
2. *Guardian*, 23 Sept. 1982.
3. *Scotsman*, 28 Sept. 1982.
4. Butler, D., Kitzinger, U., *The 1975 Referendum* (London: Macmillan, 1976).
5. Keating M., and Midwinter, A., *The Government of Scotland* (Edinburgh: Mainstream, 1983).
6. Calderwood, R., 'Gearing European Community Policies to Local Needs: How

the Local Authority Makes an Impact', unpublished paper IULA/CEM Conference, Edinburgh, Nov. 1982.

7. Keating, M., and Midwinter, A., op. cit.

8. Ibid.

9. Ibid.

10. Heald, D., 'Territorial Equity and Public Finance: Concepts and Confusions', *Studies in Public Policy* No. 75, University of Strathclyde (Glasgow, 1979).

11. *Scotsman*, 19 Jan. 1983.

12. *Glasgow Herald*, 28 June 1983.

13. Keating, M., 'The Scottish Office: An Asset in Decline?' *Scotsman*, 11 May 1984.

14. Calderwood, R., op. cit. *Glasgow Herald* 26 Jan. 1983.

15. *Scotsman*, 21 Jan. 1983.

16. Keating, M., and Midwinter, A., 'The Area Project Approach to Local Economic Development in Scotland', *Public Administration*, 62.1 (1984).

17. *Financial Times*, 6 Jan. 1984.

4

Wales in the European Community

BARRY JONES

The European connection has been a mixed blessing for Wales, presenting it with opportunities and posing it problems. The opportunities have been expressed in the form of increased inward investment to help repair the ravages of the first industrial revolution but they have been matched by a widespread concern that Wale's distinctive economic institutions and social character might be overwhelmed or distorted by the interests of the larger European political entity. The relative importance attached to these conflicting viewpoints has coloured the Welsh attitude towards the European Community. While that attitude has oscillated between cautious optimism and muted hostility, it has been persistently suspicious. The suspicion is fuelled by apprehensions that Wales does not easily fit the rationale and policy structures of the European Community because it is a small, historic, and cultural nation rather than an economic region; and, furthermore, that the liability of Wales's peripheral position would be accentuated by membership of a Community whose focus of economic development was not the south-east of England but the more remote Golden Triangle of the Rühr, Benelux, and north-east France.

Prior to the 1975 referendum wide sections of Welsh political opinion subscribed to this 'peripherality' argument. It was a view strongly held in the Welsh Labour Party[1] and produced deep divisions in a party traditionally loyal to the parliamentary leadership. The division of opinion in the dominant party in Welsh politics allied to Plaid Cymru's (the Welsh Nationalist Party) unequivocal hostility to the Common Market appeared to presage a close result in the referendum with a high level of abstentions. Yet the turnout in Wales was the highest in the United Kingdom (see Table 4.1) and the majority 'Yes' vote was significantly greater than in Scotland or in Northern Ireland. Although the subsequent devolution episode revealed a close political affinity between England and Wales, the result of the European referendum could not be interpreted simply as a reflection of geographic and cultural proximity to England. Gwynedd, the most Welsh-speaking county and the most remote, recorded a 'Yes' vote of 70.6 per cent, the second highest in Wales. In contrast the highly anglicized border county of Gwent registered only 62.1 per cent. The best result for the 'anti-marketeers' came in Mid-Glamorgan where the Wales TUC concentrated its campaign. Here 43.1. per cent voted 'No'. The evidence of the vote suggests that Wales did not divide along cultural linguistic lines but more in terms of economic interests, with rural Wales giving its enthusiastic support while industrial Wales extended a more reluctant endorsement of continued British membership.

Table 4.1.   Results – EC Referendum 1975

Counties	% Yes	% No	% Turnout
Clwyd	69.1	30.9	65.8
Dyfed	67.6	32.4	66.9
Gwent	62.1	37.9	66.4
Gwynedd	70.6	29.4	64.5
Mid-Glam.	56.9	43.1	66.4
Powys	74.3	25.7	68.1
South Glam.	69.5	30.5	66.9
West Glam.	61.6	38.4	67.2
Wales	64.8	35.2	66.7

The referendum results represented a serious rebuff for both the Labour and nationalist movements in Wales. However, the European Community's notable lack of success in developing a substantial regional development fund and positive interventionist policies, a major element in the 'Yes' lobby's campaign, contributed to a hardening of Welsh opinion against EC membership. A measure of the dissatisfaction with the European connection was reflected in the results of the 1979 Euro-election results when barely a third of Welsh electorate bothered to vote. Three of the four Welsh seats were won by Labour candidates whose electoral addresses revealed an extreme scepticism of the benefits which had accrued to Wales from EC membership and a commitment to British withdrawal.

The dramatic cut back in steel making in Wales and the closure of several Welsh steel works, associated in the public mind with the

Table 4.2. Euro Electoral Results 1979 and 1984

Euro-Constituency	% Turnout		% Winning Party Majority	
	1979	1984	1979	1984
Mid and West Wales	38.2	40.2	Lab. 5.5	Lab. 16.9
North Wales	35.9	42.4	Con. 15.6	Con. 5.6
South Wales	32.9	38.5	Lab. 6.2	Lab. 22.6
South East Wales	31.1	38.2	Lab. 24.0	Lab. 44.3

European Commission's D'Avignon Plan, together with growing concern over Britain's budgetary contributions, compounded Welsh disillusionment with the EC. In the face of this shift in Welsh opinion, the Commission launched a concerted effort to reverse this trend. Ivor Richard, the Commissioner for Employment and Social Affairs, and himself a Welshman, spoke at the 1981 annual conference of the Wales TUC and made an impassioned plea for continued Welsh membership. Later that year the Wales CBI launched a pro-Europe campaign because, according to its Director Ian Kelsall, 'the general public may have become a bit disillusioned [and] may be susceptible to the argument that the EEC has not lived up to its expectations'.[2] In the CBI's 1982 conference the principal speaker, Dr David Owen, another politician with strong Welsh connections, stressed the advantages for Wales in the European connection. But the pro-Europe campaign made little impact on the Welsh Labour movement still largely opposed to the European Community. According to a Wales TUC document published in 1982: 'Withdrawal from the EEC [is] a fundamental and indissoluble part of the economic strategy.'[3] The growing intensity of the 'in or out' debate was reflected by the Welsh Affairs Committee's decision in 1982 to investigate 'the impact on Wales of membership of the EEC'.

Welsh uncertainty over the benefits of continued EC membership was reflected in the public opinion polls taken in the spring of 1983, the only ones to test Welsh opinion on this issue. In March 39 per cent wanted to stay in, while 46 per cent wanted to come out. However, as the general election approached opinion swung round and in May a clear majority of 55 per cent favoured staying in compared with 32 per cent who still opted to come out.[4] The political parties in Wales, lacking accurate and regular measures of Welsh opinion tended to follow the line established by their British counterparts. Thus Liberals and Conservatives in Wales staunchly supported the European Community. The Welsh Labour Party reflected the British party's divisions albeit with a slightly stronger anti-EC bias because of the acute vulnerability of much of the traditional industries in Wales to EC rationalization policies. However, the most significant change was effected by Plaid Cymru. At the time of the European referendum the party was unambiguously committed to withdrawal but defeat in the European referendum and subsequently in the devolution referendum, the ebb of the nationalist tide and the consolidation of Plaid Cymru's support in rural Gwynedd, induced a reappraisal of party policy. In the 1983 general election Plaid Cymru supported continued Welsh membership of the European Community so long as Wales remained part of the United Kingdom, arguing that it would weaken the identity and structure of the British state and that EC policies would protect Wales 'from the worst of Thatcherism'.[4]

The tendency to infuse the European debate with the arguments and issues of domestic Welsh and British politics was evident in the 1984 Euro-elections. On the surface nothing changed. Wales again returned to the European Parliament three Labour members and one Conservative member. However, of Labour's three original MEPs, two had moved on to the Westminster Parliament, a route which the lone Conservative MEP had attempted, unsuccessfully, to follow. Turnout in Wales was again higher than the UK average but this was less a reflection of Welsh enthusiasm for the European Community than a measure of the strident campaign waged by the Alliance candidate in North Wales and the discontent of dairy farmers in Mid and West Wales. The general impression gained from the Euro-election campaign was that the idea of the European Community had made very little impact on the Welsh electorate. However, it would be unwise to draw any conclusions about the relationship of Wales with the European Community exclusively from an interpretation of the statistics of Euro-elections. While the Welsh connection with Brussels may not have penetrated the political consciousness of the general public, it is significant. It involves a wide range of institutions in Welsh life including central government departments, local authorities and organized interests, each of which we will now consider.

The Role of the Welsh Office

Since their creation in November 1964 the Welsh Office and the Welsh

Secretary of State with a seat in the cabinet, have been expected not simply to administer government policies in Wales but to act as a lobby for the Welsh interest. Initially, that meant winning economic advantages for Wales within the framework of British government but since January 1973 the Welsh Office role has been extended to include responsibilities for the administration of certain Community policies. The new, more widely-defined role of the Welsh Office raises expectations which can never be fully realized by a government department operating within a unitary state and lacking both the seniority and administrative experience of the Scottish Office. Furthermore, there are very few purely Welsh Office expenditures for the Welsh Secretary to control and allocate. Within the framework of the government of the United Kingdom the Welsh Office is a relatively junior government department concerned with the humdrum tasks of policy implementation and able to exercise discretion only on the margins.[5] However, it would be a mistake to dismiss the Welsh Office as merely an agency of Whitehall. In their analysis of the framework of government in Wales Madgwick and James identified four major functions for the Welsh Office—executive, overseeing, consultative, and that of spokesman for the Welsh interest. They concluded that it is in the exercise of these last three functions that Welsh government has 'edged along the scale from agency towards autonomy'.[6] The development is partly the product of external factors, the upsurge of nationalist sentiments and peripheral assertion which coincided with the creation and expansion of the Welsh Office and which helped to give it a distinctive Welsh cultural character; but it also came about because of the Welsh Office's ability to exploit its intermediate position within the framework of British government so as to establish a close and continuing relationship with Welsh local authorities. In effect, an informal network of Welsh consultative government has been created which supplements the formal departmental institutions and which has assumed considerable importance for the Welsh Office in the context of British government policies and, latterly, a significance in the administration of EC policies in Wales.

The role which the Welsh Office can play within the European Community is, however, governed by an absolute constraint. Wales is a constituent part of the United Kingdom and all communications with Brussels in respect of policy are maintained by the lead departments—Industry, Agriculture, Employment, Energy, and Environment—whose remit is functional not territorial. However, while in strict constitutional terms the relationship of Wales with the European Community is indistinguishable from that of the rest of the United Kingdom, the Welsh Office recognizes and accepts the obligations to ensure that all lead departments are fully briefed on the social and economic structures of Wales, *before* the start of discussions with the Commission in Brussels. These briefing exercises are so comprehensive that the Welsh Office has not felt the need to have its representative in Brussels. Consequently the Welsh Office presence in the Commission is slight and occasional. In the case of the ERDF, an Assistant Secretary attends the Regional Policy Committee four or five times a year; at the Fund Management Committee which meets three or four times a year, the Welsh Office is represented at principal level. Since 1978 when the Welsh Office acquired responsibility for Agriculture, an Under-Secretary from the Welsh Office Agriculture Department (WOAD) has been a member of the British delegation on Commission working parties whenever new agriculture schemes were being negotiated. No Welsh Office official has ever been seconded to work on UK REP.

Only a small proportion of EC grants and loans are identifiable at the Welsh level. Over the first ten years of British membership they amounted to £1,200m. (see Table 4.3) The Welsh Office's most significant and positive role is played in the administration of the European Regional Development Fund. Although the policy lead is taken by the Department of Industry, the Welsh Office is responsible for advising Welsh local authorities on the eligibility of their intended projects, assessing and filtering their applications and, in the final analysis, determining what applications shall be submitted to the Commission. It also maintains contact with the Commission and, if need be, can support specific cases or applications through its representative on the Fund Management Committee. Finally, it administers ERDF payments, using its formal links with Welsh local authorities and the informal consultative procedures which have evolved. Given the range of its responsibilities, the number of civil servants involved in the ERDF in Wales is surprisingly small. The Industrial Policy and Development Division with a staff of less than twelve provides back-up advice in processing ERDF applications. But the European Division which is specifically responsible for administering ERDF usually consists of no more than eight officers. Consequently the working relationship developed with Welsh local authorities is both close and personal. It contributed to breaking down the partisan suspicion with

Table 4.3. Identifiable Grants and Loans to Wales to May 1984

	£m	£m	%
ERDF		220.4	18.1
Industrial non quota grants	79.6		
Infrastructure grants	140.8		
ECSC		389.3	32.0
Grants	47.3		
Loans	342.0		
EIB		394.0	32.4
ESF		51.3	4.2
FEOGA		161.6	13.3
		1,216.9	100.0

Source: HC 410-i Committee on Welsh Affairs: Minutes of Evidence 16 June 1982. HMSO, p. 16.

which several Welsh local authorities initially regarded the EC and which inhibited the full take-up of the various grants and schemes promoted by the Commission. Over the years, the Welsh Office's European Division has fulfilled both a public relations and an educative function through regular discussions with local authority officials and the publication of a circular, detailing the financial assistance available from the EC which, updated every two years, provides a comprehensive guide through the complexities of EC procedures and an insight into the perceptions of the Commission.

In the administration of other EC policies in Wales, the Welsh Office has played a more limited and subordinate role. In the case of the European Coal and Steel Community (ECSC) policy, the lead departments of Industry and Energy are responsible for the organization, distribution and administration of funds. The Welsh Office's role is confined to that of prior consultation through the various interdepartmental committees. In the case of the European Social Fund (ESF) the Welsh Office's role is again that of an agency, subordinate to the Department of Employment. However, in addition to inter-departmental consultations, the Welsh Office has a liason function, working with Welsh sponsors, advising them and publicizing the operation of ESF in Wales. The Welsh Office also has a significant but subordinate financial role. It is the European Investment Bank's agent for the negotiation of small loans of less than £2.5m. and it provides exchange cover and guarantees for loans under the Exchange Risk Guarantee Scheme (ERGS). The Common Agricultural Policy (CAP) provides for an input from the Welsh Office. Its Agriculture Department (WOAD) administers CAP within Wales, provides advice and implements guidance measures, represents the Welsh interest in interdepartmental discussions and is represented on Commission working parties preparing advice on agricultural policy matters. It is also 'involved' on certain CAP management committees but the degree and extent of this involvement is unclear; at best limited and at worst merely token.

The Local Government Response

Welsh local authorities have been responsible for raising the salience of Welsh issues in Brussels because of the positive way they responded to the opportunities presented by ERDF. The Fund, the projects it was designed to support, and the application procedures encouraged Welsh local authorities to deal directly with the Commission. In 1981 the Welsh Counties Committee (WCC), a body representing all eight Welsh county councils, organized a deputation to Brussels to discuss the operation of the regional and social funds with members of the Commission. The following year, in October 1982, Dyfed, Gwynedd, and Powys produced a joint submission to the Commission highlighting the particular rural problems of Wales. When giving evidence to the Committee on Welsh Affairs, WCC was so enthusiastic for the European idea that it argued the need for Community 'initiatives and ideas which transcend national and regional boundaries'.[7] However, local authority enthusiasm for the European connection, or at least the perceived benefits that are presumed to flow from it, is tempered by a lack of knowledge of the precedural complexities of the Commission's bureaucracy. Visits to Brussels, while certainly a help, only partly clarify confusions in the minds of local government officials and councillors. Some local authorities, like Ynys Mon in North Wales, have prudently engaged the services, on a part-time basis of a Euro MP's researcher, to advise them on EC procedures and institutions. South Glamorgan has taken the initiative of seconding a middle-rank local government officer to the Commission in the expectation that when he returns his experience and contacts in Brussels will assist the county in its future dealings with the Commission. West Glamorgan has reorganized its management structure to co-ordinate and speed up applications to the Commission for the various loans and grants for which the county is qualified. Finally, there appears to be a general realization of the benefits of mutual help. Both Mid-Glamorgan and

Dyfed County Councils now publish regular European information leaflets which are distributed to Welsh local authorities and MPs.

Despite these initiatives, the relationship between local government in Wales and the Commission in Brussels is far from perfect. While there is no lack of information on the opportunities available to local authorities, it tends to be indiscriminate. Welsh district councils, lacking the bureaucratic expertise available to the counties, are overwhelmed by the sheer volume of information flowing from the Commission, the Council of European Municipalities and the Welsh Office. Information concerning EC funding opportunities is sometimes acquired by a process of haphazard discovery. For example, Torfaen Borough Council giving evidence to the Committee on Welsh Affairs admitted that they only discovered on their third visit to Brussels that a job subsidy scheme associated with the Social Fund was applicable to their own area, and then only as a result of a chance meeting with a Welshman employed in the Director-General's office. The Borough's spokesman conceded that the information was available in the literature issued by the Commission, but pointed out that sometimes the amount of information was so enormous that local authority officers and members did not have the time to wade through the details.[8]

Welsh local authorities are critical not simply of the system but also of the Welsh Office itself. At first sight this is surprising. The Welsh Office, using the consultative framework it has built up, provides a focus for the exchange and distribution of information on EC schemes, grants, and loans which give Welsh local authorities an advantage compared with their English counterparts. However, the central role played by the Welsh Office in the operation of the Regional Development Fund does have certain disadvantages for Welsh local authorities. The Regional Development programme submitted to Brussels, on which the ERDF allocations are based, is drawn up by the Welsh Office with relatively little local government involvement. This, together with the tendency for ERDF grants to be conditional upon existing programmes concentrates considerable power in the Welsh Office. Furthermore the Welsh Office, acting as a sieve, constitutes by far the biggest hurdle which Welsh local authorities have to surmount in pleading their case for regional aid. In the opinion of the Welsh Counties Committee the Welsh Office's central and dominant position frustrates the emergence of a tripartite regional planning system involving the Welsh Counties, the Welsh Office and the European

Table 4.4.   Distribution of ERDF Aid to Wales by Counties

Counties	Totals to May 1984 (£ mill)			
	Infrastructure	Industry	Non-Quota	Total
Clwyd	15.52	16.82	2.7	35.04
Dyfed	13.39	0.68	—	14.07
Gwent	36.27	19.97	2.7	58.94
Gwynedd	12.21	0.65	—	12.86
Mid Glamorgan	20.39	3.34	—	23.73
Powys	24.42	0.74	—	2.39
South Glamorgan	36.22	21.49	2.7	60.41
West Glamorgan	16.25	5.11	2.7	24.07
Non-identifiable	7.37	—	—	7.37
Wales	159.28	68.8	10.8	238.88

Source: EC Commission Office, Cardiff.

Commission, a development the majority of local authorities in Wales seeks to promote.

Some counties have operated the existing system with considerable success. South Glamorgan County, despite the advantage of having Cardiff, Wales's administrative capital, within its boundaries and, by Welsh standards, of being relatively prosperous, has been particularly successful in securing almost 25 per cent of the ERDF Welsh allocation (Table 4.4). In part, its success is attributable to the closure of the East Moors steelworks and the construction of the Ford engine plant, developments which made South Glamorgan eminently eligible for ERDF funding. However, the county has been able to build on this advantage by tailoring its applications to meet ERDF conditions. Thus the county's highway investment policy has been consistently oriented towards obtaining economic and social advantages rather than in achieving traffic objectives largely because the two former considerations are essential criteria in ERDF's operations. South Glamorgan's applications are also accompanied by detailed documentation which describes the economic background together with any special features such as factory closures, the package of measures planned to redevelop the area including the role of non-governmental bodies, and the precise programme which the ERDF is to be asked to support. According to the County's Director of Environmental Planning, it is crucial that 'each scheme the Commission is asked to consider is linked to previous schemes and future prospects.

Momentum can thus be built up behind the whole package.'[9] South Glamorgan's success is also the product of the county's determination to avoid public inquiries which might impede the planning process and so jeopardize ERDF support. Its chief officers sell the county hard, make frequent visits to Brussels to test the pulse of the Commission and, sensitive to the political pressures within EC, ensure that the county's applications are carefully translated and submitted in four languages (English, French, German, and Dutch) a reflection perhaps of the Welsh local authority's awareness of the symbolic importance of language.

Welsh Economic and Political Interests

The criteria for the operation of the majority of European Community schemes in Wales are determined from a British perspective and based on the presumption that the social and economic fabric of Wales is closely intermeshed with that of the United Kingdom. Furthermore, the administration of all EC schemes is achieved through the institutional framework of a British government which retains the right to co-ordinate all regional policies so as to conform to British national priorities.

However, Wales exhibits distinctive social and economic characteristics which require special treatment. A high proportion of Wales's industries are basic, traditional, and declining; much of its communications infrastructure is badly rundown and in urgent need of modernization. These general factors, highlighted by the restructuring requirements of a contracting steel industry, are responsible for the operation of the ERDF non-quota section in Wales which provides grant aid to Welsh local authorities for environmental improvement projects. Wales is also particularly well qualified for the ECSC re-adoption grants designed to help those made unemployed by the coal and steel industries. There are other important and distinctive Welsh interests in agriculture which are reflected in the volume of CAP schemes in Wales (Table 4.5). The Welsh dairy industry accounts for 45 per cent of Welsh agricultural output and represents 10 per cent of the United Kingdom's production. The Welsh sheep flocks constitute 25 per cent of the UK flock and 9 per cent of Community flocks, a dominant position which is reflected in the fact that 27.4 per cent of annual sheep guaranteed payments within the United Kingdom, are made to Wales. Welsh agriculture is heavily based on livestock and it is

Table 4.5.   CAP Schemes Administered by Welsh
Office Agricultural Department

	% of UK Total
Suckler Cow Premium	11.8
Sheep Annual Scheme	27.4
Dairy Herd Conversion	9.7
Non-marketing of Milk Premium	9.3
Agricultural and Horticultural Development	9.4
Less Favoured Areas Schemes	26.3
Individual Project Marketing and Processing } Grants	3.0
Interim Fishing Measure	

Source: HC 410-i Committee on Welsh Affairs: Minutes of Evidence 16
June 1982. HMSO, p. 16.

clearly in the interests of the Welsh farming sector to redress the
imbalance between the returns for livestock as compared to the cereals
sector. But this aspiration is at variance with the interests of English
agriculture which possesses a strong cereals sector backed by an
influential lobby. The conflict of interests causes some embarrassment
for the Welsh Office, which although having a territorial responsibility
remains a central government department with central government
obligations. The Deputy Secretary at the Welsh Office described the
position thus: '. . . although we in the Welsh Office, know and argue
for policies which will support the livestock sector, there is no sense in
our advocating policies which are disruptive to the health of the agriculture industry in the United Kingdom as a whole; it has to be taken as
one'.[10]

   The Welsh Office confronts another problem; Wales does not easily
fit the Community's criteria for the application of regional policies.
The Welsh Counties Committee have been highly critical of the Giolitti Report which in their view underestimated the seriousness of
Wales's problems by failing to identify the central fact that Wales
suffers *equally* from an underdeveloped rural hinterland and old
declining industries.[11] This dual deficiency places the Welsh Office at
some disadvantage when seeking to lobby for the Welsh interest, either
in Whitehall or Brussels. It is obliged to secure both agricultural

interests and other interests. While it might like to see more money spent on ERDF it has to be satisfied that the effects of cuts in CAP would not damage Welsh agriculture and 'simply present [it] with another kind of regional problem to deal with'.[12]

A perception that the Welsh interest was not sufficiently well articulated by the formal machinery of government was instrumental in the campaign to establish a Welsh presence inside the European Commission. The beginnings of the campaign date back to 1971, when various Welsh public bodies were attempting to evalute the possible consequences for Wales of entry into the European Community. In October 1971 the Welsh Council—an advisory body of government nominees—produced a report on *Wales and the Common Market*. While on balance favouring British membership, the report stressed it was of the greatest importance to ensure that the Welsh situation was fully understood and went on to recommend that 'arrangements should be made to secure the appointment within the delegation, the Commission and other institutions, of persons with a thorough knowledge of Welsh problems and aspirations'.[13] The government took note of the recommendation but made no move in that direction. In the spring of 1972 a Scottish Office civil servant was seconded to the United Kingdom delegation to the Commission. The development provoked widespread protests in Wales by critics who were concerned not merely that the Welsh case would go by default but that the case of its rival would be put by a Scottish spokesman based in Brussels. Welsh discontent simmered through the summer of 1972. In the autumn a *Western Mail* editorial asserted that 'a permanent Welsh representative in the EEC is essential—his role would be to state the Principality's case against those of its rivals'.[14]

The formation of the European Division in the Welsh Office did little to appease the critics for whom the problem was not how the regional development should be administered in Wales but how large the Welsh share of that fund would be. That in turn would reflect the degree of success of the Welsh lobby in Brussels. Cledwyn Hughes, then Chairman of the Parliamentary Labour Party called for a third British Commissioner—for Wales—implying that England and Scotland, in the persons of Christopher Soames and George Thomson, already had one each. Failing that, he suggested that there should be at least an assistant commissioner for Wales and advocated the creation of a Welsh unit as part of the United Kingdom permanent delegation to the Commission. These demands were rejected by the Conservative

Government's Welsh Secretary of State, who argued that the Welsh interests were equally capable of being protected by the British delegation, as were all other regional and sectional interests within the United Kingdom. However, the perceived disadvantage to Wales in the institutional arrangements for representing the United Kingdom in Brussels was resolved, but not by the initiative of the Conservative government. It came about as a result of internal changes within the Labour Party's organization. In January 1973 Gwyn Morgan, a Welshman from Aberdare, failed in his bid to be appointed Labour's General Secretary, resigned from the post of assistant general secretary and moved to Brussels to be appointed Chef de Cabinet to George Thomson. The appointment was greeted with general satisfaction in Wales and 'great glee in the Welsh Office'.[15] Wales had her man in Brussels. Subsequently the Welsh interest has continued to be represented in the Commission in a variety of ways. Roy Jenkins, in expatriate Welshman, occupied the Presidency from 1977 to 1981, and 1981 to 1985 Ivor Richard—originating from Cardiff—was Commissioner for Employment and Social Affairs with a Welsh-speaking Welshman as his Chef de Cabinet.

The Welsh presence in the Commission, although significant and influential, hardly constitutes a regularized basis upon which a lobby for Welsh interests can build. It is dependent upon political chance and the personalities of the particular Welshmen involved. While the evidence given to the Committee on Welsh Affairs indicates that Welsh officials employed by the Commission lend a sympathetic ear to visiting delegations from Wales, there are limits to the influence they can exercise. The announcement in August 1975 that a European Commission Office for Wales was to be established in Cardiff, was in part a recognition of the need to create a more tangible link between the Commission and Wales. The timing of the announcement—coinciding with a high point of Welsh nationalism and the devolution debate—reveals the European Commission's intention to maintain a harmonious relationship with Wales whatever political arrangements emerged in the wake of political devolution. When the European Commission Office in Wales was opened in March 1976 it was a unique institution and with the exception of West Berlin which occupies a singular historical and political position, the first to be located outside a capital city of a member state.

The Cardiff office was intended to accomplish similar functions to the EC office in London; namely the promotion of the Community, its institutions, policies, and ethos. But from the outset it has assumed another role, ensuring that the voice of Wales is heard loud and clear.[16] In pursuit of this objective the Cardiff office has emerged as more than a public relations office. It positively encourages Welsh local authorities and various public and private bodies in Wales to approach the Commission for financial support. It produces a regular newsletter and organizes seminars, both of which publicize the criteria and application procedures for EC grants and loans. The Office also maintains a high profile in Welsh festivals, eisteddfodau, and agricultural shows, and has become an integral part of the Welsh political scene to an extent unmatched by its London counterpart. It has developed close and constructive contacts with the Wales TUC and CBI Wales and is in constant touch with the Welsh Office and the Welsh Development Agency. The fact that most of those organizations have their main offices around Cathays Park in the centre of Cardiff further assists the development of close personal contacts. Common locale and shared aspirations have produced a flexible framework of advisory bodies, government agencies and organized interests which has done much to break down the Welsh suspicions of the European Community.

The extent to which organized interests in Wales can exploit the advantages provided by the framework of advisory bodies associated with the European Communities Office in Cardiff is dependent on their relationship with their respective British-wide organizations. In some cases this precludes an unrestricted expression of a separate Welsh interest. The National Farmers' Union of England and Wales is a typical example. Its Cardiff office co-ordinates the activities of its members in Wales and is geared to concentrate on those agricultural problems which are particularly acute in Wales, such as the small hill farmer and marginal land. A variety of approaches to the Commission are open to the Cardiff NFU office. It can communicate either through the NFU London Office, through the COPA office in Brussels or it can use its direct telex to the Agriculture Commissioner. However, it most usually operates through the London Office. While the NFU Cardiff office has the option of whether or not to communicate directly with COPA in Brussels this is denied the Farmers' Union of Wales (FUW). The FUW membership strength is concentrated amongst small hill farmers in north and West but because COPA regards Wales as an integral part of the United Kingdom it is unable to recognize a separate additional farmers' union. Thus FUW's vigorous opposition to high cereal prices cannot be formally received by COPA nor directed through normal channels to the Commission; that task remains the responsibility of the National Farmers' Union of England and Wales, which has to accommodate the disparate interests of its members before lobbying the Commission.

The CBI Wales and the Wales TUC have consistently displayed an eagerness to identify with Welsh interests and a willingness to take initiatives in support of those interests. The CBI Wales played a leading role in the campaign to ensure that Wales qualified as a peripheral area for support under the ERDF scheme; between 1971 and 1973 it sponsored the visits of numerous delegations to the Commission in Brussels to press the Welsh case. Whereas the CBI Wales has been a consistent and enthusiastic supporter of British membership the Wales TUC by contrast has been an implacable opponent. However this has not inhibited it from exploiting the procedures of the European Community in promoting the interests of its constituency, the Labour movement in Wales. It has developed close contacts with Welsh Labour MEPs and organized seminars for Welsh trade unionists to explain the operation of ERDF. It established contacts with the Socialist group of MEPs to such good effect that it was invited to give evidence to the Social Affairs and Employment Committee detailing the impact of unemployment in Wales. In April 1982 it successfully applied for a grant from the Social Fund for £250,000 (a sum matched by the Welsh Office) to set up a Welsh Cooperative Resource Centre in Cardiff. However, despite its effective lobbying and the 1983 general election results, the Wales TUC remains unconvinced that Wales will benefit from continued membership although its experience in Brussels comfirms that it can expect and receive a sympathetic hearing in the Commission. As long as Britain remains a member it is clear that the Wales TUC will continue to support a positive role for the Commission over a wide range of policies and, in particular, a campaign against multinational companies across Europe.

The initiatives taken by the Wales TUC have had repercussions within the structure of the British TUC. The British TUC took particular exception to the invitation extended by the Social affairs and Employment Committee to the Wales TUC to give evidence before it. After much heated discussion both the British and Wales TUC delegations attended. Partly because of this and other difficulties occasioned by the European connection the Wales TUC has attempted to regularize its position in relation to the British TUC.

Given that Wales is represented in the European Parliament by four MEPs and given that the EEC has a Welsh Office it is in practice impossible not to be drawn into arguments relating to Wales within the EEC, and neither would the Wales TUC wish to be any different. It is therefore proposed that, in order to legitimate current practice, it be accepted by the TUC that the Wales TUC has a proper role to play in relation to the EEC and the European Parliament and that such representations be accepted as a function and duty of the Wales TUC on behalf of the trade union membership in Wales.[17]

Taken to its logical conclusion, if the Welsh extensions of British organizations were consistently to pressure for a commonly perceived Welsh interest, a self-conscious and coherent territorial lobby would emerge. Some indications of this development are already apparent. The Wales TUC gave evidence to the Social Affairs and Employment Committee in February 1980 and CBI Wales was invited to attend as observers. Encouraged by this and the need for a co-operative Welsh effort, the CBI Wales suggested in June 1980 the creation of a 'Welsh Council' organization—in effect a joint TUC/CBI body—to promote industrial development in Wales. In 1982 a Welsh Committee for Economic and Industrial Affairs was set up, under the Chairmanship of Lord Cledwyn Hughes with the avowed intent of lobbying for Wales in London and Brussels. The South Wales Standing Conference on Regional Policy is another expression of a territorial lobby which includes all the Welsh local authorities in the area together with representatives of a wide range of public and private bodies. In pressing for the alleviation of economic and social conditions in South Wales, the Conference called on the European Community to develop an integrated regional policy and invited the Commission to initiate its own policies rather than to await submissions from member states, sentiments which suggest not only an incipient form of political regionalism but a willingness to identify with broader European aspirations rather than with the more narrowly drawn interests of a member state.

An Assessment

The evidence presented in this chapter indicates that a network of formal and informal linkages between Wales and the European Community is gradually evolving but it is still far from perfect. There is a widely shared view that communications need to be improved between Welsh local authorities, the Welsh Office in Cardiff and the Commission in Brussels. While this might be achieved simply by the Welsh

Office extending its co-ordinating role, such a development would not be unanimously welcomed by Welsh local authorities. The experiences of the first ten years of British membership of the European Community have emphasized the advantages of direct contacts with the Commission in Brussels to large numbers of Welsh organizations. Although there has been progress in developing contacts it has been on an *ad hoc*, pragmatic basis, overly dependent upon the particular initiatives of individual organizations and frequently the product of pure chance. A view is now gaining widespread acceptance that Welsh contacts with the Commission need to be organized more systematically so as to provide an institutional basis for the promotion of Welsh interests.

Welsh local authorities have been to the forefront in pressing for direct and permanent contacts with the European Communities. The Welsh Counties Commission is a member of the Conference of Peripheral Maritime Regions, but this body represents a widely disparate range of regional interests throughout Europe. Consequently during the last few years many Welsh local authorities have become convinced that a body catering specifically for Welsh interests should be set up. The idea was floated by Mr Ivor Richard's *chef de Cabinet* Aneurin Rhys Hughes when speaking at the Welsh National Eisteddfod in August 1983. Mr Hughes warned that pressures from European regions were mounting and that the Welsh case would go by default unless it could be presented more effectively through an office specifically established in Brussels to further Welsh interests and to encourage greater investment in Wales.[18] In October the Welsh Association of Community and Town Councils launched a campaign aimed at establishing a Welsh Bureau in Brussels. The Welsh Office is not yet persuaded of the advantages of setting up its own satellite office in Brussels but the Welsh Secretary of State was open-minded when confronted with a suggestion by the Welsh Affairs Committee that a Welsh Bureau in Brussels should be established and funded by Welsh local authorities and the Welsh Development Agency.[19]

Whether or not a 'Welsh Bureau' is established in Brussels, the present contacts between Wales and the European Community are significant in themselves. Welsh organizations from all sides of the political spectrum have developed a wide range of relationships with the Commission and, despite initial hostility from parts of the Welsh political establishment, the Welsh instinct to act politically, to work an existing system while anticipating its imminent demise, has asserted itself. Thus the Wales TUC while still deeply suspicious of the EC, is nevertheless prepared to advocate a positive role for the Commission in pursuit of policies which it supports. Plaid Cymru have moved from outright hostility to enthusiastic acceptance of continued membership of EC so long as Wales remains part of the United Kingdom. The partly nurtures a residual resentment for the injustice of the European Parliament's electoral arrangements, whereby the Republic of Ireland with a population similar to Wales has fifteen seats compared with only four allocated to Wales. However, it now recognizes that in certain political circumstances Brussels can act as a counterweight to London. Wales's three Labour Euro-MPs, after campaigning on an anti-Common Market ticket in the 1979 elections, were unwilling to join the group of British Labour Euro-MPs pledged to withdrawal. In the words of one of the Welsh Labour Euro MPs the proposal smacked of 'British nationalism overcoming the interests of the working class'.[20] The view reflects a general trend that is taking place in Welsh politics in relation to the European Community. The wider European context has enabled disparate groups in Welsh society to discover common interests which cross the traditional socio-economic divisions. In the long-term membership of the European Community could have a profound impact on both Welsh political perceptions and the Welsh political process.

Notes

1. See Kinnock, N., 'Regional Policy—the Presumptions and the Realities' in *The Common Market and Wales* (Cardiff: Welsh Council of Labour, 1978), p. 13.
2. Quoted in 'Britain and the Community 1973–83: Wales' (Cardiff: Commission of the European Communities, 1982), p. 23.
3. 'Planning the future economic recovery and beyond' (Cardiff: Wales TUC, 1982).
4. *Western Mail*, 17 May 1983.
5. Kellas, J. G., and Madgwick, P. J., 'Territorial Ministries: The Scottish and Welsh Offices', in P. Madgwick and R. Rose, *The Territorial Dimension in United Kingdom Politic* (London: Macmillan, 1982).
6. Madgwick, P. J., and James, M., 'Government by Consultation: The Case of Wales', Studies in Public Policy no. 47 (Glasgow: University of Strathclyde).
7. Committee on Welsh Affairs 1981–82: Minutes of Evidence, HC410 p. 115.
8. HC410, p. 50.
9. Parkinson, E., 'European Funding for Enterprise in the Regions', Conference paper presented to Regional Studies Association, Bristol Polytechnic, 30 Nov. 1981.
10. HC410, p. 19.
11. Committee on Welsh Affairs 1982–3: Minutes of Evidence, HC61-V pp. 191–5.
12. HC410, p. 19.
13. 'Wales and the Common Market' (Cardiff: Welsh Council Oct. 1971), p. 38.

14. *Western Mail* (Cardiff), 21 Sept. 1972.

15. *Western Mail* (Cardiff), 24 Jan. 1973.

16. 'Wales in Europe' (Cardiff: The Commission of the European Communities June 1976).

17. 'TUC Review of Organisation, Structure and Services' (Cardiff: Wales TUC, 1982), p. 18.

18. *Western Mail* (Cardiff), August 1983).

19. Committee on Welsh Affairs 1982–3: Minutes of Evidence, HC 61-1X p. 327.

20. *Arcade* (Cardiff), no. 26, Nov. 1981.

5

Northern Ireland in the European Community

PAUL HAINSWORTH

Uneasy Bedfellows? Northern Ireland and the European Community

British reservations towards the post-war European integrationist trends are legendary. As Churchill pointed out, the United Kingdom was 'with Europe but not of it'. Unwilling to join with France, Germany, and Co. from the beginning, the post-war British governments performed a sort of 'hesitation waltz' until eventually, in the 1960s, successive Conservative and Labour administrations made unsuccessful attempts to join the European Community (EC). As is well known, De Gaulle vetoed these attempts largely on the grounds that the United Kingdom was not ready for membership of Europe. Thus, not until 1973 (after De Gaulle's political exit) did the UK formally enter the EC—a decision ratified by the Conservative Government under Edward Heath, the Westminster Parliament and (later, in the 1975 Referendum) public opinion. At last, the continent took precedence over 'the open sea'.

For better or for worse, the British negotiators of the 1960s and 1970s spoke formally for the sub-national and regional units of the multi-national UK. The decision to enter Europe had important consequences for Northern Ireland. First, 'the open sea' was a 'two seas' problem for Northern Ireland—the peripheral, geographic location fostered a heightened sense of identity and distinctiveness therein. This psychology was particularly strident within those sections of the population who—more British than the British—espoused British traditions and heritage as an insurance for their constitutional status inside the UK. In short, Europe represented a potential and alien threat to Northern Ireland's existence. Second, and very much related to the first point, Northern Ireland was the only 'region' of the UK bordered by another member state of the EC. More significant, this state was hostile and, in principle, annexationist *vis-à-vis* the

109

Northern Ireland 'statelet'. As much as anything, these two factors conditioned local attitudes to the EC thereby making Northern Ireland and Europe uneasy bedfellows. More often than not, debate about the EC has been subsumed by the constitutional and geographic reality of Northern Ireland. The prism of localized, traditional, geo-political argument has made a unique contribution to Northern Ireland's *modus operandi* with the EC.

The purpose of this chapter is to situate the debate about the Northern Ireland 'region' within the localized context alluded to and, at the same time, examine the linkage between Northern Ireland and the EC. However, in attempting to explore this area, the author is mindful of Patrick Buckland's warning[1] about the complexity of local cross-currents, that anybody who is not confused about Northern Ireland does not really understand what is going on.

A European Region?

Superficially, Northern Ireland is not unlike other 'sub-national units' of the UK in its relations with the EC. The structures of representation and communication are *broadly* comparable. For instance, the European Commission has an office in Belfast, as in Cardiff, Edinburgh, and London. Increasingly, European Commissioners and their entourages meet local administrators, politicians, and pressure groups in Northern Ireland and in Brussels. Some local pressure groups—notably the Ulster Farmers' Union (UFU) and the Confederation of British Industries (CBI)—share platforms, offices, and facilities on a common basis with their British counterparts. Also, local spokespersons (for consumers, trade unions, employers) sit on the European Economic and Social Committee (ESC).

If we turn to the European Parliament, Northern Ireland is (over-) represented by three MEP's—John Taylor (Official Unionist Party), the Reverend Ian Paisley (Democratic Unionist Party), and John Hume (Social Democratic and Labour Party). These MEPs, part of the UK's eighty-one seat allocation, participate in the European Parliament's Committees and/or party groupings and function as prestigious local spokespersons for Northern Ireland's cause in Europe. Moreover, the European Parliament—notably via the Regional Committee or visits from 'interested' MEPs—takes an active interest in Northern Ireland affairs, which occasionally are debated on the floor of the EP. For example, the Martin Report (1981) originated from a Resolution proposed by John Hume and supported by Paisley and Taylor so that the Report's comprehensive plea for reforms and European aid enjoyed the support of all the major political groupings in the European Parliament. More controversially, in March 1983, the EP voted to look into the political and economic situation in Northern Ireland with a view to assessing the scope for European initiatives. Again, in 1985, there were moves to debate at Strasbourg the New Ireland Forum report as a basis for a political solution in Northern Ireland.

Within the formal pattern of EC—Northern Ireland relations, a central role is played by the UK Government and its local mouthpiece, the Northern Ireland Office (NIO). Given the 'special' problems of Northern Ireland (security, sectarianism, lack of consensus), the NIO has a higher political profile than its Welsh and Scottish equivalents. This may have consequences in European matters, where the NIO must be seen to be effectively defending Northern Ireland's corner. In the 1980s, for instance, the possibility of European moneys for housing in Northern Ireland thrust the NIO, the Northern Ireland Secretary and his Ministers to the forefront of Euro-bargaining. In a similar fashion, arguments about fishing quotas and rights would enable the Scottish Office to play a key role in European councils. Generally, there are obvious parallels between the NIO and the Welsh and Scottish Offices. Thus, as part of the UK, Northern Ireland is officially represented by the UK Permanent Representation (UKREP) in Brussels. This formal arrangement has prompted indigenous criticisms that UKREP and NIO fail adequately to represent Northern Ireland's interests in Europe. Therefore, it is worth recording both the formal *and* the informal representation for Northern Ireland in Europe.

In the 1960s and 1970s, the Northern Ireland Government (Stormont) was not represented directly on the main negotiating teams at Brussels and Northern Ireland was generally represented by Home Office officials on Whitehall interdepartmental committees and working parties on EC affairs. However, more representation was deemed essential, so Permanent Secretaries to the Northern Ireland Departments visited Brussels in the 'sixties' for talks on membership; these included Sir Douglas Harkness, Head of the Ministry of Finance and the Northern Ireland Civil Service (NICS); and the Permanent Secretaries from Agriculture, Commerce, Labour, and National Insurance. This practice began in 1962 and was to be repeated thereafter—including during the period of direct rule. In addition, Northern Ireland Ministries co-operated with United Kingdom Departments on matters of specific importance to Northern Ireland. The Ministry of Commerce consulted the main organizations representing trade and industry in Northern Ireland and the Department of Economics at Queen's University. The Ministry of Agriculture consulted local organizations and officials were invited to Brussels to discuss the details of the Common Agricultural Policy. Also, various pressure groups such as the Northern Ireland Chamber of Commerce and the Ulster Farmers' Union sent delegations to Brussels and repeated this practice during direct rule. Finally, NICS officials made numerous working visits to London to discuss EC matters. All in all, these diverse links suggested that, from the beginning, the British Government recognized the importance of involving Northern Ireland officials in the EC negotiations. The same applied to Stormont Ministers and Geoffrey Rippon (Heath's European negotiator in 1970) met the Ministers for Agriculture, Commerce, and Health and Social Services to 'discuss those issues of special concern to Northern Ireland'.[2] In May 1971 Mr R McLelland, the Northern Ireland Cabinet Officer in London, was recruited to accompany and advise the United Kingdom team in Brussels and report back to Stormont. In turn, Stormont conducted several debates on the possible consequences of membership of the EC and issued one or two statements.

In one of these Stormont debates (in 1971) the Unionist Premier (Brian Faulkner) stalled criticism of his pro-Europeanism by the promise of the expected White Paper, but this turned out to be a relatively short and innocuous document which recalled problems specific to Northern Ireland and concluded that 'the United Kingdom Government will be able to influence the future developments and the existing well-established arrangements for liaison between the Northern Ireland and United Kingdom Governments will ensure that the latter is fully aware of the particular circumstances of Northern Ireland'.[3] Direct rule put the cat among the pigeons: a new variable was added to the 'existing well established relationships' in the form of the Secretary of State for Northern Ireland, the NIO, and over 1,200 civil servants. With the establishment of the NIO, EC matters (besides financial, economic, commercial, and social policy, and transferred matters) became the responsibility of Division 2 of the NIO's London Office. (In 1981 Division 2 was renamed the Economic and Social Division.) As we have seen, Northern Ireland became represented by the UK Permanent Representation (UKREP) in Brussels. The NIO became an official go-between for Northern Ireland, the UK, and Brussels, but secondary informal relations were continued (see above). Major negotiations within the EC are, of course, the concern of the appropriate British Government Minister (the Prime Minister, Foreign Secretary, Energy Minister, Minister for Agriculture, Food and Fisheries, Trade and Industry) acting through Community institutions, the Council of Ministers or the Committee of Permanent Representatives (COREPER). In this framework, Northern Ireland Departments are sometimes invited to include a senior official in the UK Minister's team of advisers and/or various working groups and committees attached to Ministries operative in London and Brussels. However, absent from this picture is anything as comprehensive as the German procedure for representing regional interests. In 1984 the Commission's Northern Ireland representative pointed to the absence of machinery to co-ordinate responses to European policy initiatives. In particular, he argued that too often European measures were fed into local agencies whose terms of reference were narrower than the European regulations. This could hamper access to funds.

In the light of these problems, the NIO's role is an important one. The NIO arranges for Northern Ireland voices to be represented and informed, besides ensuring that the relevant Ministers attend various committees. Ideally, the NIO should fulfil the task of communicating EC news, papers, documents, and information to the Departments in Northern Ireland and, in turn, assimilate (and preferably respond to) feedback from the Departments, political forces, business interests, trade unionists, and local representatives. To assist co-ordination, there is a special unit within the Central Secretariat at Stormont but its role is limited.

The Secretary of State for Northern Ireland, therefore, is responsible for representing Northern Ireland's European interests within Cabinet. This might entail a rare visit to Brussels by the Secretary of State, Ministers of State or Under Secretaries of State at the NIO but, until James Prior's visit in November 1981, no Secretary of State had availed himself of this option—although the previous NIO Secretary, Humphrey Atkins, did brief the UK's eighty-one MEPs in order to draw their attention to Northern Ireland's interests in Europe.[4] This preoccupation with the NIO should not distract from the other channels of communication for European matters, for example, visits by Commissioners to Northern Ireland; the European Parliament;

Westminster; the European Economic and Social Committee; trade delegations to and from Europe; the Commission's Belfast Office; delegations from local councillors; political groupings, educational establishments and pressure groups. The NIO interacts with all these channels in order to represent Northern Ireland's voice in Europe. The creation of the NIO also meant Northern Ireland representation on various Whitehall committees. Further, the Secretary of State for Northern Ireland had the merit of giving Northern Ireland a voice inside the Cabinet. (In this respect, there are comparisons with the Welsh and Scottish Offices.)

During a visit to watch Northern Ireland in the 1982 World Cup in Spain, the NIO Secretary James Prior boasted that he was able to use his office to good advantage and meet various politicans and dignitaries. In turn, critics protested that the direct rule administration had failed to cash in sufficiently on the good publicity earned by the Northern Ireland football squad in order to promote marketing opportunities. Behind this criticism is the nagging accusation that Northern Ireland is badly represented on European matters.

Nevertheless, the net result of the above pattern of formal and informal Northern Ireland/EC relations is that Northern Ireland benefits as a deprived European region. For example, the Commission sees Northern Ireland as one of Europe's high-priority areas—on a par with Greenland, the Italian Mezzogiorro, the Irish Republic, French Overseas Departments, and Greece. In this context, Northern Ireland is in a position to benefit from Community resources and the various funds—the European Regional Development Fund (ERDF), the European Social Fund (ESF), the European Investment Bank (EIB), the European Agricultural Guidance and Guarantee Fund (EAGGF), as well as initiatives emerging from the Commission's Task Force (See Chapter 1). Beneficiaries of European aid include Aldergrove Airport, the Newry and Mourne Co-operative Society, the Northwest Centre for Training and Development, job-creation schemes, tourism, manufacturing industry, the infrastructure of Northern Ireland, several ports and harbours, farmers, and Kilroot Power Station. The Commission is also 'on the look out' for opportunities to maximize the benefits of EC aid; the Belfast 'integrated operations' scheme may be seen as an attempt to harmonize and rationalize all existing EC funds with the framework of a fully co-ordinated endeavour. However, it is questionable whether the integrated operation will release *extra* funding or even achieve its objectives. One problem has been Council's refusal to accept the notion of EC funding for housing renewal whilst another has been establishing the concept of an integrated operation in the EC. A further difficulty has been the delay in submitting an adequate package as a basis for an integrated operation. The idea was first mooted in 1979, but the initial attempt to draft a comprehensive programme failed to satisfy the Commission. Eventually, in February 1985 Northern Ireland minister Chris Patten and local representatives took a workable blueprint to Brussels. Besides the Commission and Council, it is worth noting that the EP and the Economic and Social Committee take an active interest in Northern Ireland.

Before we examine the impact of European initiatives and regional developments, it will be useful *briefly* to sketch some of the main features of the Northern Ireland economy.

The Northern Ireland Economy

As one European Community publication pointed out, 'At the heart of Northern Ireland's present economic difficulties is the fact that its industrial tradition dates back to the early 19th century with industries which have suffered a sharp decline'.[5] The economy of Northern Ireland is particularly vulnerable owing to the over-reliance on a narrow agricultural and industrial base. A recent study on the Northern Ireland economy maintains that 'It is a measure of Northern Ireland's structural problem that of the four main industries in crisis for which (EC) guidelines have been established, textiles, man-made fibres, shipbuilding and steel, three play an important role in the Northern Ireland economy.'[6] For instance, the shipbuilding industry has shed almost three-quarters of its 1950 work-force (24,500) and the textile industries reveal a similar percentage loss. Moreover, inadequate industrial diversification has left the local economy unable to respond to a rapidly changing economic environment.

The regional problem in Northern Ireland is not simply a child of the 1970s. Indeed, some economists date the problems to the birth of the Northern Ireland 'state' in the early 1920s. Since the 1940s, a panoply of reports, plans and studies have intermittently diagnosed the regional problem. These are beyond the scope of this paper,[7] but the conclusion of the Hall Report (1962) indicated a persistent difficulty. 'The problem is to develop new viable industries in Northern Ireland in order to absorb the labour which can be expected to become redundant in parts of the economy to provide the extra jobs which will be needed in view of the increase in the working population and to reduce the existing level of unemployment.'[8] As far as the latter was concerned, in 1981 the unemployment total passed the symbolic 100,000 mark in Northern Ireland. At present, the unemployment rate is over 20 per cent (about twice the national average) with male and youth unemployment particularly high. The problem is further complicated by the high birthrate (5.6 per cent compared to 0.1 per cent in the UK as a whole in 1981 figures) and high levels of school leavers. This is only partly 'mitigated' by the high rate of emigration: 6,500 per annum in the 1960s, up to 12,000 in the mid-1970s falling to about 7,500.[9]

The regional economic weakness of the local economy is reflected in the relatively poor living standards in Northern Ireland. By most indicators, Northern Ireland is behind other European regions. For example, housing surveys indicate a high level of houses statutorily unfit for human habitation whilst the average wage is roughly 59 per cent of the European Community average. In addition, the peripheral location of Northern Ireland adds about 10 per cent on to export and import prices. The European Commission's First Periodic Report on the social and economic situation in the regions[10] listed three major factors responsible for regional disparities: weak economic development and low industrial investment, high structural and overall unemployment and outward migration, and low employment opportunities. All these factors apply to Northern Ireland.

Rapid technological change, restructuring, sectoral decline, and economic recession have left Northern Ireland particularly vulnerable in the international economy. The more recent manifestations of this malaise are the withdrawal or collapse of large-scale companies (for example De Lorean, Courtaulds, Michelin, ICI, and Grundig) hitherto attracted by generous incentives. Unfortunately, the loss of jobs is not matched by compensatory investment. The lack of competitiveness appears to be a by-product of EC competition policy. Hence, Harvey and Rea[11] conclude pessimistically:

. . . while competition is being pushed hard at Community level with the resulting need to restructure in the weaker economies, the necessary funds to enable restructuring to take place are not at present being made available.

Unless there is a radical readjustment, Community policies as presently implemented will mean the elimination of the existing industrial base of a number of economies including Northern Ireland with nothing being put in its place.

Unsurprisingly, the authors place 'a fundamental question mark over the benefits of Northern Ireland membership' of the European Community. In view of this assertion, it is important to appreciate the actual levels of EC funding in Northern Ireland at the same time bearing in mind the overall impact of EC policies and free trading. According to Commissioner Christopher Tugendhat,[12] between 1973 and 1983 the EC aided Northern Ireland with £342m. in grants, £129m. in loans, plus £212m. under the supplementary measures rebate to the UK. However, general criticisms, notably concerning 'additionality', apply particularly to Northern Ireland. The UK takes about 24 per cent of the ERDF quota and Northern Ireland is accredited with 16 per cent of this figure, amounting to 4 per cent of the total ERDF. The non-quota section favours Northern Ireland, whose frontier regions and shipbuilding industry benefit from 'specific measures'.

Table 5.1.   EEC Regional Fund Commitments (£m)

	1975	*1976*	*1977*	*1978*	*1979*	*1980*	*TOTAL*
England	12	29	27	44	76	77	265
Northern Ireland	8	7	8	14	28	19	84
Scotland	10	15	14	25	37	28	129
Wales	6	8	6	17	22	33	92
	36	59	55	100	163	157	570

Source: Harvey and Rea.

Per capita, Northern Ireland has done well out of the ERDF compared to Scotland and Wales. Table 5.1 indicates comparative funding over the first few years of ERDF's existence.

Of course, these commitments refer to funds designated rather than received. According to Harvey and Rea, capital receipts only amounted to £40.7m.[13] However, these authors find it somewhat encouraging that the trend in ERDF investment in Northern Ireland is more towards infrastructure as opposed to industry, thereby making it likelier that European moneys are passed on to relevant bodies.

The ESF is less subject to the additionality problem. Again, Northern Ireland benefits from this fund—taking about 4.4 per cent of the total fund, with only 0.5 per cent of the Community population.

However, since most of this unemployment and retraining fund goes through the Department of Manpower Services and Government retraining schemes much of it is retained to offset government expenditure.

As regards the EIB, it would appear that Northern Ireland is not making too much usage of this lending facility. The UK has borrowed considerably from the EIB but Northern Ireland's share amounts to only 4 per cent of the UK's loans. Finally, FEOGA (Guidance) funds come directly to Northern Ireland and the local farmers benefit obviously from FEOGA guarantees.

Table 5.2 provides the Commission's estimate of European funds to Northern Ireland after a decade of EC membership. Once again, too much should not be gleaned from these statistics which refer to commitments (as opposed to receipts) and, in any case, are very liable to the 'additionality' principle. The overall impression of the EC's funding is that with the exception of farming guarantees, it is very marginal to the Northern Ireland economy. This is especially notice-able if we compare European funding with the UK's subvention (over £2,000m. per annum) to Northern Ireland. According to MEP Taylor[14] '. . . the contribution of the EEC to the fortunes of Ulster will continue to be insignificant compared with the financial benefits which we receive from London as a result of our position as part of the United Kingdom'. Significantly, the political mileage to be gained from the EC's grants appears infinitely greater than the actual effects of the various grants. Inevitably, therefore, we turn to this theme.

Political Linkage

The first thing that needs to be stressed is that entry into the EC coincided with the end of a sustained period (1921–72) of Unionist one party rule via a devolved system of administration based at Stormont. Within this arrangement, the Westminster Parliament reserved control over crucial areas such as defence, foreign policy, and monetary policy but devolved power to the Stormont administration in others (for example, housing). The semi-autonomous nature of the Stormont regime was reflected in the provision of a local parliament, cabinet structure, and administrative support from the Northern Ireland Civil Service. The local structures and practices led to wide-spread accusations of religious discrimination against Catholics, the minority population, but the Westminster Parliament remained

Table 5.2.   European Community Grants and Loans (Commitments) in Favour of Northern Ireland 1973–83 (£m)

Grants	1973	1974	1975	1976	1977	1978	1979	1980	1981	1982	73–83
Agricultural Fund	1,743	2,198	2,986	1,693	2,199	1,086	2,394	2,498	2,689	2,428	21,914
Regional Fund	—	—	7,750	7,205	9,370	14,230	27,840	19,230	28,220	25,215	139,060
Social Fund	4,080	4,950	4,740	13,580	9,570	16,400	24,229	26,932	30,022	48,408	182,911
Energy Measures	—	—	—	—	36	6	63	—	—	—	105
Total Grants	5,823	7,148	15,476	22,478	21,175	31,722	54,526	48,660	60,931	76,051	343,990
Loans											
European Investment Bank	—	2,500	167	—	18,500	—	52,300	49,240	5,000	662	128,369
United Kingdom Supplementary Measures (claimed on behalf of Northern Ireland)	—	—	—	—	—	—	—	—	94,200	117,548	211,748
Total Grants and Loans	5,823	9,648	15,643	22,478	39,675	31,722	106,826	97,900	160,131	194,261	684,107

Grand Total: Grants, Loans, and United Kingdom Supplementary Measures Claimed on behalf of Northern Ireland £684,107,000.

Source: Northern Ireland in Europe (European Commission) Jan. 1983.

reluctant to intervene in Northern Ireland's internal affairs until events of the 1960s and early 1970s made this position untenable.

We referred above to a series of reports on the Northern Ireland economy. Common to most of these reports were criticisms of the failure of local élites (economic, political, administrative) to attract sufficient new industry, create and perfect the appropriate economic structures, promote investment, improve marketing, or plan regional development. Arguably, the blame for these deficiencies lay as much with London as with the local administration based at Stormont, but the view from 'the centre' must be seen essentially as one of non-interference bordering on indifference. According to Birrell and Murie: 'Although it has usually been assumed that the extent of financial support from Westminster greatly restricted the independence of Stormont, certain aspects of the financial relationship suggested that Northern Ireland had a substantial degree of freedom.'[15] Evidently, even under the interventionist minded Labour Governments of 1964–70, the Stormont Administration exercised considerable influence over industrial development, regional planning, job creation, investment, and infrastructure. This viewpoint is confirmed by John Simpson: 'Northern Ireland has managed over the years to move the power from Whitehall by securing a commitment that Whitehall will find the finance for approved expenditure.'[16] Indeed, this became a familiar pattern of UK–Northern Ireland relations. Only after 1968, with the British Army in Ulster, direct rule, and the loss of Stormont in 1972, did the decision-making gravitate towards Whitehall and the newly created NIO.

At this point, it will be instructive to note the position of local authorities within the above power structure. Significantly, the reforms of 1972 centralised local government services under the government departments at Stormont or centralized *ad hoc* or area boards. As Birrell and Murie explain,[17] the centralization of services assumed the existence of Stormont as a top tier of authority. Consequently, the loss of Stormont via direct rule accentuated the transfer of local government powers. For the purpose of this chapter, therefore, the direct rule period left local government authorities as relatively minor *interlocuteurs* on European matters. To some extent local government representatives acquired a certain prestige in the absence of Stormont representatives but, despite the Commission's willingness to 'sound out' locally elected bodies, the European role of local government remains essentially low key in Northern Ireland.

The Conservative Government of Edward Heath introduced direct rule as a temporary expedient in order to manage a deteriorating situation of civil unrest and disorder. At the same time, Heath's eyes were on Europe. According to *The Times*,[18] 'The Common Market legislation is the Government's supreme strategic objective and everything else until the end of the present session must be subordinated to it.' Similarly, Uwe Kitzinger described membership of the EC as the main theme and justification of (Heath's) whole political career'.[19] Consequently, the Government pursued this objective ruthlessly. In this context, Northern Ireland was a distraction and, potentially, a ruination of the main business of the day. As Philip Norton observed,[20] 'the introduction of direct rule in Northern Ireland . . . added a possible serious complication . . . In opposition to Government policy, seven Ulster Unionists withdrew their general support from the Government, giving rise to fears that they could jeopardize the passage of the EEC Bill . . .' In short, the loss of Stormont and the imposition of direct rule was fiercely resented by Ulster Unionist who saw it as a humiliation and defeat. In October 1971 Ulster Unionists MPs had voted against the principle of EC membership but their traditional political reflex was summed up (previously) by Herbert Kirk:[21] 'Whatever was finally decided for the good of the United Kingdom it followed that, on balance, it was good for Ulster.' Of course, this Loyalism rested on the principle of render to Caesar what is Caesar's. Direct rule invaded this contractual premiss, thereby turning long-standing allies into opponents but, in practice, the Ulster Unionists' opposition to the EC legislation was sporadic and, 'their withdrawal of support had only marginal effect'.[22]

From this inauspicious beginning (direct rule *and* the EC), Europe got off to a bad start in Northern Ireland. Moreover, at this stage, Republican and Nationalist forces, including the Social Democratic and Labour Party (SDLP), shared an ill-defined mistrust of the EC as an alien, encroaching, or capitalist entity. Not until the SDLP realized the political mileage to be gained out of the EC was a change of heart forthcoming.

The traditional Ulster Unionist and Loyalist sympathies lay with long-standing British traditions and achievements—the the Monarchy, Protestantism, the Commonwealth, the sovereignty of Parliament, the unwritten constitution, the costly (especially for Ulster) victories in two world wars and the union with Great Britain. Potentially, Europe threatened all these values and endangered the

Unionist cause. The latter was epitomized by such rallying cries as 'a Protestant parliament for a Protestant people' and 'No Surrender'. Direct rule *and* Europe fragmented the Unionist camp in Northern Ireland. Some 'moderate' Unionist leaders—notably Terence O'Neill and Brian Faulkner—were prepared to accept the EC but their political leadership became associated with un Ulster values—compromise, cross-border dialogue with the annexationist Irish Republic, and power sharing with Republicans. Consequently, the EC's image became complicated with the debate about the constitutional arrangement for Northern Ireland.

The immediate sequel to direct rule was the short-lived Northern Ireland Assembly and Executive commonly referred to as the Sunningdale or power sharing experiment. Directly elected by proportional representation in 1973, the Assembly was toppled in 1974 by the (Loyalist) Ulster Workers' Council (UWC) political strike. This power sharing innovation united Unionists, the Alliance Party (Centrist) and the SDLP (Nationalist/Republican) but faced implacable opposition from the mainstream body of Ulster Loyalists and Unionists. The Executive reflected a pro-EC bias, out of tune with the hard wing of the Unionist 'family'. According to Oliver Napier (the Alliance Party leader on the Executive), 'there is nothing sinister in the words "power sharing". Power sharing is something which is the rule rather than the exception throughout Europe.'[23] The Assembly sent a delegation to study various European parliaments to consider whether their example (power sharing, coalition government, proportional representation) offered any lessons for Northern Ireland. Moreover, on the eve of the Assembly's downfall, Premier Brian Faulkner cautioned opponents that Europe's eyes 'will be upon us to see if we can pull together'.[24] This counter-productive warning held little sway over anti-power sharing, anti-EC forces and the UWC strike consumated the anti-power sharing majority won in Northern Ireland at the February 1974 General Election.

Power sharing and Europe suffered from the complication of the two themes. Indeed, a more recent manifestation of this osmosis was seen at a dinner in Belfast to celebrate ten years of EC membership for Ireland and Northern Ireland (and Denmark). Ian Paisley boycotted the occasion owing to the presence of Garret Fitzgerald, the Irish Toaiseach. Similary, John Taylor absented himself owing to Edward Heath's presence. Neither Paisley nor Taylor wished to 'celebrate' membership of Europe or Edward Heath's 'achievements'. In turn,

Heath defended the Sunningdale agreement, at the same time claiming to the Ulster's 'best friend'. Arguably, the most telling comment on this overlap between EC and local matters was provided by the Belfast *News Letter* whose editorialist observed that 'Although the banquet . . . was essentially an EEC occasion . . . the spectre of Irish politics hovered perilously . . .'[25] Europe became part and parcel of the power sharing debate in Northern Ireland, as the equation 'soft'-on-power-sharing = 'soft'-on-Europe prevailed for many Unionists. Opponents of the 1973/4 power sharing Executive tended to oppose power sharing on all levels—within Northern Ireland, between Northern Ireland and the Republic of Ireland (the so-called 'Irish dimension') or within Europe. The cry of no surrender was applicable to all—particularly since in 1973 the SDLP endorsed the idea of a United Ireland in an EC context. This mood of unsurrendering protest was central to the Northern Ireland Get Britain Out (GBO) campaign in the 1975 Referendum on the EC. Neil Oliver, Unionist leader of the local GBO lobby, explained the position: 'Just as we are prepared to live at peace with mutual respect and toleration for our fellow country-men on one island, but never in one Ireland, we are willing to live together on one continent but not in any one Community.'[26] Hence, there was to be no surrender to foreign rule—'direct rule' from Brussels would be worse than it would from Westminster. Major decisions affecting every possible aspect of life, constitutional, political, legal, economic, and social, would be taken by 'the central Brussels' dictatorship' which would unsurp all the safeguards built up by the British democracy over 1,500 years. These themes reflected those in the UK as a whole but the distinct local relevance was para-mount. Indeed, since Westminster had already decided on the EC, many Loyalists (notably the Revd Ian Paisley's Democratic Unionist Party) resented the use of the referendum—an alien and divisive (for Unionists) European device. Thus, the Belfast *News Letter*, despite its lukewarm Europeanism, breathed a sigh of relief that '. . . the main benefit from the result . . . is that principle of representative govern-ment is sustained'.[27] The loss of Stormont and the uncertainty generated by direct rule and Sunningdale gave the sovereignty of par-liament issue an added dimension in Northern Ireland.

The referendum, at least, provided an opportunity to test local opinion on the EC. Some tentative conclusions may be drawn. The low turnout of 47.4 per cent (only the Shetlands polled lower at 47.1 per cent) suggested a degree of apathy and indifference. More likely, the electorate failed to respond to a poll in which traditional divisions appeared blurred or not particularly relevant. Furthermore, for the Northern Ireland voter, it was the seventh poll in two and a-half years, possibly leading to an understandable ballot box weariness. The 'great debate' in Britain had realized a 64. 5 per cent overall turnout with a two to one majority in favour of the Labour Party's renegotiated terms. In Northern Ireland, a 'No' vote was widely predicted as opponents of the EC hoped for a regional rejection of Europe. Nevertheless, the local press was able to report a 'shock "Yes" in the province' as 52.1 per cent provided a marginal victory.

The Northern Ireland Attitude Survey (1978)[28] revealed a decline in pro-European sentiment after 1975—with younger people, Catholics, and higher socio-economic groups predictably constituting the most 'European' cohorts. Table 5.3 provides evidence of post-1975 opinion.

Table 5.3.

Question: If a referendum was held tomorrow on whether the United Kingdom would stay in the Common Market or leave would you vote Yes (to stay in) or No (to leave)?

(a)	*ALL %*	*Catholics %*	*Protestants %*
Yes:	49.3	54.9	47.2

The same question was asked to Protestants (b) with the results showing younger Protestants more favourable to the Common Market than their elders but—according to the survey—there were no parallel figures for Catholics.

(b)	*Age group*	*Protestants %*
Yes:	Under 24	60.2
	25–34	51.0
	35–44	46.0
	45–54	50.8
	55–64	34.8
	Over 65	38.6

Catholics showed a tendency to support the Common Market if they belonged to higher socio-economic groups. This was paralleled in Protestant tendencies evidently but the NIAS reported Catholic responses only in detail (c):

(c)	Socio-economic group	Catholics %
Yes:	A	80.0
	B	66.7
	C1	68.3
	C2	52.2
	D	43.1
	E	44.4

Source: Northern Ireland Attitude Survey.

If we turn, briefly, to political parties, the NIAS study posed the following question to party supporters:

If a referendum was held tomorrow on whether the United Kingdom should stay in the Common Market or leave, would you vote Yes (to stay in) or No (to leave)?

	Yes %
Official Unionists (OUP)	47.3
Democratic Unionists (DUP)	22.4
Alliance Party (AP)	66.1
Social Democratic and Labour Party (SDLP)	59.5

Possibly these statistics may underestimate current Unionist (DUP, OUP) mistrust of Europe and Alliance Party and SDLP support *for* Europe. Certainly if we turn from supporters and look at the opinion of delegates to party conference, the so-called 'middle-level élites,' there is a somewhat different picture in 1981/2. For instance, according to a sample taken at the 1981 (October) OUP conference,[29] 68 per cent delegates thought Northern Ireland's membership of the European Community 'a bad thing' 19 per cent neither a good thing or a bad thing', and only 13 per cent 'a good thing'.

The 1975 Referendum temporarily quelled the anti-EC opposition but critics such as Enoch Powell promised to continue the fight. Powell's new home amongst the Official Unionist Party provided a base to criticize European influence. With the recruitment of Enoch Powell to the Official Unionist Westminster ranks and the rise of Ian Paisley's DUP, the anti-EC cry was to be heard time and again over the next few years. More often than not, Powell pointed to links between the USA, the Foreign Office, Dublin, and Europe evidently plotting to push Northern Ireland into a United Ireland. In this context, Europe and the Foreign Office's hand are seen behind such initiatives as Sunningdale and Anglo-Irish summitry. Consequently, Heath was seen by many Loyalists as the man who not only dragged Northern Ireland into Europe without its 'full-hearted consent' but who then proceeded to use the European backdoor to 'settle' the Northern Ireland problem. Austin Ardill's assessment of Sunningdale may be taken in this light: 'we believe . . . that in order to satisfy Mr. Heath's friends in Europe . . . EEC pressures have been exerted to get us to accede to the demands from Dublin. Every effort has been made to satisfy Europe at our expense.'[30] Similarly, Powell later developed this theme: 'For the Foreign Office, what matters much more than a small province of the United Kingdom whose people are determined to uphold their right to be British, is the goodwill of Eire, the vote catching presidents of the United States and of the European nations, with their deep anti-British and, in some cases, anti-Protestant prejudices.'[31] Powell's main bone of contention has been that Britain or rather the UK, is losing its traditional values and direction. Allegedly, the membership of the EC and the hesitations over Northern Ireland are dual testimonies to this waywardness.

Further evidence of British Government intentions may be divined from the debate about direct elections to the European Parliament. Again, Europe was cast in the role of a divisive, alien, encroaching body which hastened the dilution of cherished traditions. This debate has been examined elsewhere,[32] but some observations are worth recalling. First, Ulster Unionists protested against the contrived 'gerrymander' (with Dublin's blessing) to give the SDLP a seat—which John Hume duly won in 1979. The provision of a third Euro-seat was contrasted with the loss of Stormont seats, with no immediate compensatory rise in the number of Westminster seats for Northern Ireland. In contrast, as the Scottish Nationalist Party pointed out, Scotland was allocated only eight MEP seats for a population of 5,000,000. Northern Ireland's population is approximately 1,500,00. Second, the election to the European Parliament was proportional representation by STV which was the same system used in the South of Ireland but, significantly, differed from the British first past the post system. Thus, the European electoral system differentiated between Northern Ireland and Britain, thereby adding a new dimension of uncertainty to the constitutional situation. Consequently, before the 1984 European Elections, Unionists renewed their demands for a change in the voting system to bring Northern Ireland into line with the rest of the United Kingdom. Third, the 1979

European Election divided Unionists. Indeed, the contest between OUP and Ian Paisley was fiercer than that between Hume and the traditional Unionist opposition. Fourth, as the SDLP manifesto delighted in pointing out, for the first time since 1918, Northern and Southern Irish representatives would share the same electoral forum, on the same terms.

The effect of the European Election (June 1979) was to confirm Ian Paisley's ascendancy within the Unionist family and, at the same time, a handsome personal victory went to John Hume (SDLP). John Taylor took the third seat for the OUP but, on the whole, the election was not a huge party success for the Official Unionists. Up to 1979 European affairs played a low key role in Northern Ireland politics. Predictably, European issues were seen as secondary to more immediate and tangible problems—direct rule, the security situation, political initiatives such as the Assembly, and the 1975/6 Constitutional Convention. When 'Europe' could be utilized to prop up traditional, sectarian arguments it enjoyed significant airing. The comparatively high turnout in June 1979 (57 per cent as opposed to one-third in the UK) must not be seen primarily as a vote for Europe. Rather, it was another opportunity to elect recognizable flag bearers along traditional lines. For example, Paisley's DUP manifesto took great pleasure in quoting Shirley Williams: 'the Catholic religion will be the dominant faith and . . . the application of the Catholic social doctrine will be a major factor in everyday political life.'[33] Thus, the DUP's leader would not waste his time at the EP supporting 'the Irish Republic's interests or any of the other Roman Catholic nations of Europe.' Similarly, the Official Unionist candidates offered parallel, if less strident, messages. John Hume, too, was anxious to stress the political connotations of the vote. The SDLP manifesto (*A New Horizon*) presented Europe as a 'healing force', a means of 'peace and reconciliation', meaning that European integration could lead to Irish integration/unification.

In the 1984 European Election, Paisley's strident anti-Europeanism and Ulster Loyalism earned a significant victory. To some extent, the lessons of the 1984 vote were ambiguous.[34] Indisputably, however, the DUP leader topped the poll comfortably with a massive 230,000 votes (1979: 170,000) 33.6 per cent of the votes cast (1979: 29.8 per cent). All three MEPs were elected but the campaign was dominated by the (unsuccessful) candidature of Sinn Fein. Sinn Fein, seen widely as the political mouthpiece of the IRA, galvanized all other candidates on an anti-Sinn Fein platform, thereby illustrating the primacy of local political debate within a European umbrella.

Despite the sectarian dressing of the European electoral campaigns, the election of three MEPs from Northern Ireland provides an unsuspected opportunity for common cause. After 1979, European affairs enjoyed a new lease of life in Northern Ireland largely due to the efforts and publicity of the MEPs. All could share a general dissatisfaction with the NIO and direct rule, more particularly the NIO/UK's failure to represent adequately Northern Ireland in Europe. The list of grievances was long, and included inadequate formal representation in 'the Councils of Europe', British sluggishness in extending the agricultural Less Favoured Areas (LFAs) scheme in Northern Ireland, failure to implement of principle of 'additionality' for European moneys, insufficient enthusiasm in endorsing such European ideas as the 'integrated operations' schemes for Belfast, failure to secure European money for housing, and inadequate protection for sensitive Northern Ireland industries. Various remedies have been suggested for these failings: formal representation or observer status for Northern Ireland on EC bodies such as the Council and COREPER; a Northern Ireland business bureau in Brussels; greater involvement of local representatives in planning and presenting European requests for aid; more rapid implementation of proposals, for example the extension of the LFAs, the Martin Report, the defining of the integrated operations principle; and effective scrutiny of EC affairs through the committee structure of the Northern Ireland Assembly (elected in October 1982).

Nevertheless, potential European interest and progress on Northern Ireland matters come up against traditional obstacles. In 1981, for instance, a delegation from the European Parliament's Regional Committee visited Northern Ireland to assess the prospects for European aid for housing—but, due to 'local problems', never actually visited the housing districts on the agenda. On another occasion, the ERDF used the favoured channel of aid to promote tourism in frontier districts. However, occording to John Taylor the ERDF wasted money on developing 'bandit areas' which for security reasons nobody wanted to visit. An example of the complication between EC and local affairs occurred at the aforementioned banquet, when Garret Fitzgerald looked forward to 'a new and dynamic relationship with both communities in Northern Ireland, with the British Government and with our European friends'.[35] Unsurprisingly, this plea fell on hostile ears in the Unionist family, who pointed to the Irish Republic's unwillingness to extradite and failure to sign the European Convention on the Suppression of Terrorism. The EC, consequently, is left with the dilemma of wanting to assist Northern Ireland, but mindful of the need to trend carefully. As Tugendhat surmised: 'In Europe, the will to help exists, but people outside Northern Ireland are very conscious of the constant risk of causing offence, of being thought to take sides or to meddle.'[36]

Conclusion

The most striking aspect of Northern Ireland–EC relations is that, more often than not, political arguments appear to have asphyxiated economic ones. This is not to say that the *impact* of EC membership has not been considerable for the ailing Northern Ireland economy, but this impact does not apply qualitatively to EC structural grants.

In the light of Tugendhat's comment, the European Commission shares the embarrassment of the British Government over the EP's decision to examine the economic *and* political situation in Northern Ireland. The report drawn up by Niels Haagerup for the EP's Political Affairs Committee, is interpreted by the Conservative Government and Unionists as gross interference in domestic affairs. On the eve of Haagerup's report (December 1983) and amidst increasing tension in Northern Ireland following the assassination of a prominent Ulster Unionist politician, Ian Paisley repeated the warning against interference in Northern Ireland: 'The majority here are determined to remain British and will not be swayed in that conviction by the bombs and bullets of the IRA, (the proscribed Provisional Irish Republican Army) still less by the machinations of Europeans who understand little of the situation here.'[37]

European initiatives along these lines provoke instant reaction, heated debate and promises of non-co-operation. Arguably, economic matters are marginally less controversial except where they are sectarianized—in short, *which* section of the Northern Ireland population is to benefit most from European aid?. Nevertheless, economic measures are capable of uniting Unionists, Nationalists *et al.*— often against the NIO and British direct rule. An example of 'cross-community' support occurred in June 1983 when the Council of Ministers approved £60m. of EC funds for urban renewal in Northern Ireland in the context of the Belfast integrated operation, thereby winning the combined support of the three local MEPs. An interesting feature of this aid was the British Government's unprecedented commitment to make the money additional to public expenditure in Northern Ireland. Understandably, this breach in the additionality principle was hailed as a recipe for the future. This may be wishful thinking. To date, the £60m. stands as an oasis of 'real additionality' for, in presenting the integrated operation, Environment Minister Chris Patten precluded the possibility of any additional money in the new submission.

The debates over additionality seem likely to run and run but, without doubt, the British Government and the Commission will continue to prefer economic channels to grand political initiatives. However, one potentially fruitful by-product of EC membership is the scope for Anglo-Irish dialogue within the framework of European summitry. This diplomatic umbrella has proved useful for British and Irish Governments to discuss Northern Ireland and foster Anglo-Irish relations. For instance, in June 1983 at the Stuttgart European summit, PM Margaret Thatcher and Taoiseach Garret Fitzgerald restored Anglo-Irish dialogue and discussed Northern Ireland, following a barren phase of Anglo-Irish disagreement, including dispute over the Falkland islands. At the Athens summit (December 1983), similar discussion took place against a background of continuing unrest and Unionist misgivings about the security problem in Northern Ireland. In 1984, too, the trend persisted as Garret Fitzgerald signalled his intention to use the Irish presidency of Council to smooth the path of Anglo-Irish rapprochement.

Whilst some observers see Anglo-Irish summitry within the EC as a positive aspect of membership of Europe, others prefer to turn towards other European regions in order to examine regional adaptation to membership. Hence, the example of the German *Beobachter* and the fate of Greenland have attracted some local interest. There is a deep-rooted belief that improved local structures would help secure more accountability and moneys. Inevitably, this is part and parcel of the debate about devolution and the new Northern Ireland Assembly. In this respect, the controversial Assembly committees flexed their muscles quickly. For example, the Finance Committee initiated a scrutiny of the additionality problem, the Agriculture Committee lobbied for the extension of the LFAs, and the Environment Committee promised to examine the 'integrated operations' idea. It is, of course, unlikely these channels will suffice. There is a fair degree of frustration with the EC in Northern Ireland, notably over the failures to secure European aid for housing and agriculture. This mood is evident in the local press, political party speeches, the trade union and small farmers' lobbies. In part, this reflects widespread frustration with the constitutional position but, in part, it concerns the apparent slowness of decision making procedures in the EC. Also, it must be attributed to the otherwise commendable united purpose of the three MEPs and allies. A major concern of the latter is to embarrass the UK Government and NIO but, inevitably, the MEPs promise the earth and are unable to deliver. This conflict laden situation often involves the Commission cast (unwillingly?) as an accomplice to encourage the UK Government to attract European financial aid which in turn necessitates increased public expenditure in Northern Ireland.

In conclusion, the Northern Ireland example represents a complex case study of EC/regional relations and the evidence, to date,[38] suggests that 'a Europe for the regions' is still a far cry.

Notes

1. Buckland, P. A., *History of Northern Ireland* (Dublin: Gill and Macmillan, 1981).
2. Northern Ireland and the European Communities, Cmnd. 563, Nov. 1971, p. 6.
3. Ibid., p. 16.
4. Quoted in Hainsworth, P., 'Northern Ireland: A European Role?' *Journal of Common Market Studies*, vol. xx, no. 1, Sept. 1981.
5. Stemman, R., 'What Next for Northern Ireland?' *Europe*, Nov. 1981, pp. 3–6.
6. Harvey, S., and Rea, D., *The Northern Ireland Economy with Particular Reference to Industrial Development* (Berfast: Ulster Polytechnic Innovation and Resource Centre, 1982) p. 42.
7. For details, see ibid., p. 3.
8. 'Report of the Joint Working Party on the Economy of Northern Ireland.' Cmnd. 446, Belfast 1962, pp. 57–58.
9. Stemman, op. cit., p. 3.
10. *The Regions of Europe*, Com (80) 816 (final), 7 Jan. 1981.
11. Harvey and Rea, op. cit., p. 52.
12. *The Irish News*, 28 Jan. 1980.
13. Harvey and Rea, op. cit., p. 46.
14. *News Letter* 1 Sept. 1980.
15. Birrell, D., and Murie, A., *Policy and Government in Northern Ireland: Lessons of Devolution* (Dublin: Gill and Macmillan, 1980), p. 20.
16. Quoted in ibid., p. 23.
17. Ibid.
18. *The Times*, 24 Jan. 1973.
19. Quoted in Norton, P., *Conservative Dissidents* (London: Temple Smith, 1978), p. 223.
20. Ibid., p. 76.
21. *News Letter*, 10 Oct. 1971.
22. Norton, op. cit., p. 76. cf. Hainsworth P., 'Direct Rule in Northern Ireland: the European Community Dimension, 1972–1979' *Administration*, vol. 31, 1983.
23. Quoted in Hainsworth, 'Direct Rule in Northern Ireland'.
24. Ibid.
25. *News Letter*, 29 Jan. 1983.

26. *Belfast Telegraph*, 12 May 1975.

27. *News Letter*, 7 June 1975.

28. Moxon-Browne, E., *Nation, Class and Creed in Northern Ireland* (Aldershot: Gower, 1983), chapter 9.

29. The survey was conducted within the framework of the 'Middle Level Élites Project' based at the University of Mannheim, directed by K. Reif and R. Cayrol and supported by Stiftung Volkswagenwerk, the Commission of the European Communities and the European Parliament. In Northern Ireland, the project was managed by A. Aughey, P. Hainsworth and C. McIlheney.

30. *Northern Ireland Assembly Official Report*, vol. 1, 15 Oct. 1973, col. 1982.

31. *News Letter*, 29 Sept. 1980.

32. Cf. Hainsworth, P., 'Linkage Politics: the European Election in Northern Ireland', *Parliamentary Affairs*, vol. xxxii, Nov. 4, 1979.

33. Quoted in ibid.

34. Hainsworth, P., 'The European Election in Northern Ireland', *Parliamentary Affairs*, vol. 34; no. 4, 1984.

35. *Belfast Telegraph*, 28 Jan. 1983.

36. *The Irish News*, 28 Jan. 1983.

37. *Belfast Telegraph*, 9 Dec. 1983.

38. Cf. The Regions of Europe, COM (84) 40 (final), 4 Apr. 1984. This document, the second Periodic Report of the regions provides a summary of Northern Ireland's unfavourable socio-economic status *vis-à-vis* other areas of the European Community.

6

English and Welsh Local Government and the European Community

JOHN MAWSON and JOHN T. GIBNEY

Introduction

Local authorities contemplating access to EC funds for the first time, are faced with a bewildering and complex array of organizations and decision making structures. In seeking to illustrate the difficulties faced by local authorities in their efforts to influence EC policy making and secure EC aid it is useful to refer to the case of the European Regional Development Fund which is a financial instrument of particular interest to local authorities in the UK Government's assisted areas.[1] The chapter draws on the experience of English and Welsh authorities and is divided into three sections. The first section sets out the complex organizational and decision making network around which decisions about the ERDF are made. This is followed by a discussion of the operational and financial problems which local authorities have faced, in receiving ERDF aid as well as the difficulties they have encountered over involvement in policy questions. Finally, attention is devoted to the administrative mechanisms by which ERDF moneys are allocated and how local authorities organize themselves to secure support. The discussion illustrates at a day-to-day operational level the tensions between central government and the Community surrounding the nature and purpose of the Common Regional Policy.

The ERDF Decision Making Network

At a *Community level*, the European Commission is required to review every three years the operation of the ERDF Regulation and to make recommendations as to its modification. In this regard the Regional Policy Committee is of particular importance, comprising as it does representatives from Member States and the Commission who have the responsibility of overseeing the overall development of the Fund through research studies, the RDPs and the Periodic report. Consultations take place with the Regional Policy Committee of the European Parliament, the Economic and Social Committee comprising employers, trade unions and consumer groups, as well as other interest group organizations concerned with commerce and industry in the private and public sectors. It is through these channels that lobbying bodies such as the International Union of Local Authorities (IULA) and the Council of European Municipalities (CEM) seek to present the local authority case. The Commission also engages in a dialogue with the national government's representatives, in the British case UKREP, as well as the collective body of representatives, known as COREPER, comprising senior civil servants backed up by specialist officials who attend as and when the agenda requires. Following various consultations and negotiations the Commission presents draft legislation to the Council of Ministers for formal ratification. In operational terms decisions about the allocation of funds and procedural matters are dealt with by the Fund Management Committee.

At a *national level*, Community affairs are dealt with by the appropriate Government Departments who are responsible for forwarding applications for support from the various funding instruments. The Department of the Environment handles the infrastructure aspects of the ERDF, while the Department of Trade and Industry has the responsibility for industrial aid, as well as taking the lead in the preparation of the UK RDP and negotiations concerning this policy area in Brussels. Some Government Departments handle all their EC matters from London (e.g. the Department of Employment where the ESF is concerned), others, such as the Department of Environment, which have a strong regional presence, liaise with local authorities and other agencies on the infrastructure aspects of the ERDF and forward applications to London. The task of the DOE regional office is to make sure that there is a regular flow of appropriate applications in order to ensure that the UK secures its maximum ERDF entitlement. This involves not only keeping local authorities up to date with the latest developments but also ensuring that other Government Departments, e.g. Department of Transport, and agencies for gas, electricity and water, are aware of the possibilities for funding. In practice, each regional office is allocated a broad target to aim for, and in carrying out its role it is necessary on the one hand to cajole agencies to put forward sufficient propositions and on the other to filter out the most appropriate projects for forwarding to London. In policy terms, the regional office is also responsible for preparing and updating the RDP for its area in association with the local authorities and, where necessary, as in the case of the non-quota section of the fund, to prepare a regional programme.

In a number of regions of the country, local authority associations sometimes referred to as Standing Conferences have increasingly shown an interest in EC matters. Historically concerned with physical planning matters which transcend the boundaries of a single authority, these organizations which may represent the district or county tier, or both, have become more involved in economic analysis and lobbying on behalf of their areas. Their activities include liaising with the DOE regional office in relation to the preparation of the RDP for their area, lobbying Brussels about local economic problems and supporting particular applications for aid.

Hull and Rhodes have referred to the growing significance of Community activities for regional and local authorities throughout the EC[2]. As links are further extended through the provision of EC financial aid, this influence seems likely to increase. Indeed, in the sphere of regional policy the Commission, in its proposals to reform the ERDF has, on a number of occasions sought to secure increased local authority involvement in the formulation and implementation of the policy. Local authority visits to Commission Directorates in connection with their efforts to secure EC aid for various projects have become an almost daily event in Brussels. The Commission, while recognizing the primary role of Member States in the operation of the Common Regional Policy, believes that by fostering closer links with regional and local authorities it is in a better position to understand the nature of regional problems, to develop genuine Community-wide policies and to ensure the effective use of ERDF resources including the identification of additionality. However, as we have suggested in chapter 2, Member States, including the UK Government, have proved reluctant to allow this trend to develop very far. In their efforts to retain control over the major aspects of the CRP, Member States view the emergence of a 'triangular' dialogue in contrast to existing 'vertical' power relations (see Figure 6.1) as a back door way of securing increased Community involvement in domestic regional policy.

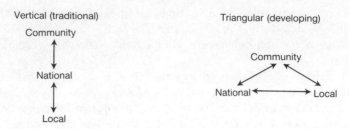

Fig. 6.1.   *Inter-Level Relations.*

Local Authority Experience of the ERDF

The tensions set out above are particularly evident in various efforts
which the Community has made to encourage Member States to introduce a programme approach both to policy matters (e.g. the RDPs),
and to access to funds (e.g. the 5 per cent of the Fund devoted to the
non-quota section and the target under the new regulation of at least 20
per cent of the Fund going to programmes within three years). By
programme approach is meant an attempt to bring together in a one
planning document an integrated package of investment projects over
a three-to-five-year time horizon, which are designed to tackle particular regional problems.[3] In recent years approximately 90 per cent the
ERDF has been spent on infrastructure investment with the bulk of the
moneys granted in the form of single investment projects. However, a
number of local authorities in Scotland, Wales and the English regions
have experienced ERDF aid in the form of programmes through the
non-quota measures, and more widely local authorities have engaged
in a dialogue with central government concerning the RDP for their
region. This experience has been extensively documented in three
separate inquiries undertaken by the House of Lords Select
Committee on the European Communities between 1981 and 1984
into the operation and revision of the European Regional Development Fund[4]. It is instructive to examine some of the evidence
presented to the Committee as it highlights not only the tensions
between the Community and the UK Government concerning the role
of local authorities in regional development, but also the debate about
the need to introduce regional programmes, exposing some of the
operational difficulties which local authorities have faced to date,

under a system based largely on the financing of single investment projects.

Perhaps not surprisingly evidence presented to the House of Lords Select Committee on the European Communities indicates that individual authorities and their representative organizations strongly support the Commission's efforts to introduce a programme approach. Underlying this enthusiasm is undoubtedly a desire to have a greater say in the formulation and administration of regional policy in the UK. In recent years local authorities have developed considerable expertise in various aspects of infrastructure and local economic planning and certainly possess the local knowledge and administrative capacity to prepare specific types of programmes (see, for example, evidence of local authorities in Lancashire to House of Lords Select Committee on European Communities 14th Report, Session 1980–1)[5]. Within local authority circles there is a view that given this experience, a more direct relationship with Brussels through the programme approach and measures such as those designed to foster indigenous development potential, would provide the opportunity to develop policies more specifically tailored to the needs of individual areas than dependent on 'broad-brush' national regional policies as at present (see evidence of the Association of District Councils)[6]. More specific reasons why local authorities are keen to see the emergence of a programme approach relate to the desire to secure genuine additionality in projects supported by the ERDF.

The financing of development under the ERDF

The two principal sources of funds for local authority economic programmes in England and Wales at present are local rate income and central government grant obtained through the annual Rate Support Grant Settlement. The Settlement is governed by the Block Grant Scheme introduced as part of the Local Government Planning and Land Act, 1980, and subsequent targets and penalties introduced by the Secretary of State for the Environment. There is no specific provision in the Block Grant Scheme for expenditure on economic development and it thus has had to compete with other key services for an ever diminishing pool of resources. Further problems have arisen through the capital control scheme introduced under the 1980 Act which has had a serious impact on the capital allocation available for all local authority activities including economic development.

Bearing in mind these increasing pressures on local authority finance, it is perhaps not surprising that many authorities have not regarded ERDF assistance, particularly on smaller projects, as worth the time and effort of putting forward proposals. Under the present system, ERDF aid is limited in practice to schemes which are fully committed and which have either already started or on which expenditure will be incurred in the calendar year of application. Because of the government's capital control system, authorities are unable to undertake borrowing for additional schemes. Thus local authorities use ERDF moneys to reduce the amount which has to be borrowed to finance an existing committed project and hence reduce interest charges and debt service costs which they would otherwise have to pay. In financial terms, as the leader of Humberside County Council recently pointed out, there is often little incentive for local authorities to take account of Community assistance particularly where there may be more attractive joint sources of funding through, for example, the Inner City programme (75 per cent funding of projects, which are also excluded from capital controls).[7] In the case of a large authority in an assisted area, the preparation of projects might not prove too demanding in terms of staff time and resources. However, for smaller authorities, and those located in areas of lower regional priority, where the probability of securing assistance may be less, it is open to question whether seeking ERDF assistance is a cost-effective exercise.

The Chief Executive of West Yorkshire Metropolitan County Council, for example, pointed out in recent evidence to the House of Lords Select Committee on the European Communities that: 'The history of our applications has been entirely erratic. We have submitted about 120 applications of which 88 have been rejected and only 24 have been accepted. . . . Those that have come through have come in an entirely unpredictable and certainly totally unrelated to the value or otherwise of the project. They have been related being blunt to the extent to which the United Kingdom Government had enough schemes around to make up its quota.'[8] He also pointed out that because: 'Any grant we get from the regional fund is then deducted from our own capital allocation by the Government . . . we could not submit to Europe any schemes which we were not already committed to doing, because that would mean knocking something else out of the programme.'[9] Thus in their memorandum of evidence to the Select Committee the County Council concluded that ERDF grant support '. . . have been treated as a windfall. It has never been taken into account in forward planning, and the ERDF cannot, therefore, claim to have influenced either the location, level, or type of projects undertaken. . . .'[10] In earlier evidence given to the Committee in 1981 the council pointed out that because of the variability of support, 'coupled with the absence of any forward commitment beyond the next calendar year makes it impossible for local authorities to devise any coherent or long-term programme for the regeneration of particular areas.'[11] For these sorts of reasons both local authorities and the Commission have been keen to see the introduction of a programme approach. Commission officials believe that if Community institutions were sufficiently involved in the preparation of programmes, they would be able to establish how far projects/developments were expanded or accelerated because of the Fund's assistance.[12]

The views of Greater Manchester Council are fairly typical of attitudes in local government about the recent decision to enhance the role of programmes in the operation of the ERDF:

Certainly it should be easier to determine the extent to which additionality is being applied. Projects which may be uncommitted at the application stage, can now be included in a programme; the implementation of which can now be seen as being largely dependent upon the level of ERDF support. Furthermore the commitment to support a programme of action would enable local authorities to bend their capital programmes towards areas of Community interest, run programmes at higher levels and also initiate new activities. In addition, a programme would allow the authorities to provide staff resources to effectively implement the programmed actions.[13]

However, it is also recognized in local government circles that, even though additionality could be established in a particular programme through a financial section which outlined separately the local authority, central government, and EC contribution (as required under the new Community programmes), central government could always, in retrospect, take into consideration past grants to local authorities when deciding upon future capital expenditure allocations, thus negating the effect in global terms.

Aside from the possibility of securing additionality, local authorities foresee other operational advantages arising from the introduction of a programme approach, in particular greater flexibility in the use of ERDF funds, which would enable them to tailor the measures more closely to the needs of the locality. Such a view is conditioned by the contrasting experience which local authorities such as Tyne and Wear,

Merseyside, and West Yorkshire have had in implementing their non-quota programmes (steel, shipbuilding, and textiles) as against measures funded under the quota section. While the definition of infra-structure projects eligible for assistance under the quota section of the previous ERDF regulation was fairly wide, in practice it was not inter-preted by national governments and the Commission as sympathe-tically as it could have been. The Fund has been more orientated towards overcoming constraints on physical expansion rather than counteracting problems associated with industrial decline. Thus the major beneficiaries of ERDF support have been the largely rural 'underdeveloped' areas in Southern Italy, Ireland, and South West France which are deficient in basic infrastructure. However, much of the investment required in older industrial areas like Merseyside is of a different type requiring renewal, repair, refurbishment, and replacement—just as important as new investment on greenfield sites which has automatically qualified in the past.

Local authorities such as Tyne and Wear, Merseyside, West York-shire and Lancashire County Councils have repeatedly advocated the introduction of a programme, approach in order to allow them to develop a coherent, relevant, and flexible range of measures of the type operated under the non-quota section.[14] Such measures include support for major infrastructure replacement renewal programmes, for example, transport infrastructure, and outworn Victorian water and sewerage systems; they also involve refurbishment conversion of redundant buildings to factory units, environmental improvements, as well as feasibility studies for smaller firms about new products and technology, and consultancy services in fields such as marketing. When dealing with the complex interrelated nature of urban renewal in the older industrial areas, a medium term investment programme designed by local agencies is infinitely preferable to support for single isolated infrastructure projects with a bias towards greenfield development.

Local authority involvement in the formulation of ERDF measures

The discussion so far has largely focused on the financial and develop-mental aspects of the ERDF. However, other important reasons underlying the Community's efforts to secure a programme approach have included the desire to involve local authorities in the formulation and implementation of Community regional measures and to assist the

Commission in securing the co-ordination of regional policies across Europe. Bearing in mind the recent charges to the ERDF regulation set out in chapter two, it is instructive to consider the experience of local authorities to date in the preparation of the UK Regional Development Programme and the non-quota measures.[15]

The major rationale underlying the decision of the Regional Policy Committee to establish the system of Regional Development Programmes in 1975 was to provide the Commission with an overview of regional problems and policies. To achieve this objective Member States were required to prepare and update their RDPs on the basis of a common format devised by the Committee. The RDP outline required that for each assisted region information should be provided on: (1) present and future problems including obstacles too, and potential for regional development, (2) the development objectives, (3) the measures to be adopted, (4) the financial resources to be employed, and (5) a timetable for implementation. To give teeth to the system, the ERDF regulation stated that investments could only qualify for fund assistance if they fell within the framework of a regional development programme. However, as was suggested in chapter two, the fact that Member States are not required to give detailed information about investment projects within the documents has undermined the basis of the legislation. It is not surprising therefore that the first round of documents, completed by the beginning of 1978, was a disappointment.

The UK document was no exception in this regard. Indeed it was made clear in the RDP that because of the nature of the institutional and administrative structure of government, particularly in the English regions, it was difficult to achieve a co-ordinated form of expenditure planning at the regional level. This is a reflection of the fragmented departmental approach to expenditure planning (particularly on infrastructure) and more fundamentally a lack of commitment to regional programming within central government.[16]

The reaction of British local authorities to the first UK RDP prepared in 1977 cannot be described as enthusiastic. There was a general feeling that there had been insufficient consultation with local authorities, that the programmes prepared for each region were weak as regards content, and that they failed to follow the outline suggested by the Commission guideline. Undoubtedly these criticisms related to a wider view that the approach to regional development planning in the English regions at that time, based upon strategies prepared by the Economic Planning Councils and/or the tripartite machinery (central government, local authorities, and the ECPs) was inadequate. There was disquiet that the programmes should in part be based upon these documents, but perhaps even more significant, was a sense that the RDP provided a vehicle to challenge the existing approach to regional development in each region and to regional policy in general.

In Yorkshire and Humberside feelings were so strong that the constituent members of the Strategic Conference of County Councils prepared their own more detailed programme which closely followed the Outline structure proposed by the Commission. County Councils in the Northern region produced individual County profiles to supplement the RDP and the exercise received tacit support from Brussels. In other regions local authorities also took steps to supplement the information. In 1978 the Association of Metropolitan Authorities (AMA) presented to the United Kingdom government a critique of the individual sections of the first RDP, based upon the comments of its members. It requested that adequate opportunity should be given for consultations between local authorities, including any regional groups of local authorities, and the DOE on the individual sections of the RDP. Subsequently the Commission published its own review of the first round of RDPs which contained a formal statement of the Commission's own opinion on the RDPs and recommendations to Member States concerning preparation of the programmes.[17]

In the light of these developments, the United Kingdom government has made some effort to respond to the criticisms made by local authorities and the Commission in the recent update of the United Kingdom RDP, which is now regarded by officials as one of the better documents. The changes introduced in the process have included a specific focus on the preparation of programmes for assisted areas rather than standard regions in order to provide more detailed background material on the areas receiving ERDF assistance. The changes have also involved increased local authority participation through the preparation of statistical and financial information for various sections of the RDP. However, local authorities have complained that insufficient time has been given for the drawing up of the relevant material (as little as three weeks in certain cases) or for the local authorities to engage in discussion with regional offices about policy matters. A question mark must therefore hang over an approach which implies that increased involvement is about providing more data rather than greater participation in the formulation of policy. It is symbolic of attitudes in central government that local authorities were asked by

DOE to undertake a 'collation' of the objectives set down by the various infrastructure agencies in their area which is not the same as a process in which the relevant organizations come together on a regular basis to devise and develop an integrated set of investment programmes backed up by formal administrative mechanisms at the regional level to ensure their implementation.

In written evidence given to the House of Lords Select Committee on the European Communities in May 1984, the Member of the European Parliament for South Wales stated: 'At the moment local involvement appears to be considerable—they are consulted—but in effect it is negligible. Local authorities are asked to react to plans drawn up by civil servants who then make arbitrary use of these comments and often distort the position given by local authorities in the first instance.'[18] In oral evidence Mr Griffith went on to say: '. . . whilst local authorities are asked to give their opinions, essentially the programme is drawn up by the civil servants—in the case of Wales by the Welsh Office—and they then ask the local authorities what they think about it and it is entirely up to them whether they accept any of the comments of the local authorities or not. The influence of local authorities is marginal, yet the schemes that come forward, particularly for infrastructure, are overwhelmingly from local authorities, so they ought to have a bigger say.'[19] Against this background the weak reference to local authority involvement in the preparation of RDPs in the revised ERDF regulation does not augur well for the future. Turning to the experience of the non-quota programmes, there have also been problems with local authority involvement. The first series of non-quota measures was launched in 1980 and the UK benefited from programmes assisting areas with major steel and shipbuilding interests. The second series of non-quota measures was agreed by the Council of Ministers in January 1984 with the UK entitled to receive at least 155m. ECU's under three of the six specific measures. The measures for the steel and shipbuilding areas was extended and a new five-year programme for areas affected by the decline of employment in the textile and clothing industries was introduced.[20]

The non-quota programmes have been welcomed by local authorities as providing a small but nevertheless flexible form of regional aid, which can be tailored to the needs of declining industrial areas. Taking Wales as an example, the counties of Clwyd, Gwent, South Glamorgan, and West Glamorgan have been given assistance under the steel programme (1980–5) with a second round of measures up until 1989, extending the geographical coverage of the measures. Under the first steel programme, Wales was allocated £10.5m. including £8.4m. for environmental works and the upgrading of disused premises for use by small firms, and £2.1m. for other measures of support of the small firms sector (provision of common services, feasibility studies, consultancy services etc.)[21]

While the measures themselves have proved to be effective and relevant, there nevertheless have been problems about local authority involvement. In the first round of non-quota programmes local authorities were given relatively short notice to prepare and submit projects. Little substantive guidance was provided either by central government or by the Commission. Evidence submitted by the North of England County Councils Association to the 1981 House of Lords Enquiry on EEC regional policy illustrates the problems encountered:

After lengthy discussion in Brussels, local authorities were suddenly told by DOE to produce bids (within 3/4 weeks)—despite the fact that some of the work was anticipated it was still a very short time to get local authority commitment. DOE guidance was helpful within the Northern Region but DOI was lamentable. No information was made available by DOI—the private sector was not properly informed of the fund and no guidance given as to what was wanted or when it was wanted and it remains to be seen whether local authorities will be told why any of the projects are to be rejected.[22]

It is apparent from recent local authority evidence presented to the Select Committee that such problems persist. For example, Strathclyde Regional Council stated in written evidence: 'Local authorities have had little control or influence over the operation of the non-quota measures, with the European Commission initiating the schemes and the United Kingdom Government disbursing the funds according to their own priorities.'[23] Looking to the future the experience of the ERDF review process documented in Chapter two suggests, that despite greater reference to local authority involvement in the new regulation, national governments including the British Government remain reticent in this direction, and thus it is likely that problems will persist.[24]

Securing ERDF Support: a local authority perspective

The chapter so far has focused on the procedural and administrative problems which local authorities have faced over the introduction and development of the programme approach, as well as some of the wider operational problems concerning the infrastructure side of the ERDF. We now go on to consider the factors which are important in determining the allocation of ERDF moneys, including questions of organizational capacity which influence the success or failure of local authorities in securing aid. In this discussion it is important to make a distinction between, on the one hand, the more formal legal aspects of the process revolving round questions such as eligibility criteria which are set out in the Fund regulation, and on the other hand, informal aspects such as the discretionary administrative procedures operated by central government and its regional offices.

Projects receiving ERDF aid fall into three categories: infrastructure (such as water, electricity, and transport schemes); industrial projects; and projects which assist less-favoured rural areas and mountainous regions. All projects supported by the quota section are capital investments with payments usually made in stages as projects move towards completion over a period of up to five years. In the case of infrastructure, assistance is only available for investments wholly or partly financed by public authorities, for the creation of schemes for common use.

Each infrastructure project submitted by local authorities has three hurdles to cross. First, central government departments at various levels weed out those applications which are clearly ineligible for ERDF grants or where there is doubt as to eligibility. Second, the departments take part in a rationing process by region to ensure that each part of the UK receives roughly 'its share' of ERDF grants (English regions receive about 45 per cent of available grants, Scotland 25 per cent, with Wales and Northern Ireland sharing the remainder).[25] Third, the Department of Trade and Industry decide how many projects by value it wants to submit in Brussels in excess of the United Kingdom's fixed quota allocation. Applications for ERDF aid outside the quota section are handled far more on an *ad hoc* basis. Because there is greater Commission involvement in, and approval of, integrated operations and non-quota programmes, there is scope for lobbying in Brussels by local authorities, even though national government approval is also required.

Turning to consider the specific sifting mechanisms which operate in regard to project applications, the main formal criterion for fund assistance is the relative economic circumstances of the area or region in which the project is located and on the project's direct or indirect effect on employment prospects. Applications for assistance must be consistent with the Regional Development Programme submitted by Member States. Fund aid may only be put towards projects which are sited in areas which national governments determine for aid. In the case of Great Britain these are the assisted areas defined by the Department of Industry (see table 1. Regional Distribution of ERDF Assistance 1975–82). Within this categorization lower priority is given to projects in Intermediate Areas, which often exceed by a considerable margin the total amount of grant available. Because of the rationing system operated at regional and national levels, project applications of a similar type may by accepted for forwarding in one year and rejected in another (see evidence of the Chief Executive of West Yorkshire County Council). In deciding between Intermediate area projects the most important criterion used by the Department of Environment is the relative level of unemployment in the area concerned compared with national and regional averages.

The application of discretionary procedures sometimes leads to frustration and confusion on the part of local authorities. For example, Lancashire County Council in evidence to the 1981 House of Lords Enquiry stated:

The County Council were recently successful in attracting ERDF aid for two relatively small road junction improvements on the route from the M55 to Fleetwood. The Department presumably supported the applications because of the level of unemployment in the area. However, because of the comparative low unemployment rate in North East Lancashire the Department were not prepared at the same time to submit to Brussels an application in respect of the major waste disposal project at Rowley, Burnley. In terms of the respective merits of the projects and their contribution to the economy of Lancashire, it is extremely difficult to explain to the public why certain projects are supported by the ERDF and others are not.[26]

The Department of Environment issues written guidance to local authorities in England about eligibility and offers detailed advice on individual applications through its regional offices. It would appear, however, that the quality of this back-up support varies between regional offices. The most recent House of Lords Enquiry into the operation of the ERDF commented that local authorities are often doubtful about what sorts of projects to put forward for consideration and how long will elapse before the fund grant comes through.[27] Undoubtedly one of the greatest causes of difficulty concerns the

Table 6.1. Regional Distribution of ERDF Assistance (Quota Section) 1975–82 (Commitments—ECU Millions)

Area	Industry and Services		Infrastructure		Total (excluding studies)		
	No. of Projects	Amount of Aid	No. of Projects	Amount of Aid	No. of Projects	Amount of Aid	%
England	254	243.83	1,800	509.20	2,054	753.03	44.1
North	(112)	(124.32)	(695)	(229.36)	(807)	(353.68)	20.7
Northwest	(62)	(03.40)	(501)	(126.13)	(563)	(229.53)	13.4
Yorkshire & Humberside	(39)	(9.14)	(392)	(99.63)	(431)	(108.77)	6.4
West Midlands	(—)	(—)	(8)	(0.54)	(8)	(0.54)	0.0
East Midlands	(11)	(2.13)	(56)	(13.60)	(67)	(15.73)	0.9
South West	(30)	(4.84)	(148)	(39.94)	(178)	(44.78)	2.6
Scotland	132	87.31	857	375.31	989	443.62	26.0
Wales	93	87.85	711	198.18	804	286.03	16.8
Northern Ireland	111	84.48	274	130.66	385	224.14	13.1
United Kingdom	590	503.47	3,642	1,203.35	4,232	1,706.82	100.0

Source: Derived from 8th Report on the ERDF.

narrowness of the eligibility criteria. For many authorities in areas of urban and industrial decline only a small proportion of their capital expenditure has been unequivocally eligible for ERDF support; a point referred to earlier in the discussion surrounding the experience of Merseyside, West Yorkshire, and Lancashire County Councils. Projects which are perceived to be marginal are likely to be filtered out at the regional or national level since central government is unlikely to risk projects being turned down by the Fund Management Committee thus putting at risk the UK's annual quota entitlement.

The types of projects which have been most successful to date have been large schemes, particularly those providing basic services and communications for an industrial area. Projects generally not regarded as being eligible have included advance factories, social infrastructure, and cosmetic and very small schemes. In evaluating applications the DOE, recognizing the position taken by the Fund Management Committee, has been keen to establish a clear and demonstrable link with the economic development of the area concerned and specifically that the development has a beneficial impact on the employment situation. In the case of tourist infrastructure projects, for example, the schemes must be situated in an area where tourism is a significant component of the local economy and it is necessary to demonstrate that the project will contribute directly to the increased usage of tourist-related service industries or result in a significant extension of the tourist season. In recent years Merseyside County Council has had a number of schemes turned down on the grounds that the area was not a recognized tourism location.

Looking to the future, it is interesting to note that the revised ERDF regulation contains for the first time a 'List of categories of Infrastructure which the Fund may not assist'.[28] If it is the Commission's intention that any type of project which does not appear on the list would be eligible for a grant, then this goes at least some way to making the Fund more relevant to the type of social and economic development programmes drawn up in areas of urban/industrial decline. For example, the maintenance and replacement of outworn physical infrastructure, modernization of public transport equipment, and capital investment in industrial premises are not excluded by the list. However, it is far from clear how the new system will operate in practice. The exclusion list appears to leave considerable room for interpretation and it could be the case that the Commission or UK Government continue to set priorities for the selection of projects

Table 6.2. Swansea City Council Projects Supported by the EC,
1976–83

Purpose	Amount %	Date
ERDF – QUOTA SECTION		
Lower Swansea Valley		
Roads and Sewers, Rose Site	39,000	1976
Roads and Sewers, Morfa	10,500	1976
Roads and Sewers, Winchwen	39,000	1976
Roads and Sewers, Beaufort Road	15,300	1977
Roads and Sewers, Lower Gasworks	99,900	1979
Roads and Sewers, RTZ II	182,300	1979
Roads and Sewers, Nantyffyn	31,500	1979
Foul Sewer, Phases I and II	66,600	1981
Feasibility Study, River Tawe Barrage	25,200	1982
Infrastructure, Enterprise Zone	562,900	1982
Infrastructure, Enterprise Zone	767,600	1983
Environmental works, East Side	50,000	1983
	1,889,800	
Maritime Quarter		
Renovation, Swing Bridge	28,500	1979
Repairs and Improvements, Museum	26,400	1979
Infrastructure, South Dock	101,200	1979
Removal of mound	51,000	1980
Foul sewer and repairs	88,500	1981
Marina Development	1,381,200	1982
	1,676,800	
ERDF – NON-QUOTA SECTION		
Lower Swansea Valley		
Landscaping, Enterprise Zone	200,000	1983
SOCIAL FUND		
Work Enterprise Project	4,700	1982

Source: Paper presented at a Conference on 'EC Aid and Local Authorities', Oxford
Polytechnic, Mar. 1983.

which, in the view of local authorities, do not reflect the needs of
declining industrial areas.

Organizing and lobbying for EC aid: Case studies

The previous discussion has pointed to some of the uncertainties and
bureaucratic complexities which local authorities experience in

gaining ERDF aid. Clearly some authorities are better than others in mastering such difficulties. In order to identify some of the critical variables in this context it is useful to refer to the experience of two local authorities outside the areas of highest regional priority, namely Swansea City Council and West Yorkshire County Council both of which have managed to secure a reasonable measure of ERDF support.[29]

The City of Swansea is a commercial and administrative centre lying at the heart of industrial west South Wales. In recent years the area has experienced a devastating run down of its traditional economic base centred on the steel industry. The area was downgraded from Development Area to Intermediate Area status in 1982. However, it is eligible for support from the steel non-quota programme and the quota section of the ERDF. (Between 1976 and 1983 the council received nearly £4m. from the ERDF and ESF.) One of the major elements in the council's programme has been the industrial regeneration of the lower Swansea valley—once a major centre of iron and steel production but latterly the largest area of industrial dereliction in the country. With support from the ERDF (quota and non-quota sections) a major reclamation exercise has been undertaken and part of the area has been designated as an enterprise zone. Another focus of the council's economic strategy is tourism since the city is located on an attractive coastline with the Gower Peninsula designated as an Area of Outstanding Natural Beauty. One of the major projects embarked upon with some support from the ERDF has been the development of the Swansea Maritime Quarter comprising a new marina surrounded by housing, shopping, a leisure centre, maritime and industrial museum, luxury hotel, and other amenities aimed at the tourist industry.

While Swansea City Council has assisted area status and this has to a large extent enabled the area to benefit from EC aid, its success is also based on an effective organization structure and lobbying programme. In this context, it is useful to refer to the way the City Council is organized to secure ERDF monies.

Applications for aid from the EC are handled by a 'Projects Co-ordinator' located in the Chief Executive's and Town Clerk's Department. The role of the Co-ordinator is to liase with the Welsh Office about EC matters and to inform appropriate Departments about changes in legislation and, new opportunities. The task also involves ensuring that the key Departments, Treasurers, Engineers, Planners, Architects, and Valuers, successfully work together in putting forward applications.

In order to keep Commission officials informed about problems in the area, the City Council has engaged in a lobbying strategy with neighbouring local authorities. In 1980 a delegation of Councillors from the District Councils in West Glamorgan visited the EC offices in Strasbourg to explain the problems resulting from the run down of the steel industry. The four District Councils submitted a strategy document entitled 'Steel, Crisis in South West Wales' which set out a comprehensive programme in industrial, tourism, housing, youth aid, and environmental schemes, the combined object of which was to secure the economic and social regeneration of the area. This was followed up by an officer-level visit to Brussels where the various schemes were discussed in detail with EC officials. This type of initiative, setting out various investment schemes in the context of a regional programme, is welcomed by Community officials, since although it is not always possible to fund the full range of measures suggested, it does provide a more detailed indication of the problems of the area than is provided in the official RDP and moreover gives a clearer view of the potential contribution of ERDF funded measures.

The importance of local authorities developing a direct relationship with Community institutions and officials when seeking to secure ERDF aid is exemplified by the experience of West Yorkshire Metropolitan County Council, which is another area which has seen a dramatic collapse in its manufacturing base in recent years. In relation to the ERDF, West Yorkshire's activities have taken the form of periodic grant applications, inputs into the policy revision process and advocacy for support for the textile industry. Contacts with the Commission and other EC institutions since 1975 have been achieved by regular officer/member trips to pursue issues surrounding a particular project(s) or wider policy questions. Initially the visits focused on three main objectives: developing and maintaining close contacts between the County Council's officers and those of the Commission, determining the most effective means of keeping in touch with Community thinking and maintaining a dialogue with the Community during the process of policy formulation and investigating the availability of financial assistance to West Yorkshire from the Community. Later lobbying activities have covered a widening range of topics including: the possibility of establishing an EC information office for the North of England, access to funds from the ERDF and ESF, the problems of the local textile and coal industry, funds for the Leeds-Bradford airport, and securing and extension of the ECSC Coal Closure Area within West Yorkshire.

By way of illustration is useful to examine in more detail some of the issues which the Council has taken up with the ERDF in mind. One matter that has been a continuous source of concern to West Yorkshire has been the fact that the UK government has had the sole responsibility for the submission of ERDF applications. In November 1975, for example, local MPs were contacted about the methods adopted in the selection of ERDF applications. As the Commission bases much of its judgement in policy development and project evaluation on information provided by Member States, the County Council recognized the need to provide Brussels directly with detailed information on the situation in West Yorkshire. In this respect it was recognized that the UK Regional Development Programme (RDP) was of critical importance. Working through the Strategic Conference of County Councils, a body representing the County Councils in the Yorkshire and Humberside region, a decision was taken to prepare an alternative more detailed regional development plan for the region. In May 1978 the document was presented to Commission officials and received a favourable response. While it was recognized that it did not carry official status, nevertheless, the Regional Policy Commissioner stressed the usefulness of the document in regard to providing background information about the problems of the area and assisting officials in making decisions about the allocation of aid.

In the wider aspects of the operation of the ERDF, West Yorkshire has taken full advantage of the ERDF review process as a means of lobbying for new policy and precedures. In January 1980 West Yorkshire prepared a set of propositions for the second review of the ERDF which were submitted to the Commission, MEPs, MPs, and the Association of Metropolitan Authorities. The proposals pressed for changes in the system which would ensure that there was up-to-date statistical information in respect of eligibility for aid; that there was greater local authority involvement in the preparation of the RDP; that the criterion for eligibility from the ERDF was widened; and that the non-quota section of the ERDF was made available to textile areas in the Community. These views were discussed with Commission officials in February and April of 1980 in visits to Brussels and with the Department of the Environment during the same period. The Commission's first set of proposals for the revision of the regulation were published in

November 1981 and included under the 'concentration' heading the suggestion that Yorkshire and Humberside would be denied access to ERDF funds. This decision reflected both the status of West Yorkshire in UK regional policy and the EC's outdated statistical base drawing on 1977 figures which did not fully reveal the deteriorating economic situation in the area relative to other parts of the Community. Local MEP's in West Yorkshire were mobilized to lobby on the question of the use of out of date statistics and two visits in 1982/3 to the Commission stressed concern about the region's exclusion from the quota section. Similar points were made in evidence to the House of Lords Select Committee on the European Communities. In the event these pressures, combined with those from other quarters, were to have their effect in the Commission's second round of proposals and in the final regulation.

Turning to the question of the textile industry, the notion of securing EC financial support for one particular industrial sector of the County was first mooted during a meeting with the Commission in 1975. It was recognized that the problem of declining textile industries was one which was shared by many areas of the Community and thus could be interpreted as an EC-wide regional problem. It was therefore felt that there was a possibility that sectoral aid for the textile industry would find favour within the Community. In 1978 the idea was developed further through informal talks with the Commission. The Scheme for Textile Area Regeneration (STAR) was produced by the County, showing how the economy of the West Yorkshire textile area could be improved through additional EC support. The initial intention was to get money from a proposed industry restructuring fund. STAR was discussed with Commission officials in October 1978 and it was agreed that a second plan—STAR 2—would be produced to incorporate possible ERDF assistance including examples of types of project which might be assisted. The decision announced in 1979 to withdraw Intermediate Area status from much of the County held back the initiative and textile areas were not included in the first round of ERDF non-quota funding, although it was recognized that this did not prohibit such allocation in a subsequent round. Given this backcloth the County sent a further document to the Commission, restating the case for support, and in January 1984 the Council adopted further Regulations to implement a second series of ERDF non-quota measures which included £6m. for eligible UK textile areas (including approximately £15m. earmarked for West Yorkshire).

Success in Europe: the lessons for local authorities

In coming to conclusions about the capacity of local authorities to attract EC funding it is important to recognize that the major determinant is the relative status of the area concerned in regard to the government's regional priorities. Perhaps, not surprisingly, because local authorities in the Development and Special Development Areas have a higher probability of securing support, they tend to be more aware of the opportunities, to know their way around Brussels, to understand how discretionary procedures operate, and to be better organized internally. It is also the case that those authorities with a large population base and those with second tier strategic functions are more likely to have the staff resources and range of activities to be successful in securing ERDF support. In contrast, smaller local authorities and those in the areas of lower regional priority may well be less familiar with the workings of the EC and, indeed, consider that is not worth the time and effort of putting forward applications. Nevertheless, as the discussion of the experience of Swansea and West Yorkshire has suggested, it is possible with appropriate organizational structures, thoroughness of approach, and political *savoir-faire* to have some measure of success without having the highest national regional priority. What then are the critical ingredients?

Undoubtedly local authority efforts to secure ERDF support are more likely to be successful if they are effectively organized on information, staffing, and departmental co-ordination. In terms of information, Government Departments, Community institutions, and bodies such as IULA/CEM produce a wealth of information. The more experienced authorities, however, are aware of other sources such as *Agence Europe* (daily) or *European Report* (bi-monthly) which give an 'insiders' background view of community developments. They also take advantage of contacts with local MEPs who are in a position to obtain information from the Council and Commission through the system of parliamentary oral and written questions.

Given the complexity and fluidity of European legislation and the procedures which flow from it, as well as the fact that there are a number of financial instruments which have regional implications, the more 'active' authorities tend to have an officer or officers with specific responsibility for this field. Considerable staff time and effort is spent in compiling and evaluating EC legislation and documentation. It is also the case that when seeking Community aid, project preparation, submission, confirmation and receipt of funds can sometimes prove a lengthy, time-consuming and frustrating experience. These difficulties compound the general organizational problem which local authorities face in developing their local economic policies that the activity is truly corporate in nature, cutting across the work of several departments.[30] Local authorities in regular receipt of Community support tend to nominate one Department e.g. Treasurers, Planning, or Chief Executive, to take the lead in EC matters. In the case of West Yorkshire, for example, the Chief Executive's office acts as an overall co-ordination unit for EC work including lobbying. An economic research unit in the Planning Department undertakes as part of its role EC policy-monitoring, analysis, and production of documentation.

Turning to the question of advocacy and liaison, it is important to distinguish between short and longer term strategies. In the short term, local authority activity may be focused on getting support for a particular projects or projects or securing changes in the way in which eligibility criteria are employed through discretionary procedures. In the longer term efforts may be channelled into making the case for the inclusion of the area under a specific Community measure such as the non-quota regulation or the new Community programmes. Alternatively the initiative may be targetted at influencing the periodic review of the ERDF in a favourable direction. Some local authorities who are in regular receipt of Community funding such as West Yorkshire make a point of following a carefully thought out lobbying strategy pursuing a number of different objectives. In this regard, establishing and maintaining close relationships with relevant Community officials and civil servants is seen as critical, as are frequent officer/member visits to Brussels. South Yorkshire County Council, for example, which received approximately £7m. from the ERDF between 1975 and 1983 annually sends a small high-level member delegation together with visits by officers as and when appropriate. In this context it is useful to refer to the comments of Prag, who in commenting on the strategies private companies should employ in lobbying states:

The most effective means of lobbying are likely to be the informal ones. All the effective groups in Brussels spend a great deal of time telephoning officials of the Commission, the Member State's permanent representatives, and Members of the European Parliament. . . . The contacts established do not always provide immediate results, but the goodwill created may come in handy another day . . . Informal contacts normally run parallel with whatever official consultation is possible.[31]

As far as the ERDF is concerned, informal contact with Commission officials is important in terms of understanding matters such as the way in which eligibility criteria may be interpreted or future policy shifts. However, as far as individual applications are concerned, the scope for lobbying is often not all that great because of the informal quota allocation between UK regions which means the decisions are effectively taken by the DOE. Pressure on the Commission can nevertheless be worthwhile if it provides a basis for persuading the DOE that a project is likely to be succesful in Brussels. Bradford Metropolitan Council, for example, initially faced with hostility from the DOE in regard to a tourism scheme, went to the Commission to discuss an ultimately successful bid to the ERDF in 1982 for the conversion of a building to house the National Museum of Film and Photography.

Turning to applications for support under the programme approach the scope for local authority advocacy is greater given the involvement of the Commission, as the experience of West Yorkshire has shown with the non-quota programme. Opportunities, moreover, are likely to increase with the introduction of Community programmes under the revised ERDF regulations. Experience has shown that collaborative advocacy between local authorities within a County area, or at a regional scale between counties, backed up by well-presented supporting documentation, can assist the case for support for a particular area. Across the country standing conferences of local authorities such as the North-East County Councils Association, the West Midlands and the East Midlands Forums of County Councils, and the East Anglian Consultative Committee are now preparing reports on the problems of their areas and organizing visits to Brussels. Such activity can even take place at a Community level as, for instance, in the case of the joint lobbying exercise undertaken by local authorities in textile areas for a non-quota programme.

Finally, turning to consider local authority efforts to influence broad policy shifts such as the periodic revision of the ERDF regulation, much work is undertaken in a collective manner by IULA and the local authority associations. However, as the efforts of West Yorkshire have shown in the most recent review process, there remains scope for individual local authority action. The timing of such activity is particularly important. When Community statutes are revised, both the Commission and the European Parliament seek external comment in the early stages of decision-making. The institutions are most easily approachable when draft legislation is being prepared. Once Council begins to deliberate over Commission proposals and the European Parliament and ECOSOC have supplied their official opinions, it becomes increasingly difficult for external groups to affect the decision-making process. In seeking to influence draft legislation, Prag suggests that comprehensive written briefs should be circulated to relevant institutions (COREPER, EP, Commission, ECOSOC, DOE, House of Lords) before official meetings take place over prospective legislation. Such briefs should include article-by-article commentary on draft legislation with suggested amendments.[32]

Conclusion

This chapter has charted the experience of some English and Welsh local authorities in their efforts to gain financial support from the ERDF. Within local government there is general support for the notion of Community regional policy opening up as it does, the possibility of access to funds for local economic development measures and the opportunity to enter into a dialogue with the Community and national governments about regional policy measures. However, as the House of Lords Select Committee pointed out in 1981 there has been a considerable disenchantment with the way in which the Fund has developed since its inauguration.[33] The main criticisms cited by the Committee, and supported by the evidence presented in this Chapter, surround the fact that ERDF aid does not in practice generate any new regional measures which would not have been financed from other sources; that given the way the UK government handles the issue of additionality, there is often little incentive for local authorities to react positively to the prospect of fund aid; that there has been disatisfaction with what is perceived to be the inflexible manner in which eligibility criteria have been interpreted particularly in areas of urban and industrial decline; and finally there is a feeling that there is too much national government intervention in the Fund's administration, and insufficient opportunity to be involved in policy questions. On a more positive note, however, it must be recognized that at a time of increasing pressure on local authority finances ERDF support does at least reduce the amount that would otherwise have to be borrowed to finance projects and thus particularly in the case of larger schemes and for those authorities in areas of national regional priority, the ERDF offers some reasonable benefit. Moreover, in so far as it has been allowed to develop through the non-quota programme, the programme approach has been welcomed by local authorities as presenting an opportunity to develop regional development measures tailored more specifically to the needs of the locality.

It is too soon to make a judgement about how the new ERDF regulation, as discussed in chapter two, will work out in practice. Undoubtedly the move to more funding of measures through the programme approach and the references to increased local authority involvement will be welcomed. However, the prospect of securing genuine additionality remains as distant as ever, given present government attitudes, and we have yet to see how eligibility criteria will be interpreted under the new regulation. At a broader level this chapter has indicated how the tensions between the Community and Member States surrounding the development of common policies work their way through into specific day-to-day problems at the point of implementation. Referring to the disappointments in local government about 'the meagre reality of the ERDF' the House of Lords Select Committee on the European Communities commented in 1981: 'Such disappointment, is the result of the small size of the Fund, the frustration of high hopes by the terms and conditions imposed by the original Fund regulation in 1975, and the manner in which national governments have chosen to administer the Fund.'[34] Any future evaluation of the ERDF regulation will need to consider how far the situation has changed.

Notes

1. According to the 23rd Report of the House of Lords Select Committee on the European Communities, by the end of 1982 almost £1,000m. of ERDF aid has been paid or promised to the UK for some 4,232 regional projects. This level of support accounts for less than 2 per cent of the industrial aid given by the United Kingdom in 1983 and for under 10 per cent of public expenditure on infrastructure.

2. Hull, C., and Rhodes, R. A. W., *Intergovernmental Relations in the European Community* (Saxon House, 1977).

3. For a more detailed discussion of the concept see M. Martins and J. Mawson, 'The Development of the Programme Approach in the Common Regional Policy: an evaluation of the British experience', in *Town Planning Review*. volume 54, no. 1, Jan. 1983.

4. See further, The House of Lords Select Committee on the European Communities, Session 1980–1, 14th Report, *Regional Policy*, Feb. 1981: House of Lords Select Committee on the European Communities, Session 1981–2, 12th Report, *The Revision of the European Regional Development Fund*, Apr. 1982: House of Lords Select Committee on the European Communities, Session 1983–4, 23rd Report, *The European Regional Development Fund*, July 1984.

5. See further, the memorandum of evidence submitted by the Association of District Councils to the House of Lords, Session 1981–2, 12th Report, Mar. 1982, pp. 19–25.

6. See further, The Local Authorities in Lancashire 'Presentation to the European Commission on Integrated Packages', House of Lords, 14th Report, Session 1980–1, May 1980, pp. 59–60.

7. Wheaton M., in *Local Government Chronicle*, 16 Mar. 1984. p. 314.

8. House of Lords, 23rd Report, Session 1983–4, July 1984, p. 82.

9. Ibid., p. 82.

10. Ibid., p. 82.

11. House of Lords, 14th Report, Session 80–1, Feb. 1981, p. 140.

12. Wilson, I., 'The European Community's Regional Policy', in *Local Government Studies*, vol. 6. no. 4. p. 26.

13. House of Lords, 23rd Report, Session 1983–4, July 1984, p. 151.

14. House of Lords, 12th Report, Session 1981–2, Letter from Merseyside County Council, Feb. 1982, pp. 49–52.

15. See also Martins, M. and Mawson, J. op. cit.

16. Ibid. p. 80.

17. EC Commission, 'The Regional Development Programmes' (Regional Policy Series No. 17), Brussels, 1979.

18. W. Griffiths MEP in minutes of evidence taken before the House of Lords Select Committee, Session 1983–4, Tuesday 8 May 1984.

19. House of Lords, 23rd Report, Session 1983–4, July 1984, p. 112.

20. The Legislative basis for the second series of Specific Community Regional Development Measures was contained in 11232/82, COM (82) 658.

21. Memorandum of Evidence submitted by the Welsh Office, to the House of Lords, 23rd Report, Session 1983–4, Mar. 84, pp. 18–20.

22. House of Lords, 14th Report Session 1980–1, Feb. 1981, p. 113.

23. House of Lords, 23rd Report, Session 1983–4, July 1984. p. 124.

24. See also J. Mawson and J. Gibney in evidence submitted to the House of Lords 23rd Report, Session 1983–4.

25. House of Lords, 23rd Report, Session 1983–4. July 1984 p. XXV. para. 60.

26. House of Lords, 14th Report, Session 1980–1, Feb. 1981. p. 58.

27. House of Lords, 23rd Report, Session 1983–4, July 1984, p. XXX para, 73.

28. Mawson, J., 'Organising for Economic Development,' in Young, K., and Mason, C., *Urban Economic Development* (London: Macmillan, 1983).

29. The discussion of Swansea City Councils experience is taken from a paper given by John Butler, City Treasurer, at a seminar on 'EEC Aid and Local Authorities', Department of Town Planning, Oxford Polytechnic, 18 Mar. 1983, The material on West Yorkshire's EC activities draws from a comparative study of local authority economic initiatives undertaken by M. Marshall and J. Mawson for West Midlands County Council in 1983.

30. Ibid; paper presented by G. Barrett for South Yorkshire County Council.

31. 'Lobbying the European Community', D. Prag, European Democratic Group Pamphlet, London Oct. 1983.

32. Ibid.

33. House of Lords, 14th Report, Session 1980–1. Feb. 1981. p. XIV para. 35.

34. Ibid. p. XIV. para. 36.

7

Italian Regions in the European Community

FRANCESCO MERLONI
(translated by Michael Keating)

Introduction

Before discussing the role of Italian regions in the EC, we must first
clarify the meaning of the term 'Region' and its implications in strictly
juridical terms as well as on the more general political plane. Italian
regions are general-purpose political and administrative bodies in
receipt of decentralized powers from the central state. Unlike the
special-status regions of the post-war period, they are not instruments
for specific types of intervention or a mere recognition of existing forms
of cultural and political autonomy, but a universal and general level of
government, exercising functions of which the central government has
divested itself. This basic feature—the 'rolling back' of the centralized
state—has focused attention on the ways in which the autonomy of the
new bodies, endowed with legislative powers as well as the ability to
interpret and articulate the general interests of their populations, is to
be guaranteed.

In this respect, Italy bears comparison both with those European
countries where the need for decentralization has been recognized
(France, Belgium, Spain) and with the federal states (German Federal
Republic, Switzerland, Austria), which possess a substantial intermediate level of government, between centre and localities. By the same
token, the Italian experience differs from those types of regionalism
which have not involved a devolution of political power either because
functions are already substantially devolved to local government
(Britain, the Scandinavian countries, the Netherlands) or because the
centralized model has prevailed (as in the case of France before 1981).
In these countries regions are recognized only through special-purpose
interventionist agencies (like the Scottish Development Agency) or
through programmes aimed at specific economic sectors (as in the case
of the pre-1981 French regions). In the first group of countries the

regional problem manifests itself in institutional terms; in the second in the form of the need for 'regional policies' aimed at underdeveloped or declining areas, and involving the co-ordination of the existing functions of the various levels or government or the creation of *ad hoc* agencies.

The Italian experience, now going back more than a decade, provides an interesting illustration of both types of problem. For as well being a means of increasing citizen participation in political and administrative life, the regions have an important planning function. We could spend a long time discussing this latter point; I shall confine myself to noting that one of the basic reasons for the creation of regions—twenty years after the constitution had provided for them—was the need for a workable level of territorial planning and integration after the failure of global planning under the first centre–left governments. Indeed, this role was explicitly laid down in all the regional statutes as a means of drawing together functions which otherwise might appear excessively sectoral and disparate.

While these functions might not include comprehensive powers of economic regulation—monetary and credit policies remain rigorously centralized—or of industrial intervention, the regions can none the less mobilize their other powers, including control of infrastructure, public services (transport, environmental matters, energy), and social services (health, social security) behind their planning programmes.

This dual role explains the fluctuating fortunes of the regions in terms of establishing their institutional credibility. It also explains why the question of their role in the European Community has been debated sometimes as a purely institutional issue and at others as a more substantial problem of the relationship between the goals and means of the regions' own policies and programmes and the 'regional policies' determined at national and community levels.

The Italian Experience of Regionalism

The process of regionalization in Italy has been neither brief nor simple for, after the establishment of the regions in 1970, it was still necessary to transfer functions to them from the central state. This happened in two stages; the first transfer in 1972 was incomplete and rather fragmentary. The second transfer decree, in 1977, followed a long series of regional demands and conflicts, a clear demonstration of the natural tendency for political bodies to seek their own aggrandizement and of the need, in order effectively to carry through administrative reforms, to rely on the pressures of interested parties within the political system. The list of regional powers and functions, summarized in the previous paragraph, remains incomplete and contradictory, but we can nevertheless say that the great bulk of functions and public services are now decentralized to the regions or to subregional entities (provinces and communes).

While complete on the formal, institutional level, the regional reform is far from complete in terms of the effective capacity of the regions to forge their own policies and carry them through. Many difficulties remain, the major ones being:

a. the heavy financial dependence of the regions on the state; 90 per cent of their funds are transfers from central government and most of these are earmarked for particular functions or specific policies;

b. the prevalence of functional linkages between the state and the regions; the regional reform, in fact, has failed to modify, even at the regional level, the functional fragmentation of the central administration. Rather, there has developed in the various sectors a series of direct links between individual ministries and the relevant regional councillors, serving to reinforce the power both of the ministry and of the councillor *vis-à-vis* his colleagues;

c. the weak powers of strategic planning and intervention, notably in industrial policy, manpower planning, major infrastructure (telecommunications, motorways, railways, trunk roads), and resource planning (energy, water, etc.);

d. while the regions have, as noted, major functions in important areas, health and social security, transport, housing, planning, and care of the environment, these tend to be exercised in a manner subordinate to the state, and not only in the financial sense; often it is national sectoral laws, notably, recently, on health, transport, water, professional training, and tourism, imposing duties on them which initiate much of the regions' own legislative and administrative activity;

e. the regions, from the outset, have been hampered by their dependence on an inefficient system of local government, many communes being too small and both communes and provinces suffering from limited powers. This has held back the delegation of functions from the regions to the lower levels, leaving the regions over-burdened with operational tasks. Together, these factors have contributed to the 'low profile' of the regions, their reduction,

Ita

Regions i

164

discrete are

internati

of the

sub

indeed, almost to the status of enlarg
agencies for a political and legislative

The Institutional Role of the Regions i

The International Capacity of the Regions

From the institutional perspective, the
regions in the Community can be consider
more general issue of their international c̲ᵤ̲ₚₐ̲c̲ᵢ̲ₜᵧ̲.̲ So all the constitutional rules on the distribution of powers between Government and
Parliament with respect to international relations apply. To the former
belongs the 'foreign power', the capacity to conduct foreign relations
and negotiate treaties; to the latter belongs only the power to ratify
treaties and to call the Government to account. So there is a separation
in principle between the decision-making (negotiation of the treaty)
and its execution in the form of adaptation of domestic laws to the new
international obligations. This has tended to centralize in the Government all matters with international repercussions, so affecting the
distribution of powers among the various levels of government and in
particular between the central government and the regions, adding to
an already complex and contradictory process.

To simplify, we can see the process of regional decentralization in
Italy in two distinct phases. The first stage was decidedly one of
conflict, with the regions, elected in 1970, seeking to obtain the
maximum functions and the central administration trying to restrain
them. This phase also saw a tendency to the rigid separation of powers
following the federal model, albeit with the preponderance of powers
going to the central state. The second phase started with the second
series of transfers of powers in 1977, in which the balance of powers
tended more to favour the regions but, to allow central co-ordination, a
series of procedures was laid down regulating state-regional relationships which effectively reduced the rigid separation of powers. So for
the great bulk of public functions it is not possible to specify one level of
government which is uniquely competent; rather, several levels of
government, with their various powers, must jointly decide and
execute policies.

The question of the international capacity of the regions, including
their role in the EC, is inevitably affected by this. So in the first phase,
of rigid separation of powers, 'international relations' were seen as a

, reserved completely for the state, not only in respect of
nal agreements or foreign representation but also in respect
implementation of agreements irrespective of whether their
ject matter involved national or regional functions. In the second
phase, which we might describe as 'co-operative regionalism', there
was a weakening of the original rigid separation of powers. The DPR
616 of 1977, which can be considered as a 'charter of regional
functions', on the one hand explicitly confirms the reservation of
'international relations' to the state even with respect to regional
functions, but on the other hand allows the regions to carry out certain
types of activity abroad and, above all, endows the regions with the
task of applying EC regulations and directives. We shall now examine
more closely these latter two provisions.

The International Activities of the Regions

Article 4 of the DPR 616 stipulates that the regions 'cannot undertake
any promotional activities abroad in connection with their functions
except with the previous agreement of the Government and within the
scope of its coordinating activities'. So we can see that some international activity is allowed on the part of the regions, provided that it
comes within the scope of the Government's control mechanisms. The
regions, for their part, have sought to extend the concept of promotional activities to cover fact-finding visits, investigative missions to
foreign administrations, membership of interregional organizations
(such as Alpe Adria or Arge Alp), and even some limited agreements
like that between Lombardy and Somalia for co-operation in health
and tourism. Central government in effect tolerates these initiatives
and, as long as it is able to exercise its powers of ultimate control,
condones activities such as the international agreements which,
according to the letter of the law, should not be allowed.

The International Capacity of the Regions in the EC

The area in which the rigid separation of powers and the centralization
of foreign affairs in the hands of the Government have been modified
most considerably is that of relations within the EC. Again, we must
emphasize the separation between the process of decision-making in
the Community and the implementation of those decisions.

Regions and Policy Execution

As there is an obvious need for coherence in a system like the Italian which provides for a regional level with its own legislative and administrative functions, we must make an overall evaluation of the regions' role in handling matters within their competence, within the broad framework of regional policies. It should be inconceivable for the regions to be mere executors of policies decided elsewhere, with a consequent loss of their own powers. The reality, however, has been different. The division of powers which characterized the first phase of regionalization forced the regions to concentrate on the executive aspects of Community policies. Here they drew attention to the delays which the mediation of the State inflicted on matters within their purview. The rigid separation of roles could have led to the absurdity of having two separate administrative apparatuses for the same regional functions; a State one for the implementation of Community policies and a regional one for the implementation of ordinary policies. To some extent, indeed, this has happened, for example in agriculture policy where the guarantee system is the responsibility of national agencies such as the AIMA (Agricultural Intervention Agency), the Intendenza di Finanza (Customs), the Cassa Conguaglio Zucchero (Sugar Market Fund), and Ente nazionale risi (State Rice Agency).

For their part, the regions pointed to the unique features of Community rules which often, unlike most international agreements, do not reguire national legislation in order to be effective. Not only are regulations directly applicable in member states, but the detailed directives and decisions of the Community might also be interpreted as binding on national decision-makers at whatever level. In all these cases, the regions argued, there exists a specific Community policy which must simply be implemented according to the normal distribution of functions between the State and the Regions.

For its part, the State has moved away from the doctrine of rigid separation and the insistence on its own monopoly in international affairs, including self-executing Community rules, and is seeking, rather, guarantees of the timely implementation of Community rules in view of the delays arising from regional responsibilities. At first, this took the form of delegating rather than devolving functions, to allow the state reserve powers to intervene or even revoke the delegation. In the second phase, a mechanism was introduced allowing the State to substitute for defaulting regions, with a forcible transfer of responsibilities as the last sanction.

The present system provides for

a. the direct application by the regions of regulations (and detailed directives) on matters within their competence;
b. the application of Community directives, within the framework of national laws adapting them to Italy;
c. a power of substitution by the State in the case of default on the part of the regions.

Of course there are problems with this. The most important is the question of how much discretion will be left to the regions in the implementation of directives, given that these will already have been defined at two higher levels. Nevertheless, it is a step forward, albeit a small one, in that it opens up the whole question of the role and influence of the regions in Community decision-making.

Regions and Community decision-making

Here too, the debate has proceeded by steps. The first has to do with the modification of State–region relations within the Italian constitution. This is vital because, despite the moves towards making the Communities a real level of government, notably through the role of the European Parliament and proposals for an executive answerable to it, at present decision-making powers are still concentrated in the hands of member states. So the first requirement is a means whereby the regions' policies and objectives can influence the European policies of the Italian government. This is more important than the establishment of direct links (though informal contacts do exist largely for gathering information), so that the issue has become subsumed in the more general question of State-region relationships. We have already noted the major problems with this, notably the tendency for sectoral integration to prove stronger than territorial. This has spawned a series of special agencies—about a hundred in number—and joint procedures in which the regions tend to be reduced to a subordinate role.

Privileged links have developed between the central ministries and relevant regional councillors, with the national Parliament and the regional councils reduced to the role of ratifying their decisions. The great problem is how to overcome this, to re-establish a generalized and reciprocal relationship between the State and the regions. Solutions which have been proposed include the unification of the mixed agencies into a general intergovernmental structure with its own legal powers; and the strengthening of forms of horizontal co-ordination among the regions themselves, either on a sectoral or on a comprehensive basis. Such co-ordination would produce not legal decisions but political agreements to be implemented by the various participants. Both models represent forms of 'co-operative federalism' but, while the former has an institutional and decision-making form and emphasizes vertical integration, the latter is nearer to the pure form of co-operative regionalism found in federal states (especially the USA and Germany) where the conference of governors or prime ministers has its own independent existence, with representatives of the central government attending by invitation.

The question of regional participation in the formulation of Community policies provides a good illustration of this debate. There have been repeated calls for the creation of a mixed agency within the Prime Minister's department, from the AICCE-Regions proposal of 1974, to that of the Giannini commission on the second transfer of functions in 1977 and the 1982 proposals for the reform of the Prime Minister's department. The latter proposal, for a centre for State-region relationships, could develop into a forum for consulting the regions on Community policies within the regions' competence.

Apart from the usual objections which supporters of pure co-operative regionalism have to this idea, such as its excessive centralization of powers in the executive and the loss of regional autonomy, there are more general criticisms. The tendency for the elected assemblies at both national and regional levels to lose power would be reinforced. The Commission could become bogged down in detailed matters, preventing a proper consideration of general issues such as Community policies. Finally, one can criticize the restriction on consultation to matters within the regions' competence; such an eminently political body should have the ability to consider the wider impact of Community policies in general.

These proposals all assume a continuation of the present system whereby the national government is pre-eminent in Community matters. In the event of a reinforcement of the independent powers of the Community institutions, of course, other patterns could emerge. Already, the Community can act directly to change national laws, reducing regions' powers to the minimum, even on matters within their competence. There are few checks on this at national level and none at the Community level. This is particularly true where policies are effectively formulated and carried out by the Commission, albeit approved and even amended by the Council of Ministers. This unique feature of Community regulations makes them, in those cases where they impinge on regional competences, a complete system spanning three levels of government and overriding the strict demarcation of functions.

There is, indeed, an analogy between the system of State–region–local government relations and the system of Community–State–regional relations. In the first place, regional institutions such as the Italian regions and, even more so, the German *Länder*, exercise a general co-ordinating role over local government, interrupting the direct channels between the State and the localities. This, however, does not remove the State's concern with the general condition of local government, its efficiency, and its ability to carry out national policies. Hence the existence of direct political links between the State and local government and of national legislation on the local government system. In Italy central government also has an array of powers over local government in matters such as finance, the status of local officials and supervision of 'non-regional' functions.

Our second system of relationships in the Community could be developed along analogous lines. The State would continue to be responsible for the co-ordination of its own and the regions' policies and, hence, remain the main interlocutor. So the compatibility of Community and regional policies would be decided between the State and the EC. This would not, however, prevent the development of institutional relationships between the regions and the Community for the purposes of exchanging information. Knowledge of the regions' plans and access to the data gathered on the ground could be a vital element in the development of independent Community policies, though the problem of reconciling these with national policies would remain.

Italian Regional Policies and the Role of the Regions

So far we have been considering the institutional relationships among the three levels of government. We now turn to the relationship of Community and regional policies. It will be useful to distinguish the 'regional policies' of the Community from its other policies, as the former raise particular problems. Since 1950 Italy has had regional policies aimed at countering the economic and social imbalances between the Mezzogiorno—covering eight of the twenty regions—and some other, mainly inland and mountainous, disadvantaged areas, and the rest of the country. For this purpose, a decidedly centralist agency, the Cassa per il Mezzogiorno, was established, though this was before the creation of the regional councils. Exceptional both in its form and its resources, it was responsible both for infrastructure development, including agriculture works, irrigation projects, provision of drinkable water and roads, and industrial expansion, through a system of control and financial incentives. It is beyond our scope to evaluate the impact of these policies. What is more relevant to our theme is the fact that they had to be modified considerably with the establishment of the regions. The Italian regions have fairly extensive powers in land-use planning and physical development as well as more limited functions in relation to economic development. While these have had little impact on national industrial policy, they have progressively reduced the scope of the Cassa. At first, the Cassa was allowed to undertake directly a range of large-scale works knows as 'special projects'. Now a policy review has suggested that the Cassa should no longer play an active administrative role but, concentrating its operations on smaller areas—for example, the metropolitan areas of the south—should limit itself to the technical and administrative co-ordination of projects on the basis of programme agreements. The various levels of government would each contribute to these integrated operations according to their functions. These programmes would thus return to being 'extraordinary' in the original sense, the use of exceptional financial measures and accelerated procedures but not in the sense of the surrender by regions and local councils of their functions.

Community Regional Policies and the Regions

While the debate on the reform of the Cassa per il Mezzogiorno was still taking place, Community regional policies, at least as regards the quota section of the ERDF, were taking a step backwards. Despite the general intention to reduce the role of the Cassa to special projects, the procedures for the ERDF envisage a decisive role for it in preparing applications for the Ministry for the Mezzogiorno which will select those to be forwarded to the EC. The regions are to be confined to collecting the applications and doing a preliminary evaluation which is in no way binding on the State or the Community. Considering that 80 per cent of the funds are used for infrastructure projects—a regional responsibility—rather than industrial development—largely but not wholly the province of the State—the distorting effect of Community policies on the already precarious position of the regions is obvious. The same applies to the non-quota section of the ERDF, although this is as yet of modest dimensions (see chapter 2). Identical precedures are followed, with the added aggravation that the matters involved are firmly within the regions' purview, including help for small and medium-sized firms, crafts, and rural tourism. Yet the non-quota section was introduced in 1979 precisely to aid 'specific Community initiatives' outside the national quotas of the rest of the Fund and aimed at alleviating the adverse side-effects of other Community policies and the particularly grave situation of certain regions. This implies a capacity on the part of the Community to formulate its own policies, while the quota section is simply a device for supporting the regional policies of individual states. So the role of the State is crucial, both in absorbing Community regional policies within its own ambit and in centralizing matters formally devolved to the regions.

A greater capacity for independent policy-making on the part of the Community, and therefore a need for a new set of relationships, is likely to emerge from the reform of the ERDF (see chapter 2), notably:

a. the increase in the non-quota section of the ERDF;
b. the greater geographical concentration of aid, putting in question the system of national quotas;
c. the move from the financing of single projects to the financing of programmes. This is intended, according to the Commission, to encourage the integration of Community, State, and regional aids.

Particularly important are the 'integrated operations', bringing together public and private ventures, with co-ordinated contributions from the Community, the member state and local authorities. As can be seen, this comes close to the model of intergovernmental co-operation proposed for Italy itself in the form of 'programme agreements'. Such a system would respect the independence of regional and local authorities which, in collaboration with a more independent Community, would decide on policies and see to their implementation.

A similar distortion of internal constitutional arrangements can be observed in other fields. In agriculture, for example, there is a potential conflict between regional functions, which include all matters of agricultural structure, and the Guidance Section of the FEOGA (the Community agricultural fund). On the other hand, the State has reserved to itself 'matters of national interest in the regulation of the agricultural market' and all matters of price intervention. Given the imbalance (95 to 5 in 1980) between price intervention and structural spending, there is an inbuilt centralizing tendency here.

Similar considerations apply to the European Social Fund where, as can be seen from the table, many of the Fund's activities fall within the regions' sphere of responsibilities. Yet the Italian system provides for bids to be made directly to the Ministry of Labour without any participation by the regions. Despite having their own legislative and administrative powers, they are reduced to the status of applicants for Community funds, just like any other public or private body.

Conclusions

It is not easy to define the present role of the regions in the Community. From the early phase of sharp differentiation from central government in which almost any regional initiative, except perhaps to implement its own policies, was ruled out, the Italian system has moved to a collaborative phase allowing a little scope for regional interventions. These include a role in the implementation of Community policies and the forging of informal international links. Central government, however, remains the dominant influence in both domestic and international policy. Indeed, in some respects, the effect of the Community has been an encroachment by central government on regional responsibilities. This is particularly noticeable in regional and social policies and in the price support part of the Common Agricultural Policy. There is not likely to be any rapid change in the situation; that would require changes in Community institutions. Only an increase in the powers of the European Parliament and the emergence of a European Government at the expense of member states could produce a more formalized system of relationships justifying closer links between the Community and regions. This could, on the one hand, give the Community the information needed to refine and evaluate its own policies and, on the other, allow the regions more influence in the formulation of those policies.

Table 7.1.   European Social Fund (Dec. 71/66/CEE)

Section	Kind of intervention	Regional Competence
People quitting agriculture	Training	Training
Textile and clothing workers	Training	Training
Immigrants	Education of children Training	Training
Young people	Training Employment	Training Young people employment policies (L. 285/77)
Regions	Training Job starting	Training
Technical progress	Training	Training
Small and medium size enterprises	Technical innovations introduction	Handicraft
Miners	Training Jobs adjustment Employment	Training Social benefits

8

German *Länder* in the European Community*

HANS-GEORG GERSTENLAUER

Several member states of the European Community have been confronted with regionalizing tendencies, exemplified by demands for autonomy by various individual regions or ethnic groups[1] but the Federal Republic of Germany is the only existing federal system in the EC. It alone has had experience of subnational, autonomous units within the larger supra-national European Community system. It thus provides pertinent evidence of the effects of the supranational decision-making on the subnational level. This question will be 'of particular significance, since the desire for autonomy is, or may be linked with efforts to achieve a more direct relationship between a particular region or autonomous units and the Community. In so far as such efforts make up an element in strategies for gaining regional autonomy, they might be at the expense of the national political system and its decision making apparatus.'[2]

In the Federal Republic of Germany there are three levels of governmental decision-making the communal or 'local' level—the subnational or 'regional' level represented by the *Länder*, and the national level represented by the *Bund*. From a constitutional point of view, the spheres of influence of each of the three levels are clearly demarcated, and the relationship between the three is very disciplined. Yet each level can be seen as one element of a unitary decision-making system which is highly complex. At the same time, each level has responsibility for certain areas of decision-making and has a certain amount of freedom to formulate its own policy; for example, the *Bund* is not allowed to intervene in the exclusive areas of the *Länder*.

The existence of the European Community now adds a fourth, supranational level of decision-making. However, the EC can

* For help on an earlier draft of this essay, I wish to thank J. Buhaenko and R. Hrbek. The author would also like especially to thank C. Wallace for help and comments on this easay. Any remaining errors or omissions are the responsibility of the author.

173

intervene at all levels of decision-making by means of directly applicable and enforceable law. So we must investigate both the interaction between national and regional levels, and that between supranational and regional levels.[3] In this latter case there is a possibility of the national level being completely by-passed. The influence of the EC supranational decision-making on the *Länder* (and vice versa) has not been fully investigated. Although there are many publications on this topic, they usually stress constitutional and legal questions, take a normative approach and tend to neglect political factors. Because of this latter tendency the state of the literature is unsatisfactory and makes it difficult to undertake a fully detailed analysis of the political factors.

Trends in the federal system of Western Germany

In order to avoid misunderstanding about the 'regional' character of the German *Länder*, it is necessary to note the specific conditions of their origin. The *Länder* in their present outline were oriented neither according to the historical *Länder* territories nor according to lines of economic, geographical, and cultural factors. Primarily they reflect the division of Germany into occupation zones and only Hamburg, Bremen, and Bavaria have retained their traditional boundaries.

The significant pre-1933 differences in their socio-economic structures have been to a large extent blurred by two post-war developments; high mobility and the integration of 10m. refugees and expellees from the East. Apart from the Danish minority in Schleswig-Holstein, there are no territorial minority ethnic–linguistic groups in Germany. Moreover, the high level of economic prosperity provided by the so-called economic miracle enabled the Germans to establish an interregional redistributive system to diminish residual disparities.[4] After 1945 a strong 'unitary' approach in public opinion was reinforced by socio-economic unification tendencies associated with a sense of common national destiny, and an anti-traditional, 'modernist' attitude. Since the 1950s and the elimination of regionalist parties, regionalism no longer registers in the inter-party conflict. Apart from the special case of the Bavarian CSU[5], parties are constituted at the federal level although in candidate nomination there remains a strong local and regional influence. *Land* branches have subordinated their aims and activities to those of federal policy, so that even in the *Land* parliamentary elections, federal personalities and issues frequently dominate.

Within this developing framework of the federal system in Western Germany three main tendencies in the relationships between *Bund* and *Länder* can be indentified. First, as a consequence of the principle of 'unity of living conditions'[6] set down in the Basic Law, there has been a shift in the balance of power in favour of the *Bund*. As early as 1962 this process was interpreted as a development towards the unitary federal state, and illustrates the fact that the scope of the *Länder's* own policy-making activities is not only small but has tended to get smaller. Second, this trend led to an increase in the *Bundesrat's* power. Here the executive authorities of the *Länder* are able to influence federal policy-making even though the *Bundesrat* has a right of veto in the last resort. It is the *Land* parliaments which suffer primarily from this development, as they lose more and more of their control functions. The third tendency, 'co-operative federalism', has resulted in a loss of power not only for the *Land* parliaments, but also for the federal parliament, the *Bundestag*. Since the foundation of the Federal Republic of Germany there have been a lot of co-ordination forums and informal relations both horizontal and vertical between the different levels. The most obvious manifestations of 'co-operative federalism' can be seen in the co-operative between the *Bund* and the *Länder* in the planning, financing, and implementation of a wide range of policies.

It is important here to note that Germany was one of the few West European countries not to have a regional protest movement in the last years but in contrast to those EC member states with decentralizing tendencies, the Federal Republic has seen a shift of power from the regional level to the national level. The way in which this development affects the relationship between the Community and the *Länder* is the concern of this chapter.

Subnational level and European Community: The impact of supranational decision-making on the federal system

The rights of the *Länder* within the federal system are affected by the EC in two different spheres; their exclusive competence to legislate in certain matters at the *Länder* level, and their right to participate in the formulation of federal legislation through the *Bundesrat*.[7] *Bundesrat's* members are delegated by the *Land* governments and more and more decisions require *Bundesrat* approval, though in particular cases the

Bundestag has the power to overrule the vote of the *Bundesrat* by a qualified majority. Most EC interventions have implications for federal
legislative competences. However, the *Bundesrat* is not represented in
the Council of Ministers, which is the major decision-making institution in the EC, and it has no right of participation in Community
affairs. Germany is represented only by the Federal Government,
which alone defines and presents the German position. Therefore in
EC matters the *Länder* have also lost influence in areas of their exclusive
legislative competence, where they have been directly affected by
Treaty articles, and Community decisions and efforts to harmonize
laws. A few examples will illustrate the point. In education and vocational training, there are various articles in the Treaties which allow
the Community to take initiatives. In 1963 ten general principles for
implementing a common vocational training policy were established.
In 1974 the EC Council, for the first time, accepted a resolution on the
co-operation in certain areas of education policy. Two years later, the
co-operation was extended to eight areas laying down the guide-lines
for an action programme.

In environmental protection, the *Länder* are especially concerned in
the field of protection of the sea and inland waters, where a Community action programme and several directives have been approved. As
regards regional policy, the *Länder* have to communicate their own
regional policy programme to DG IV (Competition Policy) of the
Commission which checks that it is in accordance with articles 92 ff. of
the EEC Treaty. The special importance for the *Länder* may be
illustrated by the fact that 'in all such cases the Community takes
decisions which the *Bund* could not have taken under domestic German
Law'.[8]

To sum up; first, in federal legislation, the shift of competences to
the supra-national level has resulted in the *Bundesrat*, as the representative of the *Länder* losing its right to participate in the legislation
process. Second, in the case of the *Länder's* constitutionally assigned
competences, the Federal Government through the German representative in the Council, has gained a right of decision over subjects
which under domestic German law, it had no right of influence at all.
Thus the *Land* parliaments have tended to lose the influence they had
through their powers of legislation and scrutiny. Moreover, with the
introduction of the *de facto* unanimity principle in the EC Council in
1966, the position of the Federal Government, as of each other national
government, has been strengthened. This, together with the fact that

the *Länder* have no formal right of participation in the European supra-national decision-making process explains why the trend within Germany towards the 'unitary federal state' mentioned above, has been reinforced by the shift of power towards the supranational level. As a consequence there has been a series of attempts by the *Länder* to compensate for and even to counteract this trend.

Participation of the *Länder* in the national and supranational decision-making:[9] The *Bundesrat*

As early as 1951 the *Bundesrat* realized that in the long term the EC integration process would cut across the federal division of power and lead ultimately to a loss of its own power. On the occasion of the ratification of the Rome Treaties, two demands were made; that the *Bundesrat* should be able to send some of its members to the European Assembly and that it should be able to participate in a significant way in defining the German position in the Community Council. From a juridical point of view, however, the *Bundesrat* has in practice achieved little. Its only right is to be informed by the Federal Government about Community affairs, but a question remains concerning the degree of real participation the *Bundesrat* can achieve in EC affairs. The *Bundesrat*, as well as the *Bundestag*, receives all EC proposals on Community regulations, directives and other documents (reports, programmes, memoranda, etc.) communicated by the Commission to the Council of Ministers.[10] The EC documents are debated at length by the *Bundesrat*, usually in its committees and the results frequently presented to the Federal Government in a formal statement. In most cases the *Bundesrat*'s point of view is in accordance with the Federal Government's approach and the Federal Government often takes into account the suggestions of the *Bundesrat*, particularly on technical details where the *Länder* and their bureaucracies have superior administrative expertise at their disposal.[11] How far the Federal Government defends the opinion given it by the *Bundesrat* in decision-making at the supranational level, has not been systematically investigated. Indeed, it is difficult to assess the *Bundesrat*'s real influence. On the one hand, the execution of this procedure is seen merely as a way of satisfying the formal obligation of informing the *Länder*[12] but on the other hand, its real influence, through informal channels, may actually be considerable.

Most of the time the *Bundesrat* meets at civil servant level. Those federal civil servants who are members of the German delegations in the working-groups of the EC Council of Ministers frequently take part on behalf of the Federal Ministries. At this stage the final approach has not yet been established. Thus there is a 'considerable informal influence' on the federal civil servants.[13] In many cases, the latter will accept an opinion expressed by one or several of the *Länder*, and agree to take it into account in negotiations with Brussels. Therefore, there is not only a detailed, mutual exchange of information and opinions on EC affairs, but also an opportunity for the *Bundesrat* to influence positions taken by the Federal Government. Moreover, the Federal Government in 1979 specifically pledged to improve the flow of information to the *Bundesrat* so that its position could more fully be taken into account during the EC Council's negotiations.

Before 1979 attempts by the *Bundesrat* to nominate members to the European Parliament had failed, and the German parliamentary delegation in Strasbourg were drawn exclusively from the *Bundestag*. This pattern of representation ended with direct elections. However, the European Parliament had some contacts with the *Bundesrat* before 1979, and subsequently they have been intensified. In 1980 the then President of the EP, Mme Simone Veil, visited the *Bundesrat*, and in February of 1982, Members of the European Assembly attended for the first time a meeting of the *Bundesrat* Committee for EC Affairs. Further meetings are planned.[14] The Committee has contacts with the European Parliament, informs all German MPs of its activities and opinions on EC matters and communicates all European Parliament resolutions, reports, and opinions to the members of the *Bundesrat*.

The first effects of the co-operation are already apparent. During a plenary session the European Parliament resolved, that 'the Community has to take care that those Member States which are not part of the geographical scope of the quota-section will not be hindered with regard to their national regional development policy'.[15] These activities illustrate the way in which the *Bundesrat* had sought with some success to promote its interests in the Community by finding 'allies' on the supranational level.

The *Länder*

The *Bundesrat* is a federal institution whose role is confined to federal affairs. So apart from the *Bundesrat*'s opportunities to infiltrate supranational decision-making, the *Länder* have had to find other ways of countering the increasing influence of the EC, especially where it affects their exclusive powers. There are two options; they can act either as a group or individually.

In the case of the first option we have the *Länderbeobachter* 'Observer from the *Länder*' who is a higher civil servant, responsible to the governments of all *Länder* and nominated by the Conference of *Länder* Ministers for Economic Affairs (*Länderwirtschaftsministerkonferenz*).* The Observer has his office at the Baden-Württemberg Representation to the *Bund* in Bonn. His main task is to collect information about Community affairs which are of interest to the *Länder*. In this capacity—and not in that of representing the *Länder*—the *Länderbeobachter* can attend the Council of Ministers as a 'non-speaking' member of the German delegation, is allowed to join in the preparatory meetings for the sessions of the Council held in the Federal Ministry for Economic Affairs, and receives the orders to the German delegation of the COREPER. Moreover, he obtains all documents on EC matters from the secretary of the Council, and he informs both the various ministers in the *Länder* co-ordination conferences and the Bundesrat committees of their contents. Finally, he has to keep in touch with the Commission and has a special distribution task within the recently established '*Länderbeteiligunsverfahren*'. As the Observer from the *Länder* attends the Council of Ministers, his role is frequently, *prima facie*, overestimated. Of course, he is able to control the extent to which the Federal Government is representing the *Länder* opinion, but on the other hand, his staff is very small and, because of pressures on his time, he cannot attend all the meetings or be well informed about all the policies concerned.[16]

Taking the second option the *Bund* and the *Länder* have arranged for *Länder* representatives, to participate in the German delegation in various Community forums. For the spheres of appointment of *Land* representatives there is no exact rule, but we can agree with Hull and Rhodes that 'it is generally true . . . that whenever a proposed Community decision will substantially affect the States, and particularly in instances where technical expertise in the Federal Republic is to be found predominantly or exclusively at the State level, the States will be invited to join a Federal Government delegation to the appropriate

---

* In 1958 this institution was established by an *ad hoc* arrangement used during the negotiations for the Rome Treaties. It is based on an informal agreement which may be revoked by the Federal Government at any time.

drafting committee.'[17] Although the precise arrangements vary from case to case, *Länder* nominees have occasionally been allowed to vote in Brussels as part of the German delegation. There are other examples of individual *Land* participation.

One *Land* civil servant is a member of the Permanent Agricultural Structure Committee; another is deputy representative in the Committee for Regional Policy; yet another represents the *Länder* in the Committee for Regional Policy; yet another represents the *Länder* in the EC Advisory Committee for Medical (Vocational) Training. As the *Länder* are, to a certain extent, concerned with EC environmental protection policies there are two *Länder* representatives appointed by the Federal Government, not only to the working groups but even the Council itself.

The *Länder* are also keen to participate directly in the field of education and vocational training. In addition to the *Bund's* two or three delegation members, including one civil servant from the German Permanent Representation, the *Länder* are pressing to have three or four delegates of their own. In the Committee for Education Affairs, the *Länder* are represented by the Chairman of the *Länder* Ministers Conference on Cultural Affairs (*Kulturministerkonferenz der Länder*).

Summing up, we can say that the *Länder* have achieved representation not only on delegations to the EC Council but also in numerous other administrative and advisory committees. While there have been no systematic case studies to show 'the real scope they enjoy for infiltrating the supranational decision-making process'[18] a wide range of pragmatic arrangements have evolved which reflect the 'co-operative federalism' of the Federal Republic of Germany. For example, in the field of regional policy the relevant *Länder* civil servants concerned are regularly informed of EC proceedings in a sub-committee of the Planning Committee of the (*Bund/Länder*) 'Joint Task for the Improvement of Regional Economic Structures' (*Gemeinschaftsaufgabe 'Verbesseurung der regionalen Wirtschaft-struktur'*). The *Länder* were kept in touch with negotiations concerning the establishment of the ERDF. In the field of environmental protection, the *Länder* participate at three levels; in the *Bundesrat*; in the *Bund/Länder* Directorate Committee for Environment Affairs; and at a lower civil servant level as delegates to the Council working-groups. So, based on the principle of mutual trust and loyalty (*Bundestreue*), the *Bund* and the *Länder* co-operate on EC policies on various levels.

It is, however, still to be investigated how effective this exchange of information and co-operation is. The *Länder* are not entirely satisfied with the practice and are pressing for a formal structure. In some exceptional cases, for example, the negotiations on the 1972 agricultural socio-structural directions the *Länder* were not informed by the Federal Government. More important, however, at the beginning of the 1970s the *Länder* were confronted by increasing EC interventions in areas where they were constitutionally competent or in spheres where they had to bear financial burdens. This problem stimulated the *Länder* first to try to solve the constitutional conflict between itself and the Federal Government, and subsequently to conclude a formal agreement guaranteeing their right to participate in those EC matters which concerned their interests.

In this constitutional conflict, the Federal Government claimed the constitutional right under Article 24(1) to transfer its own powers, as well as those of the *Länder*, to international organizations.[19] The *Länder*, however, argued that the constitutional integration power never intended a shift in the domestic power balance in favour of the *Bund*. After long negotiations which ran from November 1977 to April 1980, the *Bund* and the *Länder* came to terms. Both sides refused to compromise on the constitutional question, but settled instead for an *ad hoc* arrangement. This so-called '*Länderbeteiligunsverfahren*' (procedure securing fair participation of the *Länder*) concerns the direct co-operation between the federal and *Land* governments in areas which cover the exclusive powers and essential interests of the *Länder*. It provides the latter with information at an early phase of the EC legislation procedure and contains a unilateral commitment on the part of the Federal Government to take into account, as far as is possible, the *Länder's* views. At this preliminary phase of the EC legislative process, the Observer from the *Länder* distributes all documents and proposals from the Commission to the *Länder* even before they are submitted to the Council. The *Länder*, after a series of conferences, formulate an agreed position which the Federal Government tries to present and to put into effect 'as far as it is possible'. Only for reasons of foreign or integration policy will it dissent from the *Länder* decision. Finally, the Federal Government will, 'if it is possible', allow two *Länder* representatives to participate in those EC affairs which concern the exclusive legal power of the German *Länder*. It is worth noting here that this complicated procedure does not seem to have been very effective.

The evidence indicates that the *Länder* do participate directly or indirectly in various procedures in both national and the supranational decision-making on EC affairs. In all these cases they act as a group.

But many EC issues concern each *Land* in different ways. In these instances the procedures are insufficient to represent disparate interests. Consequently there is considerable direct contact between individual *Länder* and the Commission. There are numerous examples. In the case of Baden-Württemberg we can cite the visit of the *Land* Prime Minister (*Ministerpräsident*), Mr Späth, to the EC Commission in June 1981, the visits of the Minister of Agricultural Affairs to the Commission in Brussels in January 1981 and to the European Parliament in Strasbourg in May 1981; and the visits of the Baden-Württemberg representative to the Federal Government, to the European Parliament in Strasbourg in June 1980 and to the Commission in Brussels in September 1980. The initiative, is not always taken by the *Länder*. Official visits by individual Commissioners may sometimes be of more than symbolic significance,[20] but it is too early to assess the significance of these contacts and the extent to which the *Länder* try to bypass the Federal Government. In this context it may be interesting to note that in 1979 the Bavarian Parliament considered proposals to establish a Bavarian *Land* Representation to the Community.[21] Although the proposal was not approved, the case indicates that some *Länder* are looking for ways of representing their individual—and often diverging—interests.

Finally, it should be noted the *Land* parliaments were excluded from the arrangements made to compensate for the effects of EC intervention on the *Länder* affairs. So the shift of balance towards the executive was strengthened by the European integration process. The problem has been recognised by the *Länder*. In February 1983 the directors of the *Land* parliaments (*Landtage*) proposed to extend the general obligation of the *Land* government to inform its parliament about those EC issues which concerned *Länder* functions, hoping thereby to influence the early stages of the decision-making process on these issues. Up to the present the *Land* governments have not responded. Nevertheless, *Land* parliaments are now more involved with EC affairs, initiating major inquiries into various EC matters and holding comprehensive debates. At the same time they have improved their relationship with the Commission and the European Parliament. For example, Baden-Württemberg has made significant progress in this area. In October 1982 an official debate was held between the *Landtag* and the twelve Euro-MPs representing Baden-Württemberg, in which it was decided that the Euro-MPs should participate in the Committees of the *Landtag* when EC issues were being considered.

Other aspects of the EC issue in the German *Länder*

The previous remarks have for the most part stressed the formal, institutional and bureaucratic aspect of the relationship between the Community and the *Länder*. The attitude of the latter is characterized by consensus rather than by conflict, not only between the *Länder* themselves but also in their relations with the Federal Government. It is still to be determined however, whether there is any conflict of interests, either between the *Länder* themselves, or between parties or interest groups at the *Land* level; or whether there is a distinctly *Land* public opinion on the issue of EC membership.

For many years in Western Germany membership in the EC has not been seriously called into question by anyone. It has been regarded as a fact which caused no fundamental controversies, either between different parties or individual *Länder*. While EC membership is not at issue in itself, conflicts over EC legislation do exist within the German federal system. The *Länder* are different in size, population, and economic structured. The 'Coal States' of North Rhine Westphalia and Saarland, are affected by ECSC legislation in a quite different manner from the other *Länder*; but there is a tendency to arrive at consensual positions as a result of the processes inherent in 'co-operative federalism'. The compulsion to compromise which is said to be inherent in the German federal system has resulted in many common behavioural patterns and informal rules among actors. The parties involved approach discussions under the assumption that they will probably modify their original position in order to minimize conflicts and to come to a compromise. The predisposition of individual *Länder* to accept a compromise and to present and defend it within the German delegation, is part of the tradition of fair play which has evolved between the Federal Government and the *Länder*.

There is no systematic research on the role of *Land* branches of political parties and interest groups in EC affairs. It is certainly the case that conflicts arise between the agricultural interest groups in the different *Länder*. The interests of southern *Länder* with small and medium sized farms do not coincide with those of the interests of northern *Länder* with large sized units. But there is no evidence that the regional branches of German interest groups play any significant individual part at the European level. If there are differences in regional interests within pressure groups, they seem to be integrated at the federal level of their respective organizations.

The MEPs are constantly confronted with claims by interests at all levels. In 1979, the German MEPs were asked to identify their priorities as between regional, national, EC, and party interests.[22] The results showed that for MEP-candidates of all parties, European interests were placed first with regional interests last. This finding suggests that the representatives of regional interest groups would be better advised not to go directly to the EP, but to use other channels.

One of the few times when a conflict of interests emerged in the European Parliament was during the discussion about the Hofmann-Report on the Rhine–Main–Danube Canal when the European Parliament called on the Commission to intercede with the German Federal Government.[23] The project, situated in Bavaria, had caused a serious domestic controversy between the Liberal–Social Democrat Federal Government and the CSU Bavarian government over whether or not the canal should actually be completed. The latter, pleading for its completion, was not only supported by the national opposition of Christian Democrats, but also by the Bavarian branch of the trade union movement (*Deutscher Gewerkschaftsbund*), and even by the then Austrian Chancellor, Mr Kreisky. The attitude of the Bavarian Social Democrats, was equivocal. In the 1983 federal election campaign they were in favour of completion while Mr Vogel the Bavarian Social-Democrat candidate for the Chancellorship, spoke against the project. The Liberals were also against it. The discussion and vote in the European Parliament reflected the German controversy with the resolution being adopted by forty-eight votes to two with three abstentions. Among the seven Bavarian MEPs who voted, all five CSU-MEPs voted pro, while the only Bavarian Liberal Member, and the only Bavarian Social Democrat who took part in the vote, were against. Of the other German MEPs, all ten Christian Democrats voted for the completion of the 'Bavarian Canale Grande'[24] as did two Social Democrats who followed the majority vote of the EP Socialist Group. The other nine Social Democrats, however, rejected the resolution in support of the position adopted by the federal party. Clearly, given the right issue, German national and partisan interests can be fractured by European-wide considerations. Where there is a conflict of interests at the European level between party, interest group, *Land* and Federal government, the European level may not only act as a forum but also become an ally of one or the other of the interests. In this instance the end result seems to show that the European forum worked in favour of the Bavarian Government and against the position of the Federal Government.

European Elections and the Regional Factor

Between the so-called established parties, CDU/CSU, SPD, and FDP, which represent about 90 per cent of the German voters, there has been no substantial difference on the European issue. Both the 1979 and 1984 election campaigns were dominated much more by domestic than by 'European' issues. The parties preferred to minimize their expenditures rather than to mobilize their voters. Despite these factors, a regional factor did emerge, although the relative turn-out between the *Länder* should not be interpreted as a vote for or against the EC. In the *Länder* with an extremely high level of participation, the Saarland (1979: 81.1 per cent, 1984: 78.5 per cent) and the Rhine Land Palatinate (1979: 78.1 per cent, 1984: 76.4 per cent), the EP elections coincided with communal elections. The relatively low participation of voters in Bavaria (1979: 58.9 per cent, 1984: 46.1 per cent) and Baden-Württemberg (1979: 59.2 per cent, 1984: 48.3 per cent) reflected above all, the traditional low turn-out in these *Länder*.

By the standard of German domestic elections the turnout at both the European elections, 65.7 per cent in 1979 and 56.8 per cent in 1984, confirmed the impression given by opinion polls of increasing indifference towards the European Community within the Federal Republic. Below its superficial pro-European stance, traditionally interpreted as 'non-committal benevolence', a more critical view of German membership of the European Community is emerging. In the results of the 1984 European Parliament elections one can see the first signs that this critical attitude may assume significant political and even regional contours.

The decrease of the turnout of 8.9 per cent from 1979 to 1984 in Germany was, after Ireland, the highest in the whole Community. This figure can no longer be exclusively interpreted as disappointment or indifference towards the process of European integration. It also reflects discontent of some social groups with particular EC policies. The low Bavarian turn-out in 1984 for example is, at least partly, caused by abstentions of dairy farmers who were vexed about the CAP 'reform' decisions made in Brussels. Moreover, the seven members of the Green party were elected in 1984 on a 'programme' not explicitly pro-European, which could be interpreted as reflecting their scepticism of the EEC institutions and procedures. Finally, it should not be overlooked that 3 per cent of the votes were given to small protest movements. Amongst these the right wing National Democratic Party (NPD) won 0.8 per cent of the votes after an anti-immigrant and anti-EC campaign with such slogans as 'No German money for European projects!' or 'Germany withdraw from the EC!'.

We should not place too much stress on these factors. The prevailing mood in the Federal Republic remains broadly pro-European. However, the general public's increased attention and concern for micro-politics has been interpreted as a 'retreat to regional dimensions' and as an 'opposition to the idea of Europe'.[25] But as the example of the Green party shows, an intensified regional identification *need* not necessarily be opposed to any support for the supranational idea and institutions. However, these trends can no longer be ignored, implying, as they do, that the pro-European consensus in Germany is at risk.

EC Financial Instruments and the problem of additionality

The EC financial instruments, ERDF, ESF, and the EAGGF-Guidance section, with their inter-European redistributive function, are not very relevant to the relatively prosperous Federal Republic of Germany. Therefore, the regional impact of other EC policies has a much greater impact in Germany relative to other member states. In this context the EAGGF-Guarantee section Competition Policy and harmonization policies are important. The *Länder* are highly concerned with these issues, which effect the *Länder* in different ways. However, this aspect has made very little impact on German public opinion. The only aspect of the budget controversy to stimulate German public opinion is the country's role as a net contributor, the paymaster.

Despite this role, however, there has been a not unimportant flow of allocations from the Community to the German subnational level (see Annex). As far as contributions of the financial instruments may be broken down, from 1973 to 1983, the *Länder* received grants of about 3,700m. Deutschmark and loans to the amount of about 7,200m. Deutschmark. Although, very often the Federal government has totally or partly taken the national contribution, in comparison to sub-national units in other member states, the *Länder* enjoy a high degree of financial autonomy and responsibility. In principle the *Länder* are free to determine their priorities and the extent of their expenditure. Further, they share with the Federal government and the local authorities the right of taxation; the Federal Government has no right to supervise or to control the budget of the *Länder*. Investigations of EC financial instruments demonstrate that the *Länder* have made extensive use of this freedom with regard to additionality, taking advantage of reimbursement and additional expenditure. Additionality operates in two areas, the direct financing of individual projects and indirectly. At the present time of austerity, in the fields with weak lobbies such as migrant workers and handicapped persons or in those of high financial risk like, demonstration projects in the energy field, measures have been initiated with the incentive of EC funds. In this way, the EC is able to set minimum standards at the German subnational level. The indirect effect is more problematic; pilot projects may influence or initiate other projects. In the long term this non-financial effect may be much greater than that of the direct financial contribution and effect the German *Länder* in varying degrees. In member states the absence of legislative and financial powers at the subnational level has meant that the national government has assumed responsibility for operating the additionality rule. However, in the case of Federal Germany the national government and the *Länder*, both have discretion to operate the additionality rule because of their respective financial responsibilities.

Conclusion

Participation in EC affairs is not intended to gain new autonomy for the *Länder* but is rather a defensive reaction against their continual loss of competence. As we have seen, the addition of the fourth European level has accelerated the existing trend towards the 'unitary federal state'. Although the basic constitutional controversy between the Federal Government and the *Länder* about the 'integration power' of the former still exists, the continual demands of the latter have resulted in a *modus vivendi*, both through the use of existing policy-making channels and the establishment of various new formal and informal institutions and procedures. It provides the *Länder* with a high degree of participation and influence in both European and federal decision-making in EC affairs, while not infringing the German Federal Government's freedom of action. Permanent conflict and daily bargaining is accepted as the basis of this pragmatic compromise. It is allied to a high flexibility and to the readiness of the participants to compromise; in short a highly developed form of 'co-operative federalism' has evolved in EC affairs. It is difficult to assess the future position of the German *Länder* in the EC because of a wide range of variables which could significantly change the present situation. For example, a decision of the Federal Constitutional Court (*Bundesverfassungsgericht*) could clarify the question of 'integration power' in favour of either the Federal government or the *Länder*. There could be a worsening of the present climate of co-operation between them. At the present, however, there are no signs of serious challenges to the existing balanced relationship. More likely the Federal Government and the *Länder* will continue to operate within the established structures and in the process continually refine the pattern of co-operation which has evolved.

Notes

1. See Hrbek, R., and Schuttemeyer, S., 'The Federal Republic of Germany', in Coombes, D., *et al., European Integration Regional Devolution and National Parliaments* (London: PSI 1979).
2. Hrbek and Schuttemeyer op. cit., p. 11.
3. See Hull, C., and Rhodes, R. A. W., *Intergovernmental Relations in the European Community* (London: Saxon House 1977).
4. Urwin, D. W., 'Germany: From Geographical Expression to Regional Accommodation', in Rokkan, S., and Urwin, D. W. (eds.), *The Politics of Territorial Identity: Studies in European Regionalism* (London: Sage 1982), p. 12.
5. Urwin, op. cit., pp. 226–7.
6. Cf. Article 72, para. 3 of the Basic Law.
7. This paper is largely concerned with the legislative power in the *Länder*. However the *Land* executives have considerable power delegated to them. See Hull and Rhodes op. cit., p. 43.
8. Action programme for environmental protection (OJ 112 of 20 Dec. 1973 and C139 of 13 June 1977); Directive 76/464 rep. protection of sea and inland waters (OJL129 of 8 May 1976).
9. Sasse C., (*et al.*), *Decision Making in the European Community* (London: Praeger 1977).
10. Sasse, op. cit., p. 44 ff.
11. Hull and Rhodes op. cit., p. 43.
12. This obligation is laid down in Act. 2, para. 2 of the Act of Ratification of the EEC Treaty in Sasse op. cit. p. 44.
13. Sasse, op. cit. p. 47.
14. e.g. the meetings of the EP Transport and budget committees with the Bundestat.
15. Resolution of the European Parliament, P.E. 77 956, No. 7 × 1, 22 Apr. 1982 (authors translation).
16. For the role of the Observer see Hull and Rhodes op. cit., pp. 34–44.
17. Ibid., p. 41.
18. Hrbek and Schuttemeyer, op. cit., p. 18.
19. Art. 24(1): 'The Bund can transfer sovereign rights by law to international

organisations'.

20. Cf. Hull and Rhodes, op. cit., p. 42.
21. Cf. Hrbek and Schuttemeyer, op. cit., p. 20.
22. Reif, K., Schmitt, H., and Schubert, K., 'Wer sind und was wollen die Deutschen in Europaischen Parlament?', in *Zeitschrift für Parlaments fragen* (No. 3/1979), pp. 332–54.
23. No. 9 of the EP resolution, OJC238 13 Sept. 1982, p. 102.
24. *Die Zeit* (Hamburg: 4.2.83), pp. 23–5.
25. For further details see Noelle-Neumann, E., 'Phantom Europe: Thirty Years of Survey Research on German Attitudes Towards European Integration', in Hurwitz L., (ed.), *Contemporary Perspectives on European Integration* (London: Aldwych Press, 1980).

APPENDIX Regional breakdown of European Communities Grants and Loans received by the Federal Republic of Germany^a in million of Deutschmarks

Land	GRANTS EAGGP-Guidance^b −1972	1973–83	Total	ERDF 1975–83	Energy 1975–83	ECSC 1973–83	GRANTS TOTAL	LOANS EIB −1972	1973–83	Total	ECSC −1972	1973–83	Total	EURATOM 1973–83	LOANS TOTAL
Schleswig-Holstein	84.1	147.4	231.5	148.7	4.0	0.9	385.1	128.3	82.5	210.8	0.0	—	—	—	210.8
Hamburg	4.7	11.4	16.1	—	6.7	0.1	22.9	119.7	87.3	207.0	—	37.0	37.0	—	37.0
Lower Saxony	165.5	246.2	411.7	232.9	33.8	23.5	701.9	119.7	87.3	207.0	95.1	635.3	730.4	—	937.4
Bremen	21.7	12.9	34.6	4.1	—	—	38.7	15.2	17.7	32.9	—	506.2	506.2	—	539.1
North Rhine-Westphalia	107.0	119.1	226.1	85.5	372.4	674.4	1 358.4	135.4	119.9	255.3	1 932.6	3 057.4	4 990.0	—	5 245.3
Hessen	79.8	116.7	196.5	70.0	12.5	1.5	280.5	6.3	168.8	175.1	10.8	17.3	28.1	—	203.2
Rhineland-Palatinate	64.3	131.8	196.1	66.5	0.6	0.3	263.5	142.0	829.7	971.7	52.5	21.4	73.9	288.2	1 333.8
Saarland	1.0	8.5	9.5	152.5	17.2	48.8	228.0	121.4	116.5	237.9	358.1	652.8	1 010.9	—	1 248.8
Boden-Württemberg	134.6	230.9	365.5	42.6	31.1	0.4	439.6	127.7	364.9	492.6	7.5	48.5	56.0	—	548.6
Bavaria	196.1	284.9	481.0	233.8	32.5	4.5	751.8	173.5	142.8	316.3	9.1	5.2	14.3	—	330.6
Berlin	—	1.5	1.5	54.9	5.7	1.8	63.9	74.7	30.0	104.7	—	1.2	1.2	—	105.9
TOTAL	858.8	1 311.3	2 170.1	1 091.5	516.5	756.2	4 534.3	1 044.2	1 960.1	3 004.3	2 465.7	4 982.3	7 448.0	288.2	10 740.5

^a It is not possible to break down all EC allocations by States; the ESF, e.g., granted from 1972 to 1983 about 1,654m Deutschmark in favour of projects situated in Germany.

Most of the figures concern commitments, but not all of them, however, were realized.

^b Only direct measures (Regulation No. 17/64, No. 355/77, No. 1852/78, No. 1938/81).

Source: Statistics of the EC Commission.

9

French Regions in the European Community

YVES MÉNY
(trans. Michael Keating)

Introduction

The creation and development both of regions and of the European Economic Community have provoked strident debates, and aroused both hopes and intense disillusionment in France. The tone of the discussion has been all the sharper in that both phenomena began to develop at the same time around 1955–60 and a link between them was soon firmly established. A school of thought evolved, especially in federalist circles, in favour of a Europe with a regional rather than a national basis. At the end of the 1960s, Denis de Rougemont, in his *Open Letter to the Europeans*, posed the question in these terms: 'Because they are too small, the Nation-States should federate at the European level; because they are too big they should federalise internally.'[1] Of course, such a perspective held few attractions for the French government, especially during the period of Gaullist dominance. From 1958 to the 1980s, Michel Debré (prime minister, 1958–62) has personified the struggle of the most intransigent nationalists against any erosion of the Nation State; regional and community policies were accepted and even supported but only as economic and financial instruments at the service of the national government. However, while the most striking example of this spirit is represented to the point of caricature by Michel Debré, the most jacobin of Gaullists, it would be wrong to think that one man or one party had the monopoly of such a reserved, even negative attitude. On the contrary, the building of Europe as of the regions encountered opposition on all sides (corporate, political, economic). From the Right to the Communist Party, from the employers to the CGT (the large Communist-dominated trade union), all organized groups more or less shared the same spirit. Because regions and Europe posed radically new problems, divisions tended to emerge within organized groups rather than following traditional cleavages.

Although this sort of opposition has died down somewhat and there has been a profound change in attitudes since the 1950s, we must still take account of such psychological and political factors in evaluating the relationships between regions and the EC. These could develop only gradually and with the greatest possible caution, given the almost pathological climate surrounding the issue.

It was not mere chance which led to the evolution of the regions and of Europe at the same time. It was the emergence of a series of factors common to both. The creation of regions as of the EC was promoted and sustained by men whose *European* consciousness was heightened because their *regions* had been the subjects of military or economic conflict between states: Adenauer was a man of the left bank of the Rhine; De Gasperi, Italian citizen, had been elected to the Austrian House of Tyrol before 1914; Robert Schuman was born in a German Alsace-Lorraine. Beyond these pioneers, the post-war period saw the emergence of new élites (business managers, trade unionists, academics) committed to fighting, first for reconstruction, then for economic development. For them, the expansion of the market at the European level and the development and economic integration of under-developed regions were two sides of the same coin, two aspects of the same fight for the well-being of their populations. The regional expansion committees set up almost everywhere in the 1950s were perfectly in tune with the building of a Europe aimed at 'reinforcing the unity of the economies (of the signatories to the Treaty) and ensuring *harmonious development* by reducing the gap between the different regions'.[2] In short, the most dynamic and innovating sectors of French society saw more that was complementary than contradictory in the development of regions and Europe. However, the two sets of institutions did not develop at the same pace: the ruling Gaullists of the 1960s saw clearly the advantages which the French economy could draw from the competition of their partners. They used their relative political strength to create an agricultural policy favourable to the interests of French farmers; in turn they had to make concessions to partners more favourable than themselves to the building of Europe. By contrast, the building of regions ran up against the phobias of the jacobins on the right, and aroused fears on an archaic left and hostility from the central administration. So by 1968 the fundamental elements of Europe were in place, while regionalization was still in its infancy.

Nevertheless, the mobilization of élites and of populations in certain regions had raised serious hopes. In response to the spontaneous creation of several dozen regional and departmental committees of expansion, the Mendès-France and Faure governments of 1954–6 tried to stem the movement by starting a dialogue with 'approved' committees, that is, those conforming to criteria of 'representativeness' laid down by the central authorities. In spite of being hedged in this way, the regional movement forced the central administration to organize itself increasingly on a regional basis (particularly in those sectors concerned with economic intervention), then constrained central government to follow a vigorous regional development policy, especially following the peasant revolts of 1960–1. Here again, there is a clear link between the need for a policy of regionalization (to transform the rural areas) and the development of Community policies (the agricultural policy). But the government intended to keep control of internal economic development to itself. *Aménagement du territoire* (covering both inter-regional and intra-regional development policies) would be a matter for central government, working through DATAR, the specific ministerial *missions* (executive terms), for example in Languedoc-Roussillon, and the privileged links represented by the prefects, particularly the 21 (later 22) prefects of *circonscriptions d'action regionale* (regional administrative units used by central government). The 1964 reform formalized this evolution, marking the victory of the central administration and prefectoral corps over the socio-professional *forces vives* (the modernizing élites) henceforth mingled with local politicians in a substitute assembly, the CODER (*Commission de développement economique regional*).

The relaunch of the regionalization policy by General de Gaulle in the aftermath of May 1968 and the failure of the referendum of 27 April 1969 seemed to mark the end of regionalist dreams, while the Europeanists gained new hopes. Everyone was aware of Pompidou's hostility to regions and all knew that he had had to purchase the support of the centrists (Christian Democrats and Giscardians) by an opening towards Europe. The year 1972 saw the ratification in terms of concrete decisions of the choices implicitly made in the presidential election of 1969. On the one hand, Britain, Ireland and Denmark entered the EC on negotiated terms which implied the creation of new transfer mechanisms, notably through the development of the regional policy. In July of the same year, Pompidou thought to finish off the regional question by the use of a law confiding the management of regional interests to his opponents, that is to say the national, departmental, and local politicians. No one was actually to be elected as a regional councillor. The prefect was to be the executive of the council which would have no staff of its own and could vote only meagre funds: 15 frs. per head the first year, 25 frs. thereafter. Further, the regions were forbidden to incur any current expenditure or any investment on their own account. They could only subsidize investments decided on by other public bodies, central government, *the département*, the communes. The trap seemed perfect; but this was to overlook the dynamic proper to any institution, the will of some regionalists and ambitious local politicians to use this new platform to the full, the turning round of restrictive rules to the profit of independent policies. One example will suffice. To be condemned to subsidize the investments of other agencies might seem an unattractive prospect and to give little by way of influence. However, the opposite can happen if the region decides to concentrate its interventions in certain sectors, giving high rates of subsidy. In other words, if a region decides to subsidize, at the rate of 30 per cent or 50 per cent, works on roads which do not come under its direct aegis, no *département* could resist such manna. The region thus found itself in the privileged position for so long enjoyed by central government; deciding policies while financing only a part of them and without having to support the burden of their execution.

So the position of the regions and their relationship with the EC is more rich and complex than appears at first sight. For on this point the rule is simple: the regions have nothing to do with Brussels where their interests are defended exclusively by the official representatives of the French government. Further, for a long time community policies have been presented in a biased manner. The negative aspects have been underlined while the benefits have been either attributed to the merits of the French negotiators (each agriculture marathon becoming a sort of epic in which the interests of the peasants are fiercely defended by the French ministers), or frankly dissimulated. For a long time, ERDF aids were not mentioned and practically no indication of European subsidies appeared on the sites where the investments were being realized (contrary, for example, to the practice in Italy). By the same token, the fear of 'supranationalism' and 'stateless technocrats' prevented for a long time any visits to the French regions by the European Commissioner for Regional Affairs. The visit of M. Giolitti in November 1979 in connection with the non-quota programme *Grand Sud-Ouest* was a 'first', surrounded by tremendous precautions and handled with great discretion. At the same time, the Giscard d'Estaing government, although hardly open to the accusation of anti-Europeanism, refused to allow an 'integrated operation' for Lorraine comparable to that for Naples or Belfast, for fear of the nationalist reactions of the Gaullists, the GCT, and the French Communist Party. So there would be little to be said were it not that, once again, the pertinent observation of de Tocqueville has proved true, according to which in France 'the rule is rigid but the practice is flexible'. For the regional élites are not simply institutional actors; they can also organise themselves as pressure groups. The prefects, representatives of the State and, until 1982, executives of the regions, are not simply transmission belts for the government's will. The regions are not simply public institutions but also a whole string of private and semi-public organizations such as the chambers of commerce whose activities and co-operation allow them to play on several fronts. The regions are also socio-professional groups organized notably in the Economic and Social Committee and the numerous consultative committees. This dense network of institutions, procedures and financial mechanisms cannot be controlled or pulled up by a veto—the fluidity of information and of exchanges can easily circumvent that. The pressures of the *fait accompli*, the significant activities of the leaders of the opposition (who have become the majority since 1981), the seriousness of the crisis and the mobilization to which it has given birth, are further elements which have served to stifle the theological quarrels on the relationships between the EC and the regions and substitute a pragmatic co-operation in which all the levels of decision-making, European, national, regional, and local, participate.

The Institutional Evolution of the Regions and Its Impact on relations with the European Communities

After the regional reform of 1972 the regional structures were as follows: the Regional Council, composed of the members of Parliament in the region, representatives of the councils of the *départments* and lastly, representatives of the communes; the Economic and Social Committee bringing together delegates of socio-professional groups and 'personalities' chosen by the government; finally, the prefect, representing the government in the region at the same time as acting as executive of the Regional Council. In the latter role, he prepared and executed the budget and other decisions of the assembly. The 36,000 communes, each with an elected mayor, remained the basic units of local government. Above these were the *départements* with elected but for which the prefect acted as the executive. The tradition of the *cumul des mandats* whereby politicians accumulate offices at all levels of the system continued and, indeed was reinforced as all regional councillors by definition hold other office. For his part, the elected president of the Regional Council (re-elected every year) in theory looked after almost nothing but protocol. In other words, neither the Regional Council, condemned to instability by its dependence on national and local elections (in ten years, its composition would change at least eight times as a result of the various electoral contests), nor the President, nor the Economic and Social Committee (with a purely advisory role) was in a position to take care of regional interests and ensure that they were defended in Brussels. Even if the more dynamic presidents had had the will to do so, the system of EC—regional relationships would have prevented them. In fact, not only did the central administration and its local representatives maintain this monopoly, they even turned to their own profit the procedures intended to allow direct contacts between the EC and the recipients of aids. The European Social Fund can be taken as an illustration of this. At Brussels, French interests are defended by the Permanent Representative while in Paris a few civil servants comprise the 'ESF unit' in the Ministry of Labour and co-ordinate the 'regional' applications. In theory, in order to increase public awareness of the EC's social policy, the Commission itself takes charge of payments to successful applicants. But France has made a secret agreement, of which there is no trace in the official publications, whereby the moneys are paid into a central government fund which then distributes the sums received. So, not only is the rule of direct payment to the applicants not applied, but the principle of parity between the national government and the Community contributions is not respected. The lack of publicity is not simply motivated by nationalist considerations. It can happen sometimes that all the partners, community, national, and regional, have an interest in passing over in silence operations whose conformity to community regulations in doubtful. In fact, because the French government uses the ERDF as a compensation fund for expenditures which it has already undertaken, it can happen that 'non-aided' operations may actually be aided. So, while certain zones in the North of France benefit from important national and community aids because of the crises in the coal, textile, and steel industries, other zones less affected (like the metropolitan area of Lille) are not eligible. However, if an important firm wants at the same time to benefit from the aids and to locate in a non-assisted area, a consensus emerges to 'forget' the rules. In this way, the French government has subsidized Rank Xerox in the Lille area while the firm has at the same time benefited from European Social Fund aid, to which in theory it has no entitlement. In the event, the partners had an interest in not drawing attention to this!

In the institutional framework of the 1972 law, then, the prefect found himself caught between his local role and his national function. He could certainly urge favourable consideration of a case but his duty of obedience forced him to give way if the government or DATAR indicated that they would rather present a different project. In fact, there is not much incentive for the government to support one project rather than another. The essential matter is to present cases which will allow it to recover the quota which is its due.

So there is no real clearing-house and there have been cases of investments already completed (Renault in the Nord for example) being presented solely to recover the State's outlay. The only real competition likely to move the administration results from the non-quota section where the projects are directly chosen by the Commission (350m. frs., for example, for the regions of the south-west). To overcome this 'nationalization' of the European regional policy, the Commission has been reduced to more or less efficacious expedients ranging from informal consultation to the passing of 'consultancy' contracts to get round the prohibition on having direct contacts with local bodies. For example, APEX (Association pour l'expansion du Nord-Pas de Calais) fulfilled the role of consultant for the Commission while at the same time being a hybrid organization, representing regional economic interests (chambers of commerce) and DATAR.

The March 1982 decentralization law brought in by the Socialist Government provides for the direct election of the regional councils and the assumption of the executive role by their presidents. Obviously, the transfer of the regional executive function from a subordinate prefect to an elected president changes the rules of the game. The government will certainly wish, as in the past, to recover its outlays but the presidents of the regions will seek by all the means available to push their own favoured projects. They will certainly have to defend them in Paris but there is nothing to stop them pleading their case directly in Brussels. There is a further possibility that internal competition will give the Commission, so often presented with a *fait accompli*, a further margin for manœuvre (because of the submission of applications corresponding to more, or less, than the quota allowed).

Recent evens in France have illustrated this. The (Giscardian) President of Lorraine, at the urging of the Christian CFTC union which is strongly established in the region has relaunched the idea of an 'integrated operation' (on the lines of those in Naples and Belfast) which the previous governments had rejected. After discussion by the regional assemblies, the case will be presented by the President of the region before DATAR as well as in Brussels. It will be difficult for the government to reject a project for an investment of 30,000m. frs in five years, 50 per cent financed by the EC. The region has lost 40,000 jobs since 1974 in iron mining and steel. For its part the Commission might not be unhappy to take advantage of these regional pressures to grant what the French government rejected a few years ago. The institutional changes of 1982 could alter the rules of the game by substituting for a hierarchical vertical relationship a 'three-sided dialogue' in which the State has lost its almost complete monopoly of power.

Lastly, it is worth noting that the Mitterrand government has adopted a much more flexible attitude than its predecessors in this regard, under the influence of 'barons' like Mauroy and Defferre who, as leaders of the regions of Provence and Nord had become exasperated with the meddlesome controls of the government and administration, before the socialist victory of 1981. The government has, for example, signed a model convention for trans-frontier co-operation while the regions of Provence and Marseille have established close links with Algiers and the Bizerte region in Tunisia. Further it has accepted an infringement of the infamous unwritten additionality rule, practised by all European governments, according to which European aids are treated as reimbursements of national subsidies. For the first time, the law of 30 July 1982 on the powers of the region of Corsica affirms the 'additional' character of community aids. It is stipulated that 'the total of the [State's] grant represents where relevant, and increase on the sums advanced by any other public body and in particular the European Economic Community'.[3]

The Weight of the Regions in European Policy Making

The French regions, in contrast to the German *Länder*, are in theory not associated in any way with the making and implementation of Community policies. However, a purely legal, institutional analysis gives only a partial view of reality. The regions make their weight felt by other means, through other channels. First, through the use of personal networks which complete or parallel the administrative ones; second, by the marked regional dimension of certain community policies. Indeed, certain of the EC's policies are as much 'regional' as national or Community-wide in their impact. Coal, steel, fishing, and wine policy all show how interests which in principle are purely *sectoral* can become *de facto* perceived as regional.

The existence of parallel communication links between the regions and the EC is not in itself surprising, given that the phenomenon is so well developed in France for the relations between central and local government. The osmosis between national and local élites, and the accumulation of mandates characteristic of the French political system extend, with their consequences, to the European level and first and foremost to the Parliament. Although the French representatives are elected from a single national constituency (both the government and the Constitutional Council having seen in the creation of regional constituencies a threat to the one and indivisible Republic!) the parties carefully choose their lists so as to ensure a balanced geographical representation. So each region is 'represented' by a political leader or known spokesman for the socio-professional groups in the region; and one finds members of the national parliament, local councillors and socio-professionals who at the same time are party representatives and spokesmen for regional interests, accredited representatives of Corsica, the overseas *départements*, of Britanny or of Alsace. Some of the socio-professional leaders are chosen for their national standing, for example Maffre-Baugé, leader of the southern wine-growers, elected as an independent on the Communist list. The regional dimension has not just become important since the election of the European Parliament by universal suffrage. From the early years of the Assembly, some of the delegates from the French Parliament pressed for a European policy which would pay more attention to the regional dimension of problems. Former Presidents of the Council of the Fourth Republic (and future ministers of the Fifth) such as the radical Edgar Faure or the centrist René Pleven, sought a Community regional policy. René Pleven took an active part in the formation of an cross-party group comprising, on the French side, centrists, socialists, and Gaullists. During the 1960s this group was behind the adoption of numerous resolutions calling for stronger action in favour of the less-favoured regions. For example, in 1967 the group met in Paris to discuss a proposal of M. Pleven, later (11 May 1967) adopted by the European Parliament. This case is a good illustration of the decision-making process and the means of influence in the French political system: M. Pleven, local councillor, president of the council of the Côtes du Nord *départément* in Britanny, president in 1964 of the CODER (commission for regional economic development), member of parliament and former minister, member of the European Parliament, president of public/private hybrid companies, is the prototype of the great 'notables' who use their varied zones of influence in a mutually reinforcing manner. The local roots provided by local elective office provide the basis for consolidating a national mandate (nearly thirty years in his case!) but the national and European mandates are helpful in obtaining more easily financial advantages, administrative privileges, symbolic benefits, for the local constitutuency. In other words, even if the administrative circle is totally closed, the parallel networks largely erode the principle. All the same, even with this corrective, it remains true that access to resources and the capacity to influence are unequally distributed. The more or less favoured position of the regions depends to a large extent on the personality and activism of the regional leaders, as well as their relationships with the central government of the day.

The weight of the regions also depends on the importance of European policies for a given region. The degree of EC intervention varies according to economic sector (for example, the motor or steel industries) and according to the rate of concentration of an activity in any one region. In France, agricultural problems have long constituted the principal element of regional mobilization. Milk, port, or poultry producers in Britanny, wine growers in Languedoc-Roussillon, fruit- and vegetable-growers in the south-west have been and still are essential actors in the formulation and application of Community rules. In the triangular game of EC, French government, and regions, the various partners are by turn threatening or manipulated according to the circumstances and the balance of forces. The French government dreads the anger of the peasants but uses it as a means of pressure against its partners and the Commission. It is noteworthy, for example, that neither Giscard d'Estaing nor Mitterrand have felt themselves strong enough to confront the opposition of the peasants of the south-west to the entry of Spain and Portugal into the Common Market. The regions of Aquitaine, Midi-Pyrénées, and Languedoc-Roussillon gain both ways, at least for the time being. They constitute one of the principal obstacles to the unblocking of negotiations and at the same time they receive, under the non-quota section of the ERDF, aid to help with the problems resulting from enlargement.

From time to time, regional pressure groups organize either at the national or at the Community level. For example, since 1973 the CELIB (Committee for the study and liaison of Breton interests) has organized a meeting of the 'peripheral maritime regions' of Europe which has been maintained through regular contacts and joint activities. Frontier and mountain regions, too, have joined forces to influence Community policies.

More recently, the crisis in the steel industry has witnessed the formation of regional coalitions bringing together unions, chambers of commerce and industry, traders, and political parties. These coalitions have been formed sometimes to prevent or slow down Community decisions on reductions in output or closure of works, sometimes to obtain the maximum public national or Community aid. Both Nord Pas-de-Calais and Lorraine have tried to mobilize all their resources to slow down or modify the effects of the crisis which comes on top of those of textiles and coal. It is interesting to note that their pressure is so strong that the State, rather than resisting, has preferred to transfer its powers. The French government, while criticizing the EC, is quite happy to shelter behind Brussels's decisions; at the same time, it is tending more and more to hand over the social management of the crisis to the regions. Recently, for example, the government has decided to allocate to the regions concerned the moneys set aside for the adaptation of the coal industry. It will be for regions to choose between subsidies to keep loss-making activities going or help towards the creation of new activities: theirs will be the choice between welfare and industrial adjustment. The State, for its part, will not—and cannot—fight on both those fronts.

This transfer of power has implications for more than the relationships between central government and the regions. In fact, the fragmentation of decision-making power and its dispersal to regional, or indeed local, levels are hardly compatible with the structure and administrative mechanisms of the Community. The latter have a definite capacity for policy initiation and decision. They are less well equipped to control the implementation of community policies administered by national governments (the Community has not succeeded in controlling 10 per cent of ERDF interventions as was initially intended).[4] This task of control is practically impossible at the regional level, because of the screen of national administrations, the multiplicity of interventions and the often obscure or disguised character of regional actions. This new division of labour risks further distortion of the competition rules and makes it difficult to apply sanctions when they are violated.

Conclusion

The role of the regions and local government in the making and implementation of community policies continues to grow despite the restraints which the central government has for a long time tried to impose. This development obviously puts at risk the role of the Ministry of External Relations, on the one hand and the technical ministries on the other. It contradicts the central and exclusive function of the Ministry of External Relations, already deeply affected by the intervention of specialized ministries in the international sphere. It also goes against the vertical division of problems by function whether internal or external (for example, the Ministry of Agriculture's responsibility for agricultural problems whether they be internal or European). The regional dimension introduces a new horizontal dimension in the management of affairs, at a sub-state level, to the detriment both of the Ministry of External Relations and of the technical ministries. This underlying tendency of pre-1981 days is considerably strengthened with the decentralization policy which has freed the latest types of activity undertaken by local authorities. Now, nearly all the big towns and regions have a service dealing with 'international relations'. The proliferation of these initiatives had led the government to intervene with a circular of 26 May 1983 and the appointment of a 'delegate for the external activities of local authorities' under the secretary general of the Ministry of External Relations. His duty is to inform the government in a 'systematic and regular manner' of the activities of local authorities and ensure that 'the initiatives of the communes, departments and regions respect the rules of the Constitution and the law and do not interfere unfavourably with the foreign policy of France'. This initiative shows clearly that the government does not seek—or is not able—to forbid all 'foreign policy' on the part of the regions but that it nevertheless seeks to avoid the upsets which the multiplicity and inexperience of the new actors lead it to fear.

Notes

1. Denis de Rougement—*Lettre ouverte aux Européens* (Paris: Albin Michel 1970), p. 157.
2. Paragraph 5 of the preamble of the Treaty of Rome.

3. Loi No. 82–659 of 30 July 1982 concerning the special status of Corsica: functions. *Journal Officiel*, 31 July 1982, p. 2459.

4. Yves Mény, 'Should the Community Regional Policy be Scrapped?' *Common Market Law Review*, Aug. 1982, 19 pp.

10

The European Regional Development Fund and the Republic of Ireland

JOAN HART

The tenth anniversay of Ireland's membership of the European Community generated a considerable amount of discussion and analysis of Ireland's experience to date together with prospects for the future. In financial terms membership of the Community has proved to be of substantial benefit to Ireland. However, the current difficulties facing the Community, in particular the near exhaustion of its own resources, the pressure on CAP and the simultaneous steps to enlarge the Community, suggest that Ireland's advantageous position within the Community may be gradually eroded.

Of the four applicants who negotiated terms of entry into the Community in the early 1970s, membership commanded most support in Ireland. This is highlighted by the referendum on accession held in 1972 the outcome of which was a majority of 83 per cent in favour of membership. The degree of public support for membership of the Community reflected the level of consensus amongst policy-makers and politicians on the desirability of accession. The two largest political parties, for example, Fianna Fail and Fine Gael, were in favour of membership. The anti-marketeers consisted primarily of the Labour Party and the Common Market Study Group although it should be noted that the preferred option of the Labour Party was associate membership.

The Government's decision to seek membership of the Community was guided primarily by economic factors. Of particular importance was the key position of agriculture in the economy. At the time of accession, agriculture accounted for approximately 20 per cent of total national income and provided 27 per cent of total employment. A further consideration for the government was Ireland's open economy and the importance of external trade in terms of promoting economic growth. Ireland was particularly dependent on the UK as an outlet for its exports. In 1970 for example, approximately two-thirds of Irish exports went to the UK—half of which were agricultural products. Consequently, the government felt that it would be impracticable and detrimental to the economy to remain outside a Community which included Britain. Furthermore, it was feared that a Community which excluded the Republic and included Britain would reinforce the border and render even more problematic any moves towards reconciling north and south. The decision to seek membership of the Community can thus be closely associated with the British decision to join. However, the Government anticipated that membership of the Community would gradually lead to more trading links with other Member States thereby reducing Ireland's traditional dependence on the British market. Thus it was envisaged that, in the long-term, membership of the Community could have positive political repercussions by loosening Ireland's links with Britain. As an example of the extent to which this has occurred, it is interesting to note that during the renegotiation of the British terms of entry Garret FitzGerald, the then Minister for Foreign Affairs, stated that Ireland would remain a member of the Community irrespective of the outcome of the British referendum. This was in marked contrast to the Government's perception of the importance of Britain in influencing its original decision to join the Community.

The level of public support for the Community in Ireland has consistently been high particularly when compared to survey evidence in the UK and Denmark (see Figure 10.1, p. 232). It should be noted, however, that survey evidence indicates that support for the Community in Ireland is based on pragmatic, utilitarian considerations rather than on any deeply-felt emotions about European integration.[1] Figure 10.1 shows a drop in the level of public support since 1979—a pattern which is likely to continue given the current difficulties facing the Community and the probable negative repercussions on Ireland.

A distinctive feature of survey evidence in Ireland on the level of public support for the Community is the impact of regional differences. Support for the Community is strongest in the western-periphery of Connacht-Ulster and weakest in the capital, Dublin. The provinces of Munster and Leinster (excluding Dublin) fall in between these two poles of support.[2] The Community thus commands most support in the poorest areas of the country. This suggests that, at least in Ireland, the Community has been regarded as a possible means of improving the lot of peripheral regions. It should be noted that despite the existence of regional differences in attitudes to the Community and considerable regional disparities within Ireland this has not led to the establishment of regional parties although certain areas have set up development organizations to improve their economic position. One of the main reasons for the absence of regional parties is the small size of the country and the under-developed state of the economy relative to other Member States. The reduction of internal regional disparities is thus perceived by politicians and policy-makers alike as requiring in the first instance an improvement in overall economic performance. This helps to explain, for example, why Irish MEPs tend to put Irish interests before specific constituency or regional interests in the European Parliament.

The purpose of this paper is to examine the impact of the principal instrument of Community regional policy, the European Regional Development Fund (ERDF), in the Republic of Ireland, and in particular the extent to which it has affected regional and local authorities. The ERDF was established in 1975 in order to reduce regional imbalances in the community. Before 1975 there existed other Community financial instruments with a regional dimension notably the European Social Fund, the European Agricultural Guarantee and Guidance Fund, re-adaptation measures of the European Coal and Steel Community and the European Investment Bank. The ERDF, however, was the first instrument set up specifically to reduce regional imbalances. As such, it constitutes one of the most tangible and important components of Community action in the area of regional policy. The paper is divided into two main sections. The first section examines the operation of the ERDF and the factors which have influenced the particular administrative arrangements decided upon by the Irish government. In the second section, the impact of the ERDF in Ireland to date will be examined.

The Operation of the ERDF

Before examining the administrative arrangements and principal features of the operation of the ERDF in Ireland, it is proposed to discuss briefly the Government's attitude to the development of a Community regional policy. Analysis of the Government's views on this issue provides a partial explanation of the highly centralized administrative procedures adopted by the Government when the Fund was eventually established in 1975.

Ireland's attitude to Community regional policy

The low level of economic development in Ireland, particularly in relation to other Member States of the Community, was one of the main factors determining Ireland's attitude to membership of the Community and specifically to the formulation of regional policy. An important aspect of membership was the possibility of access to financial resources in the Community to promote the development of the Irish economy. The Irish Government argued during the Accession negotiations that structural policies should be developed by the Community. In this context the formulation of a comprehensive regional policy designed to prevent an aggravation of regional disparities and to correct existing imbalances was regarded as fundamental. Furthermore, the Government's case for the development of a Community regional policy was strengthened considerably by the decision in 1970 to progress towards Economic and Monetary Union (EMU).

Regional policy however, was not actually a negotiating issue during the Accession negotiations. One of the main concerns fo Irish negotiators was to gain recognition of Ireland's special development problems. The strategy culminated in the negotiation of a Protocol between Ireland and the Community which recommended that 'the Community institutions implement all the means and procedures laid down by the Treaties, particularly by making adequate use of the Community's resources'.[3] The Protocol also referred to the Government's policy of industrialization and economic development designed to improve standards of living, and eliminate underemployment 'while progressively evening out regional differences in levels of development'.

The main features of the Government's regional development strategy were outlined in 1972 in conjunction with the Industrial Development Authority's (IDA) regional industrial plans.[4] The strategy was essentially formulated so that Ireland would be in a position to derive maximum benefit from membership of the Community. As the most significant statement on regional policy to date, it provides a useful indication of the Government's approach to regional policy within Ireland. The attitude of the Government to domestic regional policy is important not only in terms of its approach to the development of regional policy in the Community but also to the involvement of regional and local authorities in regional planning. The regional industrial plans prepared by the IDA have been the most important component of the Government's regional strategy. To a large extent, regional policy is inseparable from industrial policy in Ireland. While the importance of physical planning for the development of regions has been recognized, physical planning has not been central to the Government's approach to regional development.

Regionalized industrial development, as operated in Ireland, does not constitute a comprehensive regional policy designed primarily to reduce regional imbalances. Industrial policy plays a vital role not only in the Government's regional strategy but also in its policy for the overall development of the economy. Given the low level of economic development, the Government's main objective is to promote national economic development. Consequently, the reduction of internal regional disparities remains a subsidiary objective. It could be argued that in promoting national development the Government is simultaneously promoting the conditions needed for regional development. However, the promotion of national economic development does not necessarily mean a balanced development of the economy. As long as Ireland remains economically weak compared with other Member States in the Community, its development strategy is unlikely to change. The present level of economic development also means that there is no possibility of significant interregional transfers in Ireland as is the case in other Member States in the Community.

During the Accession negotiations, the Government outlined its views on the objectives that a comprehensive Community regional policy should seek to fulfil. The evidence suggests, however, that in advocating a Community regional policy, the Government did not intend the Community to have specific responsibility for aspects of that policy. The role envisaged for the Community was to co-ordinate and provide supplementary finance for Member States policies with the national policy-making arean still predominant.[5] The Government's attitude was clarified during the negotiations establishing the ERDF when it outlined the principles it would aim to have implemented. These were as follows:

1. the ERDF should be 'financed on a scale commensurate with the task it will face'.
2. resources should be 'concentrated on areas [note, not Member States] where the most severe problems exits'.
3. Member States should be allowed 'a certain measure of flexibility

and discretion in applying the measures most suited to tackling their regional problems, while at the same time, national policies should constitute a sensible whole when seen at Community level'.
4. the Community should ensure 'coordination of different policy measures with a regional dimension'.[6]

The main issues of importance for Ireland were the size of the Fund, concentration of resources, flexibility at national level, and co-ordination of all Community policies with a regional dimension. Regional policy in the Community was concerned exclusively with substantial transfers of resources from the richer to the poorer regions. This was epitomized in a statement by the then Minister for Foreign Affairs, Garret Fitzgerald: 'Regional policy is concerned with the transfer of adequate resources from richer to less developed areas in order to promote a balanced economic evolution in the Community as a whole.'[7] It is interesting to note that the Government was not prepared to accept any Community-imposed conditions on the distribution of aid which would reduce its control over national development strategy in any way.

As a result of the Government's strategy during the Accession negotiations to have the country's special development problems recognized, the entire country was designated as a region eligible for ERDF assistance. However, what the Fund eventually agreed upon did not fulfil Irish expectations in relation to its size and the concentration of resources. Agreement on the size of the ERDF proved to be a problematic issue during the negotiations establishing the Fund. Ireland was prepared to accept a smaller Fund in favour of more concentration in the distribution of resources in a compromise presented in December 1973. The compromise was not accepted and eventually Ireland had to settle for 6 per cent of a smaller Fund than anticipated. On the question of the distribution of the Fund's resources, Ireland had not opposed the use of quotas as such, provided they reflected the intensity of problems to be solved and the relative ability of Member States to solve them (i.e. not based solely on population criteria). One of its main criticisms was that the distribution key failed to take into account the financial capacity of the Member States and also the relative intensity of regional imbalances.

The Central Administration of the ERDF in Ireland

The ERDF as established in 1975 was primarily and instrument to provide financial support for Member States regional development policies. Consequently, Member States have been relatively free to administer the Fund as desired. The Fund regulation was the outcome of a negotiation process beset with difficulties in moving from principle to policy. Furthermore, the negotiation process coincided with political changes in certain Member States and political instability on the international front primarily because of the Yom Kippur war.[8] It should also be noted however, that the negotiations took place in a policy environment which was basically hostile to developments in the area of regional policy. By the time the ERDF was placed on the Community agenda, most Member States were engaged in consolidating existing regional development measures—there was little political support for any new measures. The policy environment therefore was not conducive to the development of a dynamic regional policy instrument at Community level.

Given the supportive nature of the Fund and the circumstances under which it was set up, it could be argued that the Fund Regulation had an inherent bias towards the adoption of centralized administrative arrangements at national level. In the first instance, Member States could regard ERDF receipts as a 'partial reimbursement' of expenditure already incurred by public authorities.[9] In view of the centralized allocation of finance for capital investment in industry and infrastructure in Ireland, the effect of this provision was to augment resources available for capital investment. In administrative terms, it therefore meant that the existing centralized institutional framework for determining capital allocations was also the most logical framework within which to operate the ERDF. The decision by the Irish Government to consider ERDF receipts as a 'partial reimbursement' of expenditure has been criticized by advocates at regional and local level of a more decentralized and effective Fund. Their argument is that the ERDF should be more transparent and used to finance projects of importance for the development of regions rather than simply to augment capital resources.

In addition to the 'partial reimbursement' provision, two other factors have operated in favour of a centralized operation of the Fund. These are (a) the global level of resources allocated to the ERDF in the Community budget and (b) the distribution of the Fund on the basis of quotas. The amount eventually allocated by the Council to the ERDF (1,300m. u.a. for three years) was significantly lower than the sum sought by Ireland and the other less prosperous Member States (3,000m. u.a.). The small size of the Fund, together with the fact that it was to be distributed on the basis of quotas, meant that Ireland's main priority was 'to ensure that quotas allocated are claimed and paid at the earliest possible date so that funds are available to finance further investment—especially in areas of greatest need'.[10] The main objective was to maximize receipts from the Fund. This could be achieved by submitting projects already in the course of construction for Fund assistance. The operation of the Fund therefore did not require new procedures for the selection of projects. The selection of projects on the basis of normal approval procedures was regarded as the most cost-effective way of administering the Fund. The effect of this was that the involvement of levels of government other than central in the selection of projects for Fund assistance was regarded as unnecessary.

As Table 10.1 shows, allocations to the ERDF have increased significantly since its establishment. However, its proportion of total Community expenditure still remains relatively small. It is suggested that there exists a threshold level of finance below which there is little incentive for developing the administrative framework of the ERDF. This assumes a form of calculation at national level of net benefit

Table 10.1. ERDF Allocations as a % of Total Budgetary Allocations (Commitment Appropriations)

Year	*A* *Allocations to the ERDF*	*B* *Allocations to Community Budget (plus supplementary budgets)*	*C* *A as % of B*
1975(M(u.a.)	299.8	6,316.9	4.75
1976(M(u.a.)	500.1	8,912.66	5.61
1977(M(u.a.)	501.7	10,353.73	4.84
1978(M(u.a.)	556.36	12,702.93	4.37
1979(M(EUA)	962.11	15,428.31	6.23
1980(M(EUA)	1137.78	17,491.89	6.5
1981(M(ECU)	1596.18	19,986.09	7.98
1982(M(ECU)	1759.5	23,560.1	7.5

Sources: ERDF Annual Reports and General Report on the Activities of the European Communities.

accruing to the Member State from sources of finance such as the ERDF. If estimated receipts are likely to be reduced significantly by complex administrative machinery involving several levels of government, Member States will opt for simple administrative procedures in order to maximize receipts. In Ireland, for example, ERDF receipts are included in the Public Capital Programme (PCP). Despite the increase in receipts since 1975, they still only account for approximately 3 per cent of the total PCP. When the ERDF is related to global capital expenditure (see Table 10.2) it is difficult to justify setting up separate administrative procedures since this could have the effect of reducing net receipts.

Apart from the bias towards centralized administration of the ERDF evident in the Fund Regulation, it is also important to relate Ireland's expectations of the Fund to its subsequent operation. As was discussed above, Ireland regarded the ERDF primarily as an additional source of finance to support its development strategy. Its priority was to develop the economy and thereby reduce imbalances between it and other Community countries. The reduction of internal regional imbalances was of secondary importance. When the ERDF was finally established, it was therefore consistent with the Government's expectations of the Fund to administer it centrally since economic planning was and still is a centralized function.

The pivotal role of the Department of Finance in promoting the development of the economy, meant that it was regarded as the most appropriate central government department to administer the ERDF. In the course of negotiations on the establishment of the Fund, the Department of Foreign Affairs and the Department of Finance were the two departments primarily involved. Since 1975 the Department of Finance has been the principal department charged with administering the Fund and liaising with the EC Commission. Its functions include: processing and submitting applications for aid to the Commission; preparing and submitting to the Commission the Irish Regional Development Programme; processing and submitting applications for payment to the Commission; and receiving payment from the Commission which is used to augment the resources of the Public Capital Programme (PCP) which it also formulates. The Department of Finance is dependent on other government departments to submit eligible projects for ERDF aid. With the exception of projects under the non-quota section, these are projects for which the investment decision has already been made. The availability of ERDF finance

Table 10.2.   ERDF Commitments and Receipts Related to the Public Capital Programme in Ireland. IR£m

	1975	1976	1977	1978	1979	1980	1981	1982	1983
ERDF commitments	8.3	14.7	12.6	23.62	41.1	51	62.7	68.4	70.7
ERDF receipts	1.75	8.54	8.5	11.1	25.5	46.4	54.6	64.0	56.0
Receipts as % of Commitments	21	57.8	67.5	47	62	91	87	93.5	79.2
Total public Capital Expenditure	470.3	547.5	662.7	815.8	1,022	1,305	1,766	1,898	1,748
ERDF receipts as % of PCP	0.37	1.55	1.28	1.36	2.5	3.5	3.09	3.37	3.2

does not affect the investment decision.

The Department of the Environment is the central government department responsible for transmitting to the Department of Finance projects eligible for Fund assistance which are executed by local authorities. Such projects are mainly in the areas of roads and sanitary services. It should be emphasized that although regional authorities (called Regional Development Organisations—RDOs) exist in each of the nine physical planning regions, they do not have any legal status. Their main function is to co-ordinate the physical development plans formulated by their constituent local authorities and to formulate development strategies for the region. However, RDOs are dependent on local authorities and central government to implement any development strategies formulated at regional level. Local authorities, in particular the County Council which is the basic unit of the local government system, are the main implementing agencies at subnational level in relation to physical planning.

At central level, the Department of the Environment is responsible for the organization, functions and structure of local government and also for liaison with the RDOs. Consequently, there is an important factor to consider when examining the involvement of regional and local authorities in Community policy areas. This is the perceived role of the Department itself in relation to Community policy areas and the legitimacy attached by it to sub-national involvement both in domestic and Community policy areas.

Two broad categories of Community policies impinge on the activities of the Department of the Environment:

1. Community policies involving financial transfers from the Community to the Member States. Before 1975 the principal financial instrument of relevance to the Department was the Guidance section of the European Agricultural Guarantee and Guidance Fund which provided assistance for rural water supply schemes. There was also the possibility of finance from the European Investment Bank for roads.
2. Community secondary legislation in relation to public works contracts, roads and the environment.

The implementation of Community secondary legislation necessitated close liaison between the Department and local authorities, mainly at executive level. To facilitate the co-ordination of Community matters affecting the Department and local authorities, an EEC sub-section was set up within the General Section of the Department in December 1972. Its principal functions were: to monitor the flow of information on EEC matters; to identify those items of significance for the Department and local authorities generally; to communicate this information to the appropriate sections of local authorities; to convey comments from sections to the Department of Foreign Affairs for transmission to Brussels; and to co-ordinate EEC aspects of the work of the Department and local authorities.[11] It was anticipated that the EEC sub-section would be at the core of the communication network between the Community, central government and local authorities. Of particular importance for the involvement of local authorities, was the role of the subsection in identifying items of significance for the Department and local authorities generally. The Department of the Environment was to determine the Community policy areas in which local authorities could be involved. This however, was a function of the input by the Department itself in the policy formulation process both at national level and in the Community.

One of the areas of Community activity in which regional and local authorities expected to be involved was the proposed ERDF. This expectation arose partly as a result of the Department's responsibility for aspects of regional development at central level. However, in the course of negotiations on the ERDF, the Department played only a peripheral role. Given the attitude of the Government to the ERDF and to regional policy in the Community, it was logical that the Department of Finance and the Department of Foreign Affairs would be the principal government departments involved in the negotiations. The implication of the absence of the Department of the Environment from the locus of decision-making was that it did not identify the ERDF as an item of significance either for itself or for local authorities and the RDOs. Hence the relatively dismissive attitude of the Department to all requests by local authorities and the RDOs to be involved in the administration of the Fund.

Liaison between central government and regional/local authorities on the operation of the Fund

Regional and local authorities liaised with central government both before the establishment of the Fund (pre-ERDF phase) and when the Fund was established (post-ERDF phase) in order to seek involvement in the operation of the Fund. Their efforts were largely unco-ordinated however—a concerted approach to central government on the issue did not occur. While there was consensus on the need for subnational involvement in the operation of the Fund, it was up to individual local and regional authorities to develop their own strategies on how best to influence central government.

One of the regions which most actively sought regional involvement in the operative of the ERDF was the Mid-West region. The experience of the Mid-West provides a good example of the difficulties encountered by RDOs and their constituent local authorities in seeking involvement in the operation of the ERDF. In the Mid-West, the region was regarded as the most appropriate unit to deal with Community matters despite the limitations on the powers of RDOs. While individual local authorities sought ERDF assistance for specific projects, the RDO was primarily concerned with the broader aspects of the operation of the Fund.

Before 1975 the RDO established contact with central government departments principally to ensure that it would be informed of relevant developments at Community level and in a position to influence policy-making at central level. It is interesting to note that the RDO's initial contact points were the Department of Foreign Affairs and Finance, thereby recognising their key roles in relation to the Community. However, central government departments were reluctant to establish contact with the RDO given the Department of the Environment's responsibility for guiding and informing RDOs. Consequently, the RDO's main contact point was the Department of the Environment which played a peripheral role in the negotiations establishing the ERDF.

One of the principal objectives pursued by the RDO prior to the establishment of the Fund was the establishment of a consultative committee. This objective was rejected by the Department of the Environment who argued that any discussion on arrangements for the administration of the Fund would be inappropriate in the absence of specific decisions at Community level. The line of argument used by the department indicates clearly its attitude to consultation with the RDOs. To the extent that the department was prepared to consider consultation on the ERDF, it envisaged retrospective consultation—in effect a mechanism for informing regional and local authorities of developments rather than consulting with them.

Once the ERDF was established, the uncertainties of the policy environment which characterized the pre-ERDF phase were reduced considerably. Nevertheless, the absence of systematic information-flows between central government and the RDO on the operation of the ERDF continued to be problematic for the RDOs. It was even claimed that the RDO received more information on the ERDF as operated in Ireland through contact with Commission officials than through central government officials. In the absence of systematic information-flows between central government and the RDOs, it was essentially up to each RDO to inform itself so that it could formulate a position on the ERDF. Once the ERDF was established, the RDO succeeded in solving the information problem in relation to the Community aspect of the ERDF mainly through its contact with the Conference of Peripheral and Maritime Regions (CPMR) which will be discussed below. However, the RDO still encountered the problem of insufficient information on the operation of the Fund at national level.

In the post-ERDF phase, the RDO continued in its efforts to establish a consultative committee. The arguments used by central government were no longer valid. In contrast to the pre-ERDF phase, the post-ERDF phase was characterized by the development of specific demands and discussion on the administration of the Fund. One of the principal concerns of the RDO in relation to the ERDF was the provision whereby ERDF finance would be used as a partial reimbursement of expenditure already incurred for certain types of expenditure. It was argued that this provision would lessen the purpose and concept of the Fund which the RDO and local authorities felt should be used to finance specific projects. This issue was regarded as a matter of urgency since the importance of the administrative arrangements for the first year in terms of setting a precedent for the future was recognized. The strategy of the RDO was therefore to move from a peripheral to a central role in the operation of the Fund. However, on the question of a possible input at regional or local level, no procedures had as yet been devised by central government. The only advice offered by the Department of the Environment on the question of sub-national involvement was that since the Fund 'should mean that some additional resources will be available for development projects, the aim of local authorities should be to have additional projects included in expanded capital programmes rather than to have particular projects submitted for aid'.[12] The attitude of central government differed in two fundamental ways from the RDO viewpoint:

1. There was a basic divergence between central government and the

RDO on the legitimacy and necessity of subnational involvement in the operation of the ERDF. Central government, based on its perception of the ERDF, argued that subnational involvement was not required for the effective operation of the Fund. The RDO, on the other hand, argued that the Fund should be used to finance projects at regional level and accordingly advocated subnational involvement in the selection projects.

2. There was general consensus within the RDO on the region as the most appropriate subnational unit to be involved in operating the ERDF. In contrast, the Department of the Environment view was formulated on the basis purely of local authority involvement—it did not envisage an RDO input in this particular policy area. The Department of the Environment argued that RDO involvement in the selection of projects 'would not serve any useful purpose'. The only scope which the Department envisaged for an RDO input was 'by drawing up and up-dating as necessary, lists of investment priorities within their regions for the guidance of local authorities and government departments in the making of investment decisions.'[13]

The differences between the Department of the Environment and the RDO on the two issues referred to above reflect even more fundamental differences on the status of RDOs and their input in the formulation of regional policy at central level.

Given its lack of success in both establishing a consultative committee and having its views on the operation of the ERDF accepted by the Department of the Environment, the RDO proposed that the operation of the ERDF should be transferred to the Department of the Taoiseach (Prime Minister). By transferring responsibility to the Taoiseach's Department, it was hoped to overcome the problems associated with having primary contact with a department which was not the locus of decision-making in relation to the ERDF. The choice of the Department of the Taoiseach reflected a certain frustration with departmental contact on the issue to date. However, the role of the Department of Finance remained unchanged.

An important influence on the development of the RDO's expectations of the ERDF was its participation in the CPMR which constituted its most systematic source of information on the Community dimension of the ERDF. In the period following the establishment of the ERDF in 1975, the CPMR was particularly active in two respects:

i. in informing the regions of administrative arrangements and suggesting strategies to influence the Fund through its News Bulletin and meetings of the Permanent and Executive Committees and

ii. informing the Commission of its views on the Fund.

The strategy proposed by the CPMR to its constituent regions was to exert vigorous pressure on their respective governments to ensure that the Fund's resources would be supplementary to national expenditure. It advocated that the regions should present the maximum number of demands to national governments for ERDF assistance to ensure that regions would be practically associated at state level with the formulation of Community regional policy. It is important to bear in mind that the CPMR was the only body in which the RDO was represented that sought to influence the formulation of regional policy at Community level. The CPMR achieved this by having direct contacts with the Commission and also by guiding its members on the strategy to be used when dealing with central government. As such it constituted one of the main reference points for RDO strategy in relation to the ERDF.

Commissioner Thomson expressed a keen interest in the workings of the CPMR. The upshot of this was that the RDO adopted much of what was said by the Commissioner and by other Commission officials on the operation of the Fund. Consequently, the elements of the RDO's approach to the Fund were basically similar to those expressed by Commissioner Thomson. The main effect of this particular contact point however was to strengthen and justify the RDO's expectations of the Fund. The contact also served as a useful reference point for articulating and transmitting the RDO's expectations at central level.

One of the problems associated with the use of the Commission as a source of information was the difficulty to distinguish between Commission expectations of the Fund and what was politically feasible at Community level. Thus, for example, Commissioner Thomson had consistently advocated that the definition of additionality in practical terms 'means being able to identify the additional schemes which can be pursued because of the extra resources in the regions which have been made available by the Fund.'[14] This concept of additionality had also been the policy of the RDO in relation to the ERDF. It was not the definition of additionality subsequently adopted by the Commission. In practice the Commission was prepared to accept the broader concept of additionality preferred by the central governments of the

Member States whereby Fund receipts should increase the overall level of available resources.

The mismatch between expectations and political feasibility in relation to the ERDF was eventually appreciated by the RDO. It recognized that the ERDF was not developing along the lines desired by certain elements of the Commission and the RDO itself. Accordingly, since 1978 the RDO has effectively ceased to exert pressure on central government to modify the operation of the Fund. The net effect of these developments is that the RDO appears to have down-graded its expectations of the potential input by the Community in the development of the region. A recent *Study of Industrial Location in the Shannon Estuary and Surrounding Area* has been given financial assistance by the ERDF.[15] The implementation of the proposals contained in the Study offers the possibility of extending the horizons of the RDO beyond the ERDF to include other Community financial instruments with a possible impact on the development of the region. One of the aims of the Study is to facilitate intervention by all of the Community instruments in the region—not just the ERDF. It will be interesting to assess the extent to which such Community financed studies serve as a useful mechanism for co-ordinating Community financial instruments in a specific region to promote its development. If such were the case it would constitute and important step in putting into practical effect the broader definition of regional policy currently employed at Community level.

Several factors explain the failure of the Mid-West region to negotiate change in the operation of the ERDF whereby regional and local authorities could be involved in the selection of projects. In the first instance, the failure has to be explained in terms of particular features of the relationship between central government on the one hand and regional and local authorities on the other. As stated above, the RDOs do not have any statutory powers and accordingly are dependent on their constituent local authorities to implement any regional development strategies formulated. Despite numerous attempts directed at central government to acquire statutory powers, the status of RDOs in the subnational framework has not altered. One of the implications of this is that the effectiveness of RDOs as co-ordinating bodies has varied considerably in the different regions. The problems encountered by the Mid-West RDO in seeking to modify the operation of the ERDF were instrinsically linked to the more general question of the organization and powers of RDOs in the subnational framework.

A further related factor which compounded problems for RDOs and local authorities with respect to the ERDF was liaison with central government departments. Their main contact point was a department which was peripheral to the negotiations on the ERDF and its subsequent operation. Given the special responsibility of the Department of the Environment for local government and for liaison with RDOs the perceived role of the Department in the operation of the Fund was a crucial factor influencing the involvement of regional and local authorities.

However, perhaps one of the most decisive factors preventing regional or local involvement in the operation of the Fund, was the absence of a co-ordinated strategy by regional and local authorities to achieve their objectives. There is no formal organizational structure which unites regional authorities in the Republic. The absence of such an organization means that liaison with central government has primarily been on the initiative of individual RDOs. Concerted approaches to central government have not been the norm to date. The effect of this fragmented approach to central government has been to reinforce the position of the latter in dealing with RDOs.

Liaison between local authorities and central government has also been uncoordinated at local level—despite the existence of three associations—the General Council of County Councils, the City and County Managers Association and the Association of Municipal Authorities. The Department of the Environment has operated an effective strategy of 'divide and rule'—a strategy which has been particularly successful in maintaining central control over the local government system in Ireland. Since 1980 steps have been taken with the establishment of the Irish Council of European Local Authorities (ICELA) to adopt a more concerted approach to central government on both domestic and Community policy areas. This initiative reflects the level of discontent at subnational level with existing structures for liaising with central government. It also implicitly recognizes the extent to which the fragmented approach to central government reduced considerably the capacity of local and regional authorities to achieve policy objectives.

The principal features of the operation of the Fund

The centralized institutional framework for the administration of the ERDF in Ireland has remained relatively unchanged since 1975. This is because of the lack of substantial increases in financial allocations to the ERDF in the Community budget and the failure of the Commission to introduce significant changes in the operation of the Fund. These two aspects of the operation of the Fund at Community level, help to put into context the principal features of Ireland's attitude to the Fund since its establishment.

Ireland's main priority has been to seek practical improvements in the administration of the Fund with the objective of simplifying procedures and accordingly maximizing receipts from the Fund. Analysis of its attitude during the review negotiations between 1977 and 1979 and also the current negotiations reveals the lack of support for fundamental changes in the operation and nature of the ERDF.

Ireland gave little active support to the introduction of a non-quota section which has been one of the most important innovations in the operation of the Fund. It argued that the non-quota section should be confined to already designated regions and to problems defined on a regional rather than sectoral basis. The reason for its attitude to the non-quota section lies in the nature of the measures proposed. The non-quota section was introduced primarily to prevent and correct problems arising from the operation of Community policies or international developments. However, the Irish Government feared that the operation of a non-quota section would increase the number of regions eligible for Fund assistance in the Community and thereby reduce its receipts from the Fund. This explains why the Government advocated that the non-quota section should be confined to regions already eligible for assistance.[16] At its present level of 5 per cent of the Fund's total resources, the non-quota section is not significant enough to threaten Ireland's receipts from the Fund. In addition one of the specific measures adopted was for the border areas.

The principal modifications to the ERDF which Ireland has advocated are:

1. A system of accelerated payments. This was one of the Government's three priorities during the first review of the Fund. Analysis of the ratio between commitments and receipts shows that the introduction of a system of accelerated payments has had the intended impact (see Table 10.2). In 1978 the proportion was 47 per cent. This figure had increased to 91 per cent by 1980.
2. A broader definition of infrastructure than that adopted in the 1975 Regulation. The Government also advocated a higher rate of Fund

assistance for infrastructure projects in certain cases. Both were adopted during the first review of the Fund.

3. The use of a programme instead of a project approach as proposed under the current review of the Fund.

Since 1980 Ireland has adopted the use of programmes in order to simplify the administration of the ERDF. The Road Development Plan, for example, was approved by the Commission as a framework for submitting projects for Fund assistance. Examination of the press releases issued by the Department of Finance since the establishment of the ERDF reveals a marked shift away from providing detailed information on projects financed in each County to the provision of overall figures of Fund assistance for various programmes.

On the basis of experience to date with the use of programmes, Ireland initially favoured the introduction of the use of programmes in the operation of the ERDF. However, in the course of negotiation, it has become obvious that the procedure envisaged by the Commission is considerably more complex than originally anticipated. This has given rise to fears that the introduction of programmes with procedures similar to those, for example, in the non-quota section would complicate rather than simplify approval procedures. Consequently, a more cautious attitude to the adoption of programmes by the Commission is now evident.

It is worth noting that even Commission officials in Directorate General XVI disagree on the effectiveness of programmes in the operation of the Fund. Officials who process applications advocate that the use of programmes would simplify the project approval procedure and accordingly allow the Commission to assess programmes in depth. Officials responsible for the control of the Fund, however, argue that their problems will be compounded by the use of programmes because they will make the procedure even less transparent than is already the case.

The use of programmes by Ireland to simplify the administration of the Fund since 1980, coincided with other tactics to simplify the approval procedure. An investigation of aid applications reveals two significant trends.

First, as Table 10.3 shows, the number of projects submitted by Ireland has decreased substantially from 168 in 1975 to a low of thirty-six in 1980. The effect has been to simplify the administration of the Fund in Ireland. A further implication of this trend however, is that it reduces the flexibility of the Commission in selecting projects to be

Table 10.3.   Investigation of Irish Applications for ERDF Aid

	A	B	C
	No. of Projects Presented	*No. of Projects Financed*	*B as % of A*
1975	168	105	62.5
1976	116	89	76.7
1977	78	73	93.6
1978	143	121	84.6
1979	142	135	95.1
1980	36	35	97.2
1981	69	68	98.5
1982	59	58	98.3

Source: ERDF Annual Reports.

assisted because of the existence of quotas. Second, projects costing more than 10m. European units of account (EUA), which are processed separately and are easier to administer, have accounted for a higher proportion of total approvals. In 1980 fourteen such projects were approved, while in the previous five years the total number of Irish projects approved in this category was five.

Impact of the ERDF in Ireland

It is difficult to assess the impact of the ERDF in Ireland for three main reasons related both to the Government's attitude to the development of the economy and also the operation of the Fund. As discussed in the previous section Ireland's priority has been to promote the development of the economy as a whole. Since Ireland's accession to the Community, economic circumstances have been such that the decline in its position in relation to other Member States has reinforced the need for national economic development.[17] The emphasis on developing the economy means that the reduction of internal regional disparities has been a secondary consideration. It is significant, for example, that there has been no major statement on regional policy since 1972. Furthermore, it is interesting to note that the Regional Development Programme submitted by the Government to Brussels had as its basic document the White Paper *National Development 1977–1980* which made no reference to regional policy in terms of reducing internal disparities.[18]

The operation of the ERDF in Ireland is highly centralized. Receipts from the ERDF are included in the Public Capital Programme (PCP) under a separate budget heading. Accordingly ERDF receipts supplement the finance available for capital expenditure. This centralized operation of the Fund allows a measure of flexibility in the use made of receipts from the Fund. However, the inclusion of receipts in the PCP, which allocates finance on a sectoral basis, means that a geographical breakdown of ERDF receipts is not possible. Consequently, claims to the effect that a certain proportion of ERDF finance is allocated to the designated areas cannot be substantiated because Fund aid is not distributed on a regional basis in Ireland.

An aspect peculiar to Ireland when assessing the impact of the Fund is that the entire country constitutes a region. While this has been justified by the low level of economic development, it compounds problems of analysing the impact of a Fund already centralized in its operation. Requests to have the Fund's resources concentrated on the more underdeveloped areas in Ireland have not been accepted. The argument used by the Government is that any discrimination in favour of certain areas to the exclusion of others in distributing the Fund's resources would inevitably lead to a reduction in Ireland's allocation.

Consequently, an assessment of the impact of the ERDF in terms of its contribution towards reducing internal regional imbalances is not possible. A more useful approach is to put the development of the Fund in the context of Ireland's expectations of Community membership and of the ERDF. As noted above one of Ireland's main priorities during the Accession negotiations was to have its special development problems recognized by the other Member States. This was fundamental to its strategy of gaining preferential access to Community sources of finance in order to promote economic development. The designation of the country as one region indicates a certain consensus at national level and in the Community on the need to focus in the first instance on promoting national economic development. Given this emphasis on access to financial resources, the remainder of this chapter will examine the ERDF in the context of the PCP. The main objective is to determine whether ERDF receipts can be identified with additional expenditure particularly in relation to the specific parts of the PCP financed by the ERDF. Also included is an analysis of the main categories of projects financed by the Fund.

Between 1975 and 1983, Ireland received IR£276.39m. in total

Table 10.4.   Allocations in the PCP to Programmes Eligible for ERDF Aid IR£m

Programme	1975	1976	1977	1978	1979	1980	1981	1982	1983
Roads	13.77	11.64	18.83	22.7	30.0	35.5	60.0	80.0	92.0
Telecommunications	47.18	48.0	50.5	53.5	78.3	123.4	220.0	233.5	190.0
Sanitary Services	18.71	25.93	27.03	33.17	40.4	50.75	71.57	82.4	88.1
Harbours	.16	.09	1.13	.64	3.62	7.1	3.0	2.8	.65
Industrial Development (IDA)	40.86	50.9	59.0	78.0	119.0	156.7	129.95	141.0	121.9
Post-Primary Education	1.63	2.85	2.35	2.36	1.37	2.11	26.0	22.6	18.3
Arterial Drainage	2.32	2.75	3.69	4.16	7.46	7.69	10.10	11.25	11.81
TOTAL	124.36	124.16	162.53	194.5	280.15	383.25	520.6	573.5	522.76
% of Total PCP	26.5	25.9	24.5	23.8	27.4	29.36	29.47	30.2	29.9
ERDF Receipts % total eligible expenditure	1.4	6.0	5.2	5.7	9.1	12.1	10.5	11.15	10.7

Source: Public Capital Programmes.

from the ERDF which on an annual basis has ranged from the relatively small initial sum of IR£5m. in 1975 to IR£64m. in 1982 (see Table 10.2). In 1983 these receipts accounted for over 3 per cent of all capital expenditure included in the PCP. Although this represents a substantial increase from the 0.37 per cent recorded in 1975 it is still relatively insignificant when compared to the total cost of financing the PCP. However, ERDF assistance is not allocated to all items of expenditure included in the PCP but only to those items which qualify for assistance under the Fund's rules. In 1983 these items of expenditure amounted to nearly 30 per cent of total capital expenditure (see Table 10.4). When related to these particular items in the PCP, ERDF receipts assume greater importance. In 1978, when the first breakdown of ERDF receipts was given in the PCP, the proportion was 5 per cent and by 1983 this had risen to almost 11 per cent. This indicates that the ERDF is a significant source of finance available to the Government in financing the particular areas eligible for assistance under the Fund.

The areas which have been financed by the ERDF are roads, telecommunications, sanitary services, harbours, arterial drainage, regional technical colleges, and special teacher training colleges, industrial development (IDA) and Udaras na Gaeltachta. These are all financed by the quota section of the Fund. Furthermore, since 1981, the Special Border Areas Programme has been assisted through the non-quota section of the Fund. It is proposed to examine first of all the projects under the quota section since these are financially the most significant and then to examine the non-quota section.

The Quota Section

Items included in the PCP which receive ERDF assistance can broadly be divided into two categories—infrastructure and industrial/service projects. Analysis of the allocation of Fund assistance to these two categories reveals a bias in favour of infrastructure projects. Apart from 1975, when 66 per cent of Fund aid was allocated to industrial projects, infrastructure projects have consistently accounted for over 50 per cent of total assistance. In 1980 the proportion increased to 87 per cent (see Table 10.5). The trend evident in Table 10.5 is a further indication of the importance attached to infrastructure by Ireland during the first review of the Fund. Furthermore, the Government's strategy is to submit even more infrastructure projects for Fund assistance up to the

Table 10.5.   Percentage Breakdown of ERDF
Grants to Industry/Service and Infrastructure
Projects in Ireland

	Industry/Service	Infrastructures
1975	66.3	33.7
1976	39.9	63.1
1977	45.1	55.5
1978	42.5	57.5
1979	47.4	52.6
1980	12.7	87.3
1981	17.0	83.0
1982	28.7	71.3

Source: ERDF Annual Reports.

70 per cent limit allowed. Under the revised Fund Regulation, adopted in 1979, up to 70 per cent of ERDF aid can be allocated to infrastructure projects.[19] The indications are that this limit is being interpreted as refering to the Community as a whole rather than to allocations to individual Member States. This means that individual Member States can claim more than 70 per cent of their total quota for infrastructure provided that the limit has not been surpassed as Community level. The interpretation of the 70 per cent limit in this way is of particular importance for the less prosperous Member States who have consistently emphasized the role of infrastructure in the context of regional development. It also explains why Ireland was allocated 87 per cent of its ERDF aid for infrastructure projects in 1980.

One of the reasons for the importance attached to infrastructure in claiming finance from the ERDF is that in certain priority areas including Ireland, infrastructure projects qualify for preferential rates of assistance. Furthermore, repayments have tended to be faster for infrastructure than for industrial projects. The priority attached by the Government to maximizing receipts from the Fund, thus explains the increased emphasis on infrastructure. Apart from these considerations, however, the importance attached to infrastructure reflects the poor infrastructure characteristic of countries with low levels of economic development such as Ireland.

To what extent has this bias in favour of infrastructure in the allocation of ERDF finance been evident in capital allocations for infrastructure at national level? It is significant that in the PCP, capital expenditure on infrastructure assisted by the ERDF increased at a faster rate than capital expenditure on industrial development assisted by the ERDF. Furthermore, the proportion of capital expenditure on infrastructure to total expenditure eligible for assistance rose from 65 per cent in 1977 to 73 per cent in 1981. This indicates the growing importance of infrastructure in relation to industrial development in the allocation of capital finance at central level. This pattern is also evident in the distribution of ERDF receipts (as opposed to commitments) between infrastructure and industrial development. The proportion allocated to industrial development fell from 33.46 per cent in 1979 to 18.18 per cent in 1982.

The Commission attaches prime importance to defining additionality in terms of increasing the level of capital expenditure. To what extent has the operation of the Fund in Ireland been identified with additional investment? Between 1975 and 1983, the PCP increased almost four-fold at an average rate up to 1981 of 24.8 per cent which even in real terms was substantial. More significant, however, was the fact that the part of the PCP financed by the ERDF grew at a faster rate than did the overall figure for capital expenditure in particular from 1978 onwards. If inflation and receipts from the Fund are taken into account, there was still an increase of around IR£50m. in expenditure during the period 1975–81. This indicates clearly that at least in arithmetical terms, ERDF receipts have been associated with additional expenditure under the PCP. The Department of Finance advocates that projected receipts from the ERDF are considered when formulating the PCP. Variations in levels of receipts from the Fund can thus affect overall resources available for capital investment. The Department of Finance therefore argues that ERDF finance is additional. However, evidence based on the PCP alone is insufficient to develop conclusively a casual relationship between the availability of ERDF finance and any additional capital expenditure. The difficulties involved in measuring additionality mean that the Commission does not have at its disposal any way of establishing conclusively whether the principle of additionality applies in relation to the ERDF.

The Non-Quota Section

The problem of measuring the additional element in ERDF assistance would not appear to be as problematic, however, in the case of the Special Border Areas Programme, which comes under the non-quota

Table 10.6.   Expenditure on Special Border
Areas Programme Plus ERDF Contribution
(£ Sterling)

	Outturn	ERDF receipts
1980	100,000	—
1981	2,974,000	660,000
1982	3,390,000	2,000,000
1983	1,350,000	2,000,000
1984	5,500,000	4,000,000

section. The operation of the non-quota section is more transparent than the quota section. The County Councils concerned, for example, have been directly involved in submitting projects as part of the overall programme. First receipts worth IR£0.6m. were received in 1981 and it is estimated that receipts will approximate IR£4m. in 1984 (see Table 10.6). This figure amounts to a little over 7 per cent of receipts under the quota section.

It is as yet too early to judge the impact of the Programme in the areas concerned particularly since the projects have not been checked by officials responsible for controlling the ERDF in D.G.XVI of the Commission. It is interesting to note that a divergence of views between the Commission and the Department of Finance is evident on the impact of the special measure. Commission officials suspect that little has been achieved in implementing the Programme. They argue that the introduction of a Community measure for the border areas was a political act by the Member States in recognition of the political and economic problems associated with the border. The value of the measure was political rather than a serious attempt to promote development. The Department of Finance on the other hand, claims that the special measure is having a recognizable effect on the counties in question and that local authorities can embark on certain projects now because of the extra finance available.

Given the current proposals to adopt a programme approach for the operation of the quota section, it is important to determine the effectiveness of programmes on the basis of present experience with the non-quota section. If the programmes are found to be ineffective and/or to create administrative complications, it is unlikely that they will have the anticipated positive effect in terms of promoting more involvement at regional and local level in the operation of the Fund.

There is confusion amongst officials in Ireland over the procedures proposed for operating the use of programmes in the ERDF. Ireland, for example, argues that if programmes are to operate on a similar basis to that of programmes under the non-quota section, the procedure would be too cumbersome. Consequently, Irish officials feel that Member States will be in a position to choose whether or not to adopt the programme approach. If this proves to be the case, the involvement of subnational units of government will still be at the discretion of the central governments of the Member States.

Conclusion

The centralized administration of the ERDF in Ireland has to be seen in the context of the Government's expectations of the Fund and the nature of the Fund set up by the Community. Ireland's main priority during the Fund negotiations was to seek a well-endowed Fund which would provide financial support for its development strategy. Given the low level of economic development beside that of other Member States, the Government's objective was to promote the overall development of the economy—the reduction of internal regional disparities was a subsidiary objective. There was general consensus at Community level also on the Government's strategy as is evident by the designation of the entire country as a region eligible for Fund assistance.

In relation to the impact of the ERDF in Ireland, the evidence at Community level suggests a divergence of Member States' economies and accordingly a decline in the Irish economy relative to other economies in the Community. This is despite the fact that Fund receipts have supplemented resources available for the Public Capital Programme. Analysis of the PCP reveals substantial increases in allocations for capital expenditure since 1975 particularly in those areas eligible for Fund assistance. However, because of the lack of transparency associated with the centralized operation of the Fund, it is not possible to develop a causal relationship between the availability of ERDF finance and increases in capital expenditure.

One of the most important implications of the manner in which the ERDF is operated in Ireland, is that it has reinforced the role of central government in the institutional framework for regional planning. The designation of the country as one region means that, for the purposes of the ERDF, central government constitutes the regional authority. The distribution of the Fund on the basis of quotas, together with the small size of the Fund as against total capital expenditure have rendered unnecessary the involvement of regional and local authorities in the operation of the Fund. Apart from these Community-related factors, other factors specific to Ireland explain the ineffectiveness of regional and local authorities in seeking involvement in the operation of the Fund to date. Some of the major obstacles are inherent in the nature of the local government system which is characterized by tight central control and weak organizational links between local and regional authorities themselves.

While the Commission's objective is to have regional and local involvement at national level, it acknowledges that it can but exert influence on central governments in this respect. Politically, it would not be feasible to enforce such provisions. A pre-requisite for sub-national involvement in the operation of the ERDF is the development of strong organizational links at regional and local level. Consequently it is up to regional and local authorities in Ireland to identify factors which have impeded their involvement to date and accordingly to devise a strategy the object of which would be to ensure that the spirit of the Commission's current proposals are implemented in Ireland.

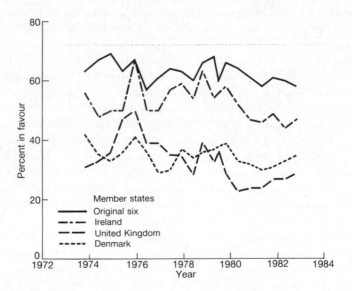

Figure 10.1. *Support for EEC Membership, 1973–1982, by Member State.*

Notes

1. John Coakley, 'The European Dimension in Irish Public Opinion 1972–1982' in David Coombes, ed., *Ireland and the European Communities—Ten years of membership*, Dublin, 1983, p. 59.

2. Ibid., p. 57.

3. European Communities, 'Act concerning the Conditions of Accession and the Adjustments to the Treaties', *Protocol No. 30 on Ireland*, 1972.

4. *Review of Regional Policy*, statement issued by the Government Information Bureau on behalf of the Government, 4 may 1972.

5. Speech by Dr Hillery, Minister for Foreign Affairs, at the Annual Dinner of the Confederation of Irish Industry, 15 Apr. 1971.

6. Ireland, *Dail Debates*, 265(1973): 1248.

7. Ireland, *Dail Debates*, 270(1974): 1852.

8. For a comprehensive account of the negotiations establishing the ERDF see Ross B. Talbot, *The European Community's Regional Fund* (Progress in Planning, vol. 8), Oxford, 1977.

9. Regulation (EEC) No. 724/75, art. 4, sec. 2(a), *Official Journal* L 73, 21 Mar. 1975, p. 1.

10. Mid-West RDO, 'Correspondence with Department of Local Government (subsequently the Department of the Environment) on the ERDF', Report prepared for Meeting of the Board, 19 Jan. 1976.

11. Department of Local Government, 'Developments in EEC Matters having implications for Local Government', Circular E 1/7, 28 May 1974.

12. Mid-West RDO, 'European Regional Development Fund', Report prepared for Meeting of the Board, July 1975.

13. Mid-West RDO, 'Correspondence with the Department of Local Government in relation to the ERDF', Report prepared for Meeting of the Board, 26 Apr. 1976.

14. Letter from Commissioner Thomson to M. Pierret, Secretary-General of CPMR, 11 Mar. 1976 in Mid-West RDO, 'Conference of Peripheral Maritime Regions', Report prepared for Meeting of the Board, 19 July 1976.

15. Mid-West RDO, *Study of Industrial Location in the Shannon Estuary and Surrounding Area*, 1984.

16. Ireland, *Dail Debates*, 300(1977): 501.

17. European Communities, Commission, *The Regions of Europe: First Periodic Report on the social and economic situation of the regions of the Community*, COM(80) 816, 7 Jan. 1981.

18. Department of Economic Planning and Development, *National Development 1977–1980*, Dublin, 1978.

19. Regulation (EEC) No. 214/79, art. 4, sec. 1(b), *Official Journal* L35, 9 Feb. 1979, p. 1.

11

Conclusion

BARRY JONES

There is a tendency to regard the European Community as having entered into a period of immobilism during which the process of integration has been brought to a halt. While it can be argued that the Community has created an economic framework which so binds them together that another European war has now become practically impossible and psychologically unthinkable, the architects of the European Community had higher and more positive aspirations. They expected that a united Europe would become more self-reliant both economically and politically and that it would be capable of taking corporate action over a wide range of policy issues. In this respect the European Community has proved less than successful largely because member states have exhibited an obstinate reluctance to submerge their historic identities within the wider European context. De Gaulle's reassertion of the primacy of member states in foreign policy matters, the consolidation of the unanimity principle in the procedures of the Council of Ministers and the continuing budgetary crisis are all symptoms of national self-interest at variance with Community values. Further dissention has been created by a world energy crisis which has placed acute strains on the economies of member states and precipitated a variety of *ad hoc* policy responses. Consequently the momentum towards integration of member states has not been maintained. However, as the chapters of this book reveal, stasis at the nation state level has not inhibited the development of a complex network of relationships between the European Commission in Brussels and a variety of subnational, regional entities extant in the member states.

One reason for this development is the evident enthusiasm of the Commission to relate directly to the variety of regional levels of government and administration within the member states. From the Commissioners' point of view there are considerable advantages in developing a relationship with these regions. They possess more detailed and up to date information which enable the Commission to adapt more readily to local conditions and changing circumstances. But the regions can also gain from the relationship not least because it provides them with an alternative avenue along which pressure may be exerted in support of regional interests. In some respects the developing relationship between the Commission and the regions reflects the regionalist strategy advocated by the European federalists. For enthusiastic federalists the strategy of direct contacts between the Commission and the regions of member states and the encouragement of regional lobbyists which would stimulate institutional developments at the regional levels provided 'the only available stepping stone to a truly federal system'.[1] However, such an aspiration would appear to underestimate the resilience of the European nation state and the evidence presented in the chapters of this book, while intriguing, hardly constitutes a basis for presuming an eventual federal solution.

The evolving relationship between the Commission and the regions, or subnational levels of member states would appear to be the product of a variety of functional and pragmatic considerations. First, there is an appreciation in several member states of the need to represent regional interests within the European Community. This is particularly evident in Britain, where the setting up of ERDF was seen as a justification for establishing direct contact between the Commission and governmental bodies responsible for regional development.[2] Second, the administrative process in member states is undergoing what Coombes has described as a 'leakage' effect.[3] Regardless of the particular constitutional arrangements in member states, national governments increasingly share responsibility for the administration of domestic policies with regional or local levels. This can either take the form of informal consultative procedures or of the delegation of administrative functions to decentralized agencies. In either case the result tends to make the regional, subnational levels more significant in the administrative process. In addition the general acceptance of the Gaullist view that foreign policy and diplomacy should be the preserve of the member states has ensured that the Community is primarily concerned with those very economic and social welfare issues,[4] which national governments tend to delegate to regional or local levels of administration.

It is virtually impossible to generalize about the nature of the relationship between the several institutions of the Community and the various sub-national levels of government and administration within member states. This is partly the product of the different constitutional arrangements which range from federal and quasi-federal structures like the German Federal Republic and Italy, to unitary systems of government which in practice delegate certain administrative functions to subordinate agencies with either a legal basis or a democratic input. But it is not only a question of different constitutional arrangements. The relationship is strongly influenced by political factors; the level of regional identity and assertion and the willingness of local authorities to initiate procedural innovations which can in practice transform the degree of legal autonomy possessed by the respective regions and local authorities. In other words the informal contacts and procedures between the subnational entities and the Commission may be more significant than the formal and legalistic framework.

Another consideration should be taken into account in evaluating the relationship; the parties involved are not always the same. At the Community level there is a measure of consistency. Almost invariably it is the officials or institutions of the Commission which are involved. A notable exception to this general principle is to be found in the German arrangement whereby *Länder* representatives might be appointed even to the Council itself. This reflects the fact that Germany is the only member state with a federal system of government but in practice the arrangement has no tangible benefit to the *Länder* and has rarely been exercised. The character of the parties to the relationship at the subnational level varies enormously. First, there are the regions, the intermediate level of government or administration which operate between the central and local authorities of member states. Within this category there are important subdivisions. Such regional intermediate authorities may have a quite explicit legal basis for the powers they exercise and the role they play within the political and administrative framework of their respective member states. Obvious examples which fit this category are the German *Länder* and the Italian Regions. Another variant is presented by the French regional councils which while having a representative basis have very limited legal powers and operate within a highly centralized political system. Finally, this broad category includes executive agencies which have quite clearly defined administrative functions at the regional level although they might well be central government departments. The Northern Ireland, Scottish, and Welsh Offices are examples of this subdivision.

The chapters have also revealed that the relationship between the local authorities of member states and the Commission is in some cases, of growing significance. It is instructive to read how some local authorities have responded to the opportunities provided by EC membership while others have not.

Finally, most of the chapters indicate that the relationship between supranational and subnational levels is not simply one involving different levels of government. Nor is it simply one in which one type of civil servant consults with another type of civil servant. Certainly the administrative dialogue is important and could have considerable significance in the long-term operation of the Community, consolidating its procedures and inculcating a common administrative perception; but the realization that many of the significant determinants of policy are to be found in Brussels has stimulated private interests at the subnational levels to organize and lobby the Commission. This type of relationship, inevitably, is highly informal and dynamic and varies considerably both between member states and from time to time within member states. It is important for two reasons; it represents an overtly political and spontaneous response from the subnational levels of member states; and it can act in concert with the equivalent administrative institutions to exert the most formidable pressures on both national governments and the Commission.

First, however, we need to review the role played by the regional or intermediate levels of government in member states. The way they relate to the Community and its policies is important in itself but it also establishes the parameters within which local authorities and private organized interests are obliged to operate.

Germany and Italy with federal or quasi-federal constitutions possess 'regional' institutions with clearly defined legal powers and a democratic basis. They are thus eminently capable of developing an articulate administrative relationship with the European Communities. Of the two the German *Länder* have been more successful in establishing their presence in Community institutions. Although the Italian regions aspire to a significant role in the EC by such means as formal enquiries into Community policies and investigatory visits to the Commission, they fall far short of the institutional opportunities and procedural devices available to the German *Länder*. The upper house of the Federal German parliament, the Bundesrat, represents the *Länder* interests; it debates EC policies and consults on a regularized basis with the Federal government and German Euro-MPs.

Länder interests are also represented by an official non-voting and non-speaking observer (*Länderbeobachter*) on the Council of Ministers. In addition, as the German chapter shows, the *Länder* have gained a *de facto* participation in most administrative and advisory bodies of the Community.

The addition of another supranational level of government appears to have altered the relationship between regional and central levels of government. In Italy the administrative imperatives of Community policies was a contributory factor to the Charter of Regional Functions (1977) which established the framework for what Merloni describes as 'co-operative regionalism' by breaking down the strict demarcation between central and regional government functions. The pragmatic arrangements which had evolved in Germany involving the Community, the federal government and the *Länder* were consolidated by a formal agreement in April 1980. The federal government undertook to keep the *Länder* informed on all negotiations with the Community and promised to take account of their views so far as was possible.

Neither the Italian nor the German chapter provides evidence of a fundamental shift of power from central to regional levels of government. Merloni cites the administrative characteristic of 'sectoriality' which militates against such a development and which has led to the seepage of effective power from regions to central government ministries. Gerstenlauer describes the long-term trend in Germany towards 'unitary federalism' in which the balance of power has shifted to the federal government. Both suggest that membership of the European Community has done little to halt these twin developments. The Community might even have accentuated the trends. For example, in Italy DPR616 of the 1977 Charter confirmed the reservation of international matters (including EC treaties and executive agreements) to the Italian central government *even in matters devolved to the regions* and the operation of ERDF has restored power to the central government ministry responsible for the Mezzogiorno. In Merloni's opinion the Community has produced new centralizing distortions within areas formally devolved to the regions. In a surprisingly parallel development the German *Länder* complained in 1977 that the federal government was misusing the constitutional 'integration power' to subordinate not only its own powers to Community regulations but also those of the *Länder*. The 1980 agreement was designed to overcome this problem. However Gerstenlauer notes that the participation and consultation procedure has not been as effective as was hoped. Thus Community membership for Italy and Germany has consolidated the position of central government at the expense of the regions.

Although France and the Republic of Ireland possess unitary systems of government, their experiences of EC membership are similar to those of Italy and Germany. In the chapter on Ireland, Hart concludes that ERDF has reinforced central government's role in regional planning. She points out that the fund is negotiated and administered by central government departments to exploit the partial reimbursement concession. The French government employs a similar centralized approach; both Social and Regional Development Funds are administered nationally. There are no direct regional payments and both ERDF and ESF are used to compensate the French government for expenditure already undertaken in so indiscriminate a fashion that, as Mény indicates it is possible for non-qualified schemes to be funded.

The regional dimension is weak in both countries but particularly so in Ireland where the Regional Development Organisations (RDO) lack a legal status and a democratic base. They fall between central government, on whom they are dependent for funds and local authorities which actually implement policies. The RDO play a central role but occupy a peripheral status. The French regions with indirectly elected assemblies and presidents have a stronger political identity and regional political élites are able to exercise initiatives; the President of the Lorraine regional council advocated a Community 'integrated operation' for his region. However Mény identifies the French regions' basic deficiency. They lack a legal role in their relationships with the Community, and are obliged to operate on an informal basis, exploiting the personal networks of regional political barons. It is an uncertain basis for promoting regional interests and one which, Mény suggests, is heavily dependent upon the benevolent indifference of a central government whose leading figures have strong regional connections.

The case studies of France and the Republic of Ireland reveal a reaction against central government. In Ireland the RDOs, critical of the centralist approach to regional planning have approached the Commission directly for information and joined the Conference of Peripheral Maritime Regions (CPMR) in expectation of better contacts with the permanent executive Committees of the regional fund. The French regions, despite their legal limitations and central government constraints are able in practice, to exercise significant powers over Community policies. Mény argues that in several instances this is because purely sectoral interests are either coincident with or are perceived as regional interests.

The French case study illustrates an important consideration relevant to all the case studies in this book. Although regional levels of government may lack a legally defined role in respect of community powers, there are alternative informal processes through which influence may be exerted. The opposition of south-west France to the entry of Spain and Portugal to the Community and Scotland's determination to defend its fishing industry are but two examples. However, as Keating and Waters point out, such a regional influence is only effective when the regional interest is clearly identified and there is general agreement between government, public bodies, and organized interests; a conjunction of interests and energies which is neither readily nor regularly attainable. *influence of Centre agree*

Strictly speaking, there are no regional authorities in the United Kingdom although the peripheral nations of Scotland, Wales and Northern Ireland have acquired administrative arrangements which in the context of the European Communities have a regional character. They share a novel characteristic; a central government department whose territorial remit grants it an intermediate status within the administrative structure of the United Kingdom. As Keating and Waters, and Jones demonstrate the Scottish and Welsh Offices perceive as one of their major roles the promotion of their respective national interests. The Northern Ireland Office operates in a more complicated environment; its national community is fractured by the sectarian divide and the Office's primary task is crisis management, responding to pressing economic and security problems. All three Offices are an integral part of central government and are represented on interdepartmental and cabinet committees. However their ability to influence EC policy areas is seriously constrained by the lead departments of Agriculture, Industry, Employment, and Environment which are responsible for conducting negotiations with Brussels. Only the Scottish Office which in practice has assumed special responsibilities for fisheries policies may be excepted from this general limitation.

Although the three nations/regions suffer from similar social and economic disabilities, the Northern Ireland problems are quantitatively and qualitatively different. It is the only part of the United Kingdom to qualify for high priority status which places it in the same category as Greenland, Mezzogiorno, Greece, and the Republic of Ireland. Hainsworth acknowledges the Northern Ireland Office's efforts in lobbying the Commission and notes its success in obtaining support for an Integrated Operations scheme in Belfast which required some subtle interpretations of the eligibility criteria to include housing. He also points out that the perception of the European Community has been distorted by the values of Northern Ireland's domestic politics; the United Kingdom's accession to membership of the Community coincided with direct rule and for many Northern Irish politicians European integration has become the touchstone for Irish unification. The Scottish and Welsh Offices confront less traumatic but no less intractable problems. Disparate interests have to be balanced. As was noted in Wales, industrial demands have to be matched by the needs of the agricultural interest. Above all the two Offices have to perform two quite diverse functions; to represent the interests of the periphery in central government and to administer policies, emanating from both the British government and the Community, in their respective nations. In this latter function a close working relationship has developed with local authorities.

The evidence presented by all the case studies demonstrates the salience of local authorities in EC regional policies and particularly so in those member states with unitary systems of government. The Community, its funds, expertise, and officials, represents a counter-balance to the established authority of central government. Two quite distinct strategies may be identified. The first one involves local authorities bypassing their national governments and establishing direct contacts with Brussels to seek information and advice and to lobby for their areas. Even in Northern Ireland where Hainsworth describes local authorities as little more than 'minor interlocutors', there is a massive interchange of local councillors and Commission officials. Several local authorities, including those from Brittany, Wales, and Ireland, have joined the Conference of Peripheral Maritime Regions (CPMR) to improve their contacts with the Commission. A more comprehensive organization, the Consultative Committee of Local and Regional Authorities was set up in 1976 to discharge a similar role. There are several examples noted in the England, Scotland, and Wales studies of individual local authorities seconding staff to the Commission in Brussels for limited periods to assist in their comprehension of the organizational norms of the Community. The second strategy is designed to create strength from unity; there is a definite pattern of neighbouring local authorities grouping themselves into *de facto* regional lobbies. Mawson and Gibney identify several such joint regional lobbies in England, the North East County Council's Association (NECCA); the Yorkshire Textile Area Action Group (YORTAG) and the East Anglian Consultative Committee (EACC) are all examples of local-authority-based regional lobbies. The Convention of Scottish Local Authorities (COSLA) and the Welsh Counties Committee (WCC) operate in a similar fashion with one important difference. They each have a 'regional' department of central government upon which they can focus their lobbying activities. All the local authorities examined in the case studies have at least a minimal role to play in regional planning but several, particularly those in the United Kingdom, demonstrate a desire to be more positively involved at an early stage in the planning process. This is apparent in the highly-centralized planning system of the Republic of Ireland, where the local authorities formed the Irish Council of European Local Authorities (ICELA) in 1980 to rectify what they saw as an imbalance in the planning process. Where local authorities are unable or unwilling to act, the Commission itself may take the initiative through such expedients as placing 'consultancy contracts' with groups of local authorities; for example, the Association pour l'expansion du Nord-Pas de Calais (APEX).

There appears to be an imbalance in the activities of regionally-based private, organized interests. Ironically, member states with federal or quasi-federal institutions show least evidence of regional pressure group activity. This could be a reflection of the relative effectiveness of the regional institutions but evidence presented in the case studies suggest that part of the explanation lies elsewhere. Gerstenlauer makes the point that with the exception of Bavaria, the German *Länder* have little sense of historical tradition or cultural identity around which interest groups might orientate their activities. The Italian chapter notes the vertical bureaucratic control induced by sectoriality in administrative procedures. In both countries pressure groups are functionally based and integrated into the political system at the national level. The unitary states provide greater evidence of regional pressure group activity. Some groups are regionally autonomous (the Farmers Union of Wales) but the majority are the regional branches of national organizations, although their enthusiastic support of regional interests need not be diminished by the national connection. In specific cases—the crisis in the steel industries of Scotland, Wales, and Lorraine being the most pertinent—a regional coalition of local authorities, employers associations, trade unions, and political parties has been brought into existence. The case studies agree that it is not only EC regional policies which have a regional impact; general policies in respect of agricultural support or industrial rationalization can produce an uneven spatial impact and provoke a regional reaction. For those regional interests such policies are *de facto* regional policies. The salience of regional interest groups may therefore be taken as a measure of the relative importance of EC policies in the regions, but there are strict limits to the role regional interest groups may play. The regions are parts of highly developed, integrated political systems. Regional interest group attitudes and the procedures which they have evolved are conditioned by the fact that they operate within the constitutional framework of their respective states, according to the rules and conventions of their parliaments and the organizational structures of their national political parties and pressure groups.

There are strong indications that Community regional policies will grow in importance. The continuing budgetary crisis and the demands for the reform of the Common Agricultural Policy could be partially resolved by the channelling of additional community funds into ERDF. The Commission is already on record as favouring the more positive promotion of regional policies. The July 1983 Report of the EC Commission foreshadowed a more interventionist role by the Commission in the formulation of regional programmes in key areas rather than in merely funding the regional policies of member states. The existence of small poor regional states, the Republic of Ireland and Greece, will ensure that lobbying for additional regional development funds will take place at the highest levels of decision-making within the EC. The accession of Spain and Portugal, while doubtless creating fresh difficulties for the Community, will also maintain pressure for an expansion of the regional development programmes.

On the evidence of past performance it seems that national governments of member states will be reluctant to concede an erosion of their sovereign powers in regional matters unless substantial financial subventions are made from the regional fund. Even then some member states confronted with the intractable problem of managing their respective public expenditures might well respond with measures which further centralize administrative and financial institutions. There would be little the European Community could do if such a development took place. The Treaty of Rome takes no account of subnational levels of government within member states. To the Community such regional and local levels of government have no legal status; all member states are regarded as constitutional monoliths. The role which the European Commission plays in regional development policies is, in the final analyis, determined by the attitudes of the national governments of member states. The reluctance of the French government to publicize ERDF support of various projects in the French regions is a salutary reminder of national sensitivity and suspicion of supranationalism, which could frustrate the interventionist role in regional development policies espoused by the Commission.

However, member states are not political monoliths. The case studies reveal a proliferation of subnational levels of government, administration, and organized groups whose interests frequently do not coincide with those of the central government. In most of the regions studied there are clearly expressed intentions to create more effective links between themselves and Brussels. Organized groups in Northern Ireland have suggested that there should be a Northern Ireland Business Bureau based in Brussels, a similar demand to that made by Welsh local authorities. Another suggestion is that the Province should be granted 'observer status' in the Council of Ministers equivalent to that of the German *Länderbeobachter*. Although the arrangements to represent the German *Länder* compare favourably with other regions of the EC, they are lacking in one important respect. They presume an identity of interests between the *Länder* which is not always present. Bavaria the *Land* with the strongest sense of cultural identity recognizing that its interests might not always coincide with those of the other *Länder*, has considered appointing a permanent representative to the Commission. The Italian regions have recommended setting up a State-Regions Conference attached to the Prime Minister's Office to provide themselves with a platform on which to play a more active role in the operation of the ERDF. For the relationship between the regions of the member states and European Community to be put on a proper footing there would have to be a substantial restructuring of government functions at the regional level. However, apart from the abortive devolution exercise in Scotland and Wales in the late seventies and the ambiguous decentralization proposals of the present French government, there is no evidence and little likelihood of institutional reforms taking place.

In these circumstances the hopes of the European ethnic minorities appear slim even though they argue that a Community based on ethnic, regional states would eliminate the problems of cultural and linguistic minorities and create what they regard as the 'True Europe'.[5] The aspirations of the European federalists also seem unrealistic. The range of powers they advocate should be allocated to the regions and to the Community[6] is on the evidence of the case studies quite unrealistic. If we look to the future there appears to be no certain conclusion to the dialogue between the regions and the Community—other than it will continue. In the long term it might result in more diffused decision-making procedures which might go some way to satisfying federalists and ethnics but the peripheral minorities might always remain disadvantaged. Galtung has argued that 'Scotland, the Italian South will remain peripheries [because] the system will not given them organic self-sustained and autonomous life',[7] and that the more regional and other interests organize to lobby the Commission in Brussels 'the more the European Community will grow in vitality'.[8] The logic of this development is a highly centralized and highly bureacratic European superpower for whom regional and perhiperal interests will be subordinate to the needs of the Community as a whole. Yet the Community has exhibited a willingness to devise special arrangements to meet the particular problems and requirements of peripheral areas. For example the Channel Islands and the Isle of Man with a combined population of almost 200,000 were granted considerable concessions in Protocol No. 3 in the United Kingdom Treaty of Accession enabling them to maintain their fiscal independence, permitting them to avoid payment of VAT and allowing them to keep all levies collected under CAP. However it is doubtful whether such a level of dispensations could be contemplated on a wider basis within the Community. The dialogue between regional interests and the Commission in Brussels is undoubtedly significant. Whether it will result in a consolidation of power in the Commission or in a progressive decentralization of administrative procedures and decision making depends on the administrative conventions now in the process of evolution and, inevitably, on the degree of proprietorial interest expressed by the national governments of the member states.

Notes

1. Wallace, H., 'Institutions in a Decentralised Community', in Burrows, B., Denton G., and Edwards, E., *Federal Solutions to European Issues* (London: Macmillan, 1977), p. 36.

2. See, for example, *The British People: Their Voice in Europe* (London: Hansard Society) 1977 and *New Hope for the Regions*. (London: Conservative Euro-Group) 1979.

3. Coombes, D., *European Integration, Regional Devolution and National Parliaments* (London: PSI 1979), p. 6.

4. Hull, C., and Rhodes, R. A. W., *Intergovernmental Relations in the European Community* (London: Saxon House 1977), p. 3.

5. Fourere, Yann, *Towards a Federal Europe: Nations or States* (Swansea: Christopher Davies, 1980), p. 133.

6. Macfarquhar, R., MP, 'The Community, the Nation State and the Regions', in B. Burrows, G. Denton, and G. Edwards, op. cit. p. 23.

7. Galtung, Johan, *The European Community: A super power in the making* (London: Allen and Unwin, 1981), p. 131.

8. Ibid., p. 25.

Index

Additionality principle 75, 86, 186−7,
  196−8, 229
Adenauer, Konrad 192
Agricultural Development Programme
  70, 72, 84
Alliance Parties 62
Alsace 199
Alsatians 5
Anglo-Irish Dialogue 130
Apex 242
Aquitaine 200
Association of Metropolitan Authorities
  142
Atkins, Humphrey 113

Baden-Wurttemberg 179, 182
Barnett formula 66
Basques 5
Bavaria 174, 182, 184−5
Belfast Integrated Operation 114, 129,
  241
Borders Regional Council 84
Bretons 5
Britanny 199
British Steel Corporation 85
Buchan, Gilbert 72
Buckland, Patrick 110
Budget refund 75, 86
Bundesrat 76−7, 237
Bureau of Unrepresented Nations 5

Cassa per il Mezzogiorno 169
CELIB 201
Central region 81, 84
CGT 191
Charter of Regional Functions 238
Churchill, Winston 109
Coal policies 6, 199
CODER 193, 200
Collins, Kenneth 70
Comité des Organisations Professionelles
  Agricoles (COPA) 67, 103
Commission 7, 8, 18, 37, 40, 44, 45, 51,
  55, 64, 65, 71, 74, 82, 101−3, 198
Common Agricultural Policy 24, 29,
  95−6, 99−101, 171

Common Fisheries Policy 63; and
  Scotland 72−3
Common Regional Policy 20−57 *passim*,
  243−4
Confederation of British Industry 67; in
  Wales 91, 104
Conference of Peripheral Maritime
  Regions 5, 69, 106, 217−19, 239−41
Conservative Party 61, 62
Consultative Committee of Local and
  Regional Authorities 241
Convention of Scottish Local Authorities
  68, 242
Coombes, David 235
COREPER 134
Corsica 198, 199
Council of European Municipalities
  (CEM) 97, 134
Council of Ministers 7, 8, 9, 10, 11, 12,
  31, 65
Court of Auditors 87

DATAR 193, 197
D'Avignon Plan 91
Debré, Michel 191
Defferre, Gaston 198
de Gasperi 192
de Gaulle, Charles 109, 224
De Laurean 116
de Rougement, Denis 191
Denmark 14, 20, 42
Department of Agriculture and Fisheries
  for Scotland 73
Department of the Environment 68
Devolution 62, 92
Directorate for Competition Policy 13
Dumfries and Galloway 69, 84
Dundee 77

Economic and monetary union 24
Economic and Social Committee: of EC
  9, 67; of France 195
Edinburgh 71
England 11; and ERDF 136−44
Enlargement of Community 20
EURATOM 22

247

Euro-Election Results: in Northern Ireland 126–8; in Wales 91–2; in West Germany 185–6
European Agricultural Guidance Fund 16, 17, 22, 24, 29, 84, 171
European Coal & Steel Community 16, 22; and Scotland 63, 85; and Wales 95, 99
European Commission 101–3
European Council 17
European Court of Justice 8
European Federalists 235, 245
European Golden Triangle 6, 89
European integration 6
European Investment Bank 13, 14, 27; and Northern Ireland 118; and Scotland 69, 80–2, 85–6; and Wales 95
European Joint Group 68
European Monetary System 16
European movement 5
European Parliament 8, 166; and additionality 87; electoral arrangements 9, 107; and ERDF 55; and France 199–200; and Italy 171; and North Ireland 110–11; and regional policy 133; and Scotland 70
European Regional Development Fund (ERDF) 11, 14, 18, 20–57 passim; and England 136–44, decision making network 133–6, and local authorities 136–44, and non-quota section 140–4, and regional allocation 145–7; and France 194–6, 201; and Ireland 206–31, and non-quota section 227–9, and partial reimbursement 210, and quota section 227–9, Special Border Areas Programme 229–30, suggested reforms 222–3; and Italy 109; and Northern Ireland 114–7; and Scotland 69, 72–4, 82, 86; and Wales 94–9, 104, 144; and West Germany 180, 186 ff.
European Social Fund 14, 18, 22, 27; and France 194; and Italy 171; and Northern Ireland 117–8; and Scotland 70, 74, 82–4; and Wales 95, 97
European Unity 1
Europeanism 1, 2, 4

Farmers' Union of Wales 103, 242

Faulkener, Brian 122
Faure, Edgar 193, 199
Fianna Fail 204
Fine Gael 204
fishermen 11
Fitzgerald, Garret 128, 130, 205, 209
France 2; and ERDF 42, 194, 196, and European Parliament 8, 9, 199; and European Social Fund 14, 196, 201; and peripheral nationalism 3; and regional government 12, 193–4, 195–6
free trade 1
French Communist Party 191
Friesland 34
Fund Management Committee (of ERDF) 15, 16, 31, 41, 49, 77

Galtung, Johan 245
Giannini Commission 167
Giolitti Report 42, 100, 194
Giscard d'Estaing, Valéry 194, 200
Glasgow 70, 82
Greece: and regional policies 20; regional trends 35
Greenland 38
Griffith, Win 143

Haagerur, Niels 129
Hainault 34
Harkness, Sir Douglas 111
Hall Report 115–16
Heath, Edward 109, 121, 126
Highland Regional Council 74, 84
Highlands and Islands Development Board 69, 70, 74, 75, 82
Hofmann Report 184
Holland 42
House of Lords Select Committee on the European Communities 136–7, 143, 146, 157
Hughes, Aneurin Rhys 106
Hughes, Lord Cledwyn 101, 105
Hull, C. 135, 179
Hume, John 110–11, 126–7

Industry Department for Scotland 75, 76, 85
Integrated Development Programmes 17, 69, 72, 74, 84
integrated operations 17, 49–50, 51, 70, 170, 195, 198
interest groups 8, 10; in Scotland 66–8

International Union of Local Authorities
(IULA) 68, 134
international role of regions: Italy 164;
France 202
Ireland 5, 11; and Industrial
Development Authority 207–8; and
Public Capital Programmes 212, 225,
228–9, 231; and Regional
Development Organisation 214–21,
239; and regional policies 13–14;
Irish Council of European Local
Authorities (ICELA) 221, 242
Irish Labour Party 204
Irish Unification: and the EC 118–29
Italy: and peripheral nationalism 3; and
regional government 10, 11, 160–71
passim

James, Mari 93
Jenkins, Roy 102

Kelsall, Ian 91
Kitzinger, Uwe 121
Kreisky, Bruno 184

Labour Party 61–2, 89–92
Länder: and competition policy 6; and
contact with Commission 182; and
liaison with federal government
180–82; parliaments of 182; and
powers of 176–8
Länderbeobachter 11, 179–80, 237
Languedoc 11, 200
Less favoured areas 63, 74
Local Authorities: in England 138 40,
154–5; in Ireland 214–5, 221; in
Northern Ireland 120; in Wales 96–7,
106
Lombardy 164
Lorraine 198, 201
Luneburg 34
Luxembourg 34

McLelland, R. 112
Madgwick, Peter 93
Maffre-Bangé 199
Manpower Services Commission 82
Mendès-France, Pierre 193
Mezzogiorno 13, 34, 38, 169
Midi Pyrenees 200
Midwinter, Arthur 65
Mitterrand, Françoise 200
Morgan, Gwyn 102
Mouroy, Pierre 198

Napier, Oliver 122
National Coal Board 85
National Farmers Union 67
National Farmers Union of Scotland 67,
71
New Community Instrument 16, 82
Nord Pas-de-Calais 201
Northern Ireland: and attitude to EC
124–5; and Community policies 6,
13, 38; and direct rule 121; and
European Parliament 8; and
nationalism 3, 6; economy of 115–18
Northern Ireland Office 12, 111–15,
240–1; and negotiations for British
entry 112
North of England County Councils
Association 144
Norton, Philip 121

Oliver, Neil 123
O'Neil, Lord (Terence) 122
Orkney and Shetland 73
Owen, David 91

Paisley, Ian 110–11, 122–3, 127, 129
Patten, Christopher 115, 130
Periodic Report 32, 45, 52, 57
Plaid Cymru 5, 89, 92, 107
Pleven, René 199–200
Pompidou, Georges 193
Portugal 20, 57, 200
Powell, Enoch 125–6
Prag, D. 155–7
Prior, James 113–14
Provan, James 70

quantitative guidelines (for ERDF) 42,
43
Quotas (for ERDF) 39, 43, 52, 76, 170,
227–9

Rate Support Grant 75
Ravenscraig 6, 85
Referendum: in Ireland 204; in
Northern Ireland 123–4; in Scotland
60–1; in Wales 89–91
regional administration 2
regional development 4
Regional Development Programmes 16,
26, 27, 31, 38, 44, 46, 47, 50, 52, 54,
56, 212
Regional expansion committees 192, 193
Regional government 4, 10; in France
193–4, 195–6; in Italy 161–9

regional lobbies 242–3
Regional policy 161; community 2, 6, 7,
  13, 20–57 *passim*; in France 193–4;
  in Italy 168–9; in UK 86; in West
  Germany 176
Regional Policy Committee 26, 27, 46,
  70
Regional Policy Directorate 15, 16
regional trends 32–7
Regionalism 1, 2
Rhodes, R.A.W 135, 179
Richard, Ivor 87, 91, 102, 106
Ripon, Geoffrey 112

Scheme for Textile Area Regeneration
  (STAR) 153
Schleswig-Holstein 174
Schuman, Robert 192
Scotland: and attitude to EC 60–1; and
  Community policies 6; and devolution
  4–5, 62, 87; and ECSC 63, 85; and
  ERDF 69, 72, 73, 74, 82, 86; and
  fisheries policy 72–3, 240; and
  nationalism 3; and regional policy 13,
  38
Scottish bench 8
Scottish Development Agency 75, 77, 82,
  160
Scottish Fishermen's Federation 71,
  72–3
Scottish Labour Party 5, 62
Scottish National Party 62
Scottish Office 12, 64–6, 71, 73, 93,
  101, 240–41
Scottish Trades Union Congress 67
Secretary of State for Northern Ireland
  114
Secretary of State for Scotland 64–6, 72
Seveso directive 63, 69
Sillars, Jim 62
Simpson, John 120
Soames, Christopher 101
Social Affairs and Employment
  Committee 104–5
Somalia 164
South Glamorgan County Council 98–9
South Wales Standing Conference
  105
Spain 20, 57, 200
Spath 182
Steed, Michael 61
Strategic Conference of County Councils
  142

Strathclyde Regional Council 63, 69, 70,
  74, 76, 84, 85, 144
Supplementary Measures 49, 75
Supranationality 2
Swansea City Council 150–1

Taylor, John 110, 122, 128
Tayside region 76, 82
textile industry 6, 11
Thatcher, Margaret 130
Thomson Report 25, 47, 101
Trades Union Congress 67
Treasury 74, 75
Treaty of Paris 13
Treaty of Rome 2, 9, 13, 25
Tugenhat, Christopher 129

Ulster Farmers' Union 110–12
Ulster Unionism 121–2
United Kingdom 2, 12, 14

Valle d'Aosta 34
Veil, Mme Simone 178
veto 2
Vogel 184

Wage subsidy schemes 82
Wales: and attitude to EC 91; and
  autonomy 3; and devolution 4–5; and
  regional policy 13, 38
Wales TUC 90–1, 104–5, 107
Welsh Agriculture 99–101
Welsh Cooperative Resource Centre 104
Welsh Counties Committee 96–7, 100,
  242
Welsh Labour MEPs 107, 143
Welsh Labour Party 89, 92
Welsh nationalism 5
Welsh Office 12, 92–7; and the
  Commission 94, 98; and the ERDF
  94, 97–8; and Welsh agriculture 100;
  and Welsh interest 100–1
Werner Report 24
West Germany: and attitude to EC
  '183–4; and ERDF 42; and federation
  3, 10, 11, 174–5
West Yorkshire County Council 138–9,
  151–2
Western Isles 69, 72, 74, 84
Williams, Shirley 127
Wilson, Harold 61
Wine policies 199, 200

Younger, George 72